# TRAILS OF BETRAYALS IN SOUTH SUDAN'S POWER STRUGGLE

GN STEPHEN BUDY ROLNYANG

*The ideas and opinions in this book are ultimately those of the author. Their authenticity is the responsibility of the author, not Africa World Books.*

*he publisher wishes to acknowledge and thank Dr Douglas H. Johnson for his invaluable help and support for Africa World Books and its mission of preserving and promoting African cultural and literary traditions and history. Dr Johnson and fellow historians have been instrumental in ensuring that African people remain connected to their past and their identity. Africa World Books is proud to carry on this mission.*



*ISBN: 978-0-6454529-5-2*



*Cover design, typesetting and layout : Africa World Books*

## Table of Contents

## About the Author

Born on November 15, 1968 in Mayom, Upper Nile Province – now Unity State in South Sudan, General Stephen Buoy Rolnyang, started attending school at the age of 9 years in Ajak-Kuac County, Bahr El Ghazal. Six years later, Gen. Buoy dropped out of school and joined the Anya Nya II Southern Sudanese insurgency. In 1984, Gen. Buoy abandoned the insurgency (Anya Nya II) camp and joined the Sudan People's Liberation Movement/Army (SPLM/A). After serving in the insurgency briefly for one year, Gen. Paulino Matip, who had recruited him established Anya-Nya II movement in Western Upper Nile in 1985 and decided to release him – where he returned to school.

Gen. Buoy proceeded to study in Khartoum where he did his Senior School Certificate and thereafter rejoined Gen. Paulino Matip in 1991. When he resumed work with the Anya Nya II movement, he was dispatched for a Special Forces Training at the Sudanese Military Training Centre in Omdurman. After a year, Gen. Buoy went for a specialized training with the Sudan Armed Forces' Signal Corp in Khartoum. On completion, Gen. Paulino Matip deployed him as a Radio Operator at his headquarters. In 1992, Gen. Buoy joined the SPLA faction led by Riek Machar and he was transferred in the same year to Machar's headquarters with the rank of Captain and as a Signal Officer.

In 1996, Gen. Buoy was again promoted to the rank of Alternate Commander (A/Cmdr.) and assigned as Chief of Signal for Western Upper Nile. However, when Gen. Paulino Matip broke away from Riek Machar's faction, Gen. Buoy was promoted to the rank of Commander in South Sudan United Movement/Army (SSUM/A) and assigned the duties as Chief of Signal. Nonetheless, he defected to the SPLM/SPLA mainstream on August 10, 1998 where he was deployed as Operations' Officer on Twic border with Upper Nile under the command of Salva Kiir Mayardit, who commanded the SPLA 3rd Front.

While working here, Gen. Buoy oversaw logistics of the 3rd Front under Salva Kiir in Bahr El Ghazal Region in 2000. He was sent for a one-year training course at the Institute for Strategic Studies at Lasu area on the Southern Sudan border with DR Congo. Salva Kiir later sent him to assist Commander Peter Gatdet with the new organizational structure of the SPLA – where he was confirmed as Commander of Western Upper Nile in 2003 – 2005. From here, Gen. Buoy was transferred from Western Upper Nile to command the 21st Infantry Independent Brigade in Eastern Equatoria (Kapoeta HQS) 2005 – 2007. He was later redeployed to Juba to establish the command of the Military Police and

Commando Units (known as Special Forces).

Between 2008 and 2014, he studied and obtained a Bachelor of Management Science (BMS) degree from Kyambogo University (Uganda). He also undertook several other certificate courses from Cambridge International College and the SPLA Senior Command and Staff conducted in Juba SPLA headquarters by American Military experts. After completion of the courses, he was redeployed from the Special Forces Unit to the 1st Infantry Division in Upper Nile Region, with its headquarters in Renk in 2013, as Deputy Commander of the Division. But shortly between 2014 and 2015 he was confirmed as 1st Infantry Division Commander when Maj. Gen. Angelo Jongkuc – the then commander was re-deployed to the SPLA headquarters, due to a crisis the country underwent in December 2013.

From 2015 to 2017, Gen. Buoy was redeployed from the SPLA 1st Infantry Division to command the SPLA 4th Infantry Division in Western Upper Nile, but shortly thereafter, he was arrested and detained before being re-assigned as Director General of Procurement in the Ministry of Defence and Veterans Affairs after he had been released.

From 2017-2018, Gen Buoy was redeployed for the second time to command the SPLA 4th Infantry Division in Bentiu. He was then further redeployed to command the SPLA 5th Infantry Division (Wau) in 2018. He was redeployed from Wau 5th Infantry Division to the SPLA headquarters as Director of Military Organization on May 22, 2018, until he was arrested on May 31, 2018, on allegations of attempting to rebel against the Government of South Sudan. However, the Military Tribunal, which heard the case acquitted him of the charges levelled against him.

# Dedication

This memoir is dedicated to all the heroes, heroines and martyrs of the South Sudanese liberation struggle, and in particular to the following martyrs from Western Upper Nile who were my Comrades during the period. Namely Commander Duay Taitai Badeng, Alternate Cmmander Peter Thoare Gatkuer, Gen. Paulino Matip Nhial, Commander Elijah Hon Top, Commander James Koang Ruac, Commander Philip Bipean Machar, Commander Maliny Kawaye Goh, Commander Francis Nyir Gatluak, Commander Charles Gaatcham Dup, Commander Peter Magey Karay, Commander Jeremiah Malith Kong, Alternate Commander Peter Goh Mathiang, Col. Peter Nor Gatwech, Col. Duol Mathiot Chan Nyaweah, Major Malek Rolnyang Kai, Capt. Michael Char Makuei, Capt. Bol Buop, also known as Bol Nyawan, Capt. Bishar Ket, Capt. Paul Thong Ruac, Capt. Bateah Wagah, Capt. Puot Ruathdheal Luoy, Capt. Duyier Kuajien, Capt. John Top Ngoang, Capt. Kuol Gatdang Manyliem, Comrade Charles Kuot Chatiem, 1st Lt. Waduay Mayang, 1st Lt. Faustino Puok Majok and 1st Lt. Lewis Gatkuer.

These soldiers, most of whom hailed from Western Upper Nile Region, and many others not mentioned here, made tremendous contributions towards the struggle for the liberation of South Sudan. Their perseverance, vision and resolve as they moved around in the jungle, dodging enemy bullets and missiles, firing on their own to suppress the enemy, in order to free all South Sudanese people from oppression, can never be quantified.

When the actual history of South Sudan is finally written, collaborators who were also traitors, will never be forgiven for squandering the immense national goodwill and resources our people needed to better their lives. Their parochial indulgences pushed us to continue fighting to the end.

I dedicate this book also to my fellow South Sudanese, who have suffered unspeakable injustices while residing in refugee camps or in exile, but resiliently hoped and fought for a new dawn. You deserve justice in our free fatherland or motherland. To you, I owe the energy to continue fighting for the total liberation of the country.

# Acknowledgments

The idea to document my experience in the liberation struggle of South Sudan initially arose during my confinement at the Juba Military Prison between May 31, 2018 and October 21, 2019. Having watched the cataclysm in our country from a close range, I felt compelled to write down my experiences for future generations.

I am grateful to the South Sudan People Defence Forces (SSPDF) Military Police Prison Guard, whose name I won't mention or who shall remain anonymous, for allowing me to use my laptop during my solitary confinement. Without him, the publication of this book would have taken a much longer.

My tribute also goes to my relatives, bodyguards and friends who occasionally visited me in jail to comfort, encourage and provide me with the moral support. I will never forget those who stood in solidarity with my family during those hard times.

To the First Vice President of South Sudan, His Excellency, Taban Deng Gai, thank you for supporting my family both materially, financially and morally during their time of need.

I am incredibly indebted to my wives and children for their unwavering support and encouragement that transcended the period that I was put under arrest, when I wrote this book.

I will not forget the many friends, colleagues and reviewers who took their valuable time to make comments and offer suggestions while I was writing this book. Special thanks to Duncan Mboya for reviewing the manuscript and ensuring that everything went as planned.

As I cannot mention each and every person who has helped in one way or the other during the preparation of the book, let me say, peace be with you all!

# Abbreviation

| | |
|---|---|
| A/CDF | Assistant Chief of Defence Forces |
| A/Cdr | Alternate Commander |
| APC | Armored Personnel Carrier |
| APMHC | Alternate Political Military High Command |
| Capt. | Captain. |
| CDF | Chief of Defence Forces |
| CDR | Commander |
| COGS | Chief of Gen. Staff |
| Col. | Col. |
| Coy | Company |
| CPA | Comprehensive Peace Agreement |
| D/COGS | Deputy Chief of General staff |
| FDS | Former detainees |
| GHQS | Gen. Headquarters |
| HPMG | High Purpose Machine Gun |
| HQS | Headquarters |
| ICRC | International Committee of the Red Cross |
| IGAD | Inter-Governmental Authority on Development |
| IGP | Inspector Gen. of Police |
| INFO | Inform/Information |
| J-1 | Juba Palace -1 |
| Jamus division | A code given to an SPLA Unit |
| KIA | Killed in Action |
| LRA | Lord's Resistance Army |
| Lt. Col. | Lieutenant Col. |
| Lt. Gen. | Lieutenant Gen. |
| M.I | Military Intelligence |
| Maj. Gen. | Major Gen. |
| MIA | Missed in Action |
| MO | Moral Orientation |
| NCO(s) | Non-Commissioned Officer(s) |
| NCP | National Congress Party |
| NPTC | National Pre-Transitional Committee |
| OPS | Operations |
| PETROL | A code given to an SPLA Unit |

| | |
|---|---|
| PMHC | Political Military High Command |
| POW | Prisoner of War |
| R/ | Repeat |
| R-ARCSS | Revitalized agreement on the resolution of the con flict in the Republic of South Sudan |
| RPG – 7 | Rocket Propel Grenade |
| RSF | Rapid Support Forces |
| RTGONU | Revitalized Transitional Government of National unity |
| RTNLA | Revitalized Transitional National Legislative Assembly |
| SAF | Sudan Armed Forces |
| SANU | Sudan African Nationalist Union |
| SPDF | Sudan People Democratic Front |
| SPLM/A-IO | Sudan People's Liberation Movement/Army in Opposition |
| SPLM/A | Sudan People's Liberation Movement/Army |
| SRRC | Sudan Relief Rehabilitation Commission |
| SSDF | South Sudan Defence Forces |
| SSLM/A | South Sudan Liberation Movement/Army |
| SSOA | South Sudan Opposition Alliance |
| SSP | South Sudan Pound |
| SSPDF | South Sudan People's Defence Forces |
| SSUM/A | South Sudan United Movement/Army |
| T55 | Tank Type 55 |
| TGONU | Transitional Government of National Unity |
| Tiger | A code given to a Unit |
| Tumsah | A code name given to a Unit |
| UDSF | United Democratic Salvation Front |
| UN | United Nations |
| UNMISS | United Nation Mission in South Sudan |
| USSLM | United South Sudan Liberation Movement |
| WIA | Wounded in Action |
| WUN | Western Upper Nile |

# Preface

The publication of this book has been a long journey that dates back to the time when I was first listed to serve in the Anya Anya II movement in various forests in South Sudan.

The incidences, which represented my transition from youth to adulthood, were marked by a profound sense of isolation brought on by the uncertainty surrounding my family, communities, and, as I would soon learn, the entire region of South Sudan. To face the world, I always rallied all of my faculties, establishing a reliant character in the process that prepared me for the hardships I would face for a long time.

Many events recounted in this book are about the past, but I have also attempted to bring them out in their proper perspective and establish continuities with what's happening in our country today. The primary source for the information is my own memory and reflections, since most of the events took place in my presence.

To get a good background of my lineage, I also took leave to visit my villagers where I had opportunity of interviewing some of my family members and elders from my community, the Bul Nuer, for a complete history of the community. I held many discussions with colleagues, elders and other informants there.

In the process of compiling the book, I realized the difficulty in narrating the story of a long war, a part of which I never personally witnessed. For that purpose, I opted to break the book into three parts – Part I, II and III – to make it easier to read.

Part I deals with my background from the moment I was born amongst the Bul Nuer people up to the time I came of age. I was born in Nyang Dhoarkan village, in Unity State. I grew up herding cattle alongside my agemates. I struggled with my early education after the death of my parents – a struggle that took me to stay with my maternal grandmother. At the age of 15 years, I had already joined the Anya Nya II movement to help liberate my country.

In Part I of the book, I have also narrated a tale of the Bul Nuer's spiritual and traditional leadership in the past and given an analogy of men from this community who joined forces in various groupings with other South Sudanese in the liberation of our country from the Arab Sudanese government.

I also give a detailed chronology of the struggle of South Sudan to independence, starting in the 1800s until the 1983 when I joined the Anya Nya II rebel movement.

I also examine some of the hardest historical moments in our country, traversing the formation of liberation movements, the constant factionalism that beset them, and the collective effort by our well-wishers, including regional and international players, to help us overcome them. The part ends in 1983, when I joined the movement and began to witness the events from a position of knowledge.

Part II, therefore, tackles my experiences within the context of evolving national politics up to the attainment of self-rule in 2005 and subsequent events.

Part III demonstrates how some politicians from my community developed enmity towards me which led to my arrest. Before my arrest, I was transferred to many work stations as part of frustrations to quit the military service.

From the moment I joined the Anya Nya II till today, I have devoted my energy and time in the liberation struggle. Along the way, I was recognized for my contributions and elevated to senior ranks within the rebel movements and the military of South Sudan upon the attainment of our independence.

However, these accomplishments came with setbacks as well. From the mid-2010s, some of my tribesmen, who were also serving in the politics and military, started pulling me backwards by raising unfounded allegations against my person. For nearly a decade, I did my best to dispel the accusations, but my detractors were so determined that they eventually succeeded in their evil schemes. I was arrested, detained, stripped of my high military ranks, and dismissed from the South Sudan People's Defence forces (SSPDF).

In both the Anya Nya II movement and the SPLA, I was always inspired by the patriotism of our people and their craving for freedom and security even in the darkest periods. The struggle was a genuine cause for the liberation of our country to which many contributed everything they could. I was, therefore, crestfallen to see myself being dragged into petty squabbling by fellow Bul politicians, who concocted stories about my rebellion from the government at the peak of my military service. I truly never expected such things to happen in an independent South Sudan.

In this section of the book, I have recorded some of the important events I observed closely during the struggle and after we attained self-rule. I have written about many issues that have not been properly documented even by journalists, given the deteriorating security situation and lack of openness that impede good reporting.

Briefly, today's problems stem from incompetent administration. The presidency, which is the symbol of our national unity, has been hijacked by individuals from the National congress party, who did not participate in the liberation struggle of the Republic of South Sudan.

In 2005, the founding father of the SPLM/A, Dr John Garang' De-Mabior signed the comprehensive peace agreement with the Sudan government under Omar Hassan El Bashir. This peace agreement ended the longest Sudanese civil war that dates back to the mid-1950s, when Southern insurgents took up arms against the Islamist successive governments in the Sudan who were oppressing the Southerners, the war which resulted in the deaths of more than two million, only between 1983 and 2005.

Unfortunately, Dr John Garang' died in a Uganda helicopter crash on 30/7/2005, and as a result of the tragic death, Salva Kiir Mayardit who was an SPLA battlefield commander and deputy to John Garang' took over. Kiir who had little knowledge of the democratic governance and rule of law, later led the South Sudan to independence. The country is a home to over 12 million people drawn from 64 tribes or ethnic groups with diverse cultures, religion and languages.

For the continuity of South Sudan, Kiir appointed Dr Riek Machar Teny Dhur-gon – his longtime rival as his First Vice President. The two leaders (Kiir/Riek) have failed to meet the expectations of the people of South Sudan who have been fighting for freedom, justice and equality. While in Sudan they felt they were being oppressed by the Arabs, but now the oppression of Kiir/Riek is worse than what they experienced from the Arabs.

The South Sudanese people thought Kiir and Riek would guide them towards a genuine path of democratic system of governance. Instead, they failed to establish a viable state and build vibrant institutions right away from the independence of the Republic of South Sudan. The only institutions that exist in South Sudan are the army (SSPDF) and the national security forces – and all of which are predatory institutions.

Despite serving two terms after the independence of the Republic of South Sudan on July 9, 2011, the report card of the two indicates that Kiir has turned to be a demi-god and dictator while Riek has become a vicious self – aggrandizer who cares only for his own interest.

In 2013, Kiir and Riek disagreed about who was going to be the leader of the SPLM/A. The fight swiftly spread across the country causing serious destruction in the country with the Dinka and Nuer being targeted on ethnic basis. There was a full–scale civil war in the country that resulted in the death of nearly 400,000, and more than 2 million people displaced. As a result, Riek formed his own movement the Sudan People Liberation Movement/Army in Opposition (SPLM/A-IO), with the reform agenda.

The two leaders caved into international pressure and signed a power-sharing deal in Addis Ababa in 2015, which was tragically violated in 2016 when combat started in J-1, dubbed the J-1 dogfight, by both leaders (Kiir/Riek). Riek was in hot pursuit for 41 days until he fled to Democratic Republic of Congo (DRC) where he was rescued on humanitarian grounds. On the way, some of Riek's fighters were found and killed.

In 2018, the peace that was violated in 2016, as a result of J-1 fight, was revitalized under the auspices of the Inter-Governmental Authority on Development (IGAD) countries. Another pact was also signed in Khartoum known as the revitalized agreement on the resolution of the conflict in the Republic of South Sudan (R – ARCSS) that reinstated Riek as 1st Vice President and this time around with other more vice presidents, which resulted in the formation of the fragile and embattled revitalized transitional government of national unity (RTGONU).

According to the peace pact, it was agreed (controversially) that elections will be held in 2022 or 2023, with the reconstitution of the revitalized transitional national legislative assembly (RTNLA). This will happen when the formation of the unified command and graduation of the unified forces as stipulated in the provisions of the security arrangement is far from over. The formation of the government of national unity was supposed to be made on May 12, 2019, but was pushed to November 12, 2019 on the request of the SPLM/A –IO, on a pretext that some of the provisions such as internal boundaries and security arrangements were yet to be resolved.

After being in power for 16 years, President Kiir has developed dictatorial and kleptocratic tendencies – which have seen him create his own paramilitary security that intimidate, torture, execute people and lynch political dissidents for crimes they have not committed. Under Kiir's leadership, corruption has flourished, as his inner circle embezzles, misappropriates, or steals state resources and millions of dollars from the United States in the form of grants and donations for the fiscal year, as well as other humanitarian aids for the over 12 million poor people of South Sudan who rely heavily on foreign aid, with impunity. In addition, president Kiir has failed to resolve the proliferation of fire arms which is the cause of rampant inter – communal violence, revenge killing, rape, cattle raiding in the countryside. This book forms part of the history of South Sudan that will be available and help inform the future generation.

No doubt there are events that I may have missed out that took place in other corners of South Sudan during the liberation struggle as I could not have been everywhere during that long uncertain period. These and others will finally be included in the coming editions once I come across the information.

The story of our struggle to self-rule shows that with determination everything is possible and our action stands out like the morning sun that rises high from the East to remind those who are still in dire need of emancipation that it can be done, no matter how long it takes.

**Gen. Stephen Buoy Rolnyang**

# Part I: The Bul Nuer

## Chapter 1
## My Lineage and childhood

I was born on November 15, 1968, in a village called Nyang Dhoarkan, in Unity State, Bieh Payam, Mayom County. My ancestry was among the Bul Nuer tribe that occupies the western part of Western Upper Nile.

The people of Bul Nuer are descendant of the Nuer tribe – a Nilotic ethnic group that lives in the Upper Nile regions of South Sudan and speak the Nuer language. Others residing in western Upper Nile region include the Nyuong, Dok, Haak, Jikany, Jagei and Leek plus their Nuer brothers in the eastern and central Upper Nile. They include Thiang, Laak, Gawaar, Lou, and Jikany Doar. Together, the Nuer are the second largest ethnic community in South Sudan, after the Dinka.

My great grandfather, Bajah, had four family lineages plus Nyal Nyang. They include Yor Chuon Bajah, Thong Kumay Both Chuon Bajah, Luer Bon Choot Bajah, Kan Nerew Giel Tum Bajah and Nyal Nyang. Bajah had two wives namely Thicien and Nyaguay. Thicien was the mother of Choot Bajah and Nyaguay was the mother of Chuon Bajah.

Chuon Bajah had twin sons who were named Yor Chuon and Both Chuon. Both had a son called Kumac who married and had a son called Thong. The other twin brother Yor had three sons namely Jul Yor, Bol Yor and Kai Yor. Jul had two sons whose names were Ngual Juol and Bang Juol.

Ngual Juol had one son called Kai Ngual Yor, while Kai also got married and had three sons and four daughters namely Rolnyang Kai Ngual, Heal Kai Ngual, Jal Kai Ngual, Mer Kai Ngual, Nyeluak Kai Ngual, Thiyang Kai Ngual and Kerker Kai Ngual.

Kai Ngual Yor's first-born son, Rolnyang Kai Ngual, who was my father, married four wives. His first wife was Nyelonyaa Tuak, followed by Nyedona Kaya, Nyagoana Kong and Achol Mayen Majak. My mother Achol Mayen Majak was from the Dinka community. His first three wives were from the Nuer Bul community.

Nyalonya Tuak, my father's first wife, gave birth to Riwluak Rolnyang Kai, Gatdena Rolnyang Kai, Nyaluit Rolnyang Kai and Nyakoang Rolnyang Kai.

His second wife, Nyedona Kaya, gave birth to Gatbel Rolnyang Kai, Thunduk Rolnyang Kai, Malek Rolnyang Kai, Nyawiika Rolnyang Kai and Nyedak Rolnyang Kai.

The third wife, Nyagoana Kong, gave birth to Gat-tuong Rolnyang Kai, Nyetuor Rolnyang Kai, Nyawah Rolnyang Kai, Nyegay Rolnyang Kai and Nyaawic

Rolnyang Kai.

My mother, Achol Mayen Majak, who was my father's fourth wife, gave birth to the two children, my elder sister Nyanuer Rolnyang Kai and I, Buoy Rolnyang Kai, and my mother died soon thereafter.

From my father's genealogy, I am the last-born child in the family of Rolnyang that has since grown and expanded into a larger family. My paternal uncle, Mabek Mayen and elder brothers gave me considerable information regarding my parentage and family. My father and mother came from the Bul Nuer and Twic Mayardit Dinka of Bahr El Ghazal communities, respectively.

In the year 1973, when I was 5, my father died. Shortly thereafter, my mother moved back to Bahr El Ghazal, her original home, where we lived in a tiny village called Akotong in Ajak Kuac.

Unfortunately, my mother died at Akotong in Twic county Bhar El Ghazal region, nobody could remember the year of her death, leaving me under the care of my maternal grandmother, NyeLok Dau Chak, who took such good care of me that I embraced her as my own mother.

During this period that I was staying at my grandmother's home, I made friends with my age mates and playmates. One such friend is Mariem Tuotlual Dau, who was a cousin to my grandmother.

The main activities that occupied everybody's time including my maternal uncles were crop farming, fishing and rearing livestock – mainly goats and cattle. My maternal uncles, Mabek Mayen Majak and his brother Gatjiek Mayen Majak were always very kind to me and often gave me attention just like one of their own. In particular, they saw to it that I learnt the skills that every young person in the village was equipped with.

Mabek Mayen was a very strong man who normally cultivated up to 10 acres of land. He liked taking me along with my cousins to help him plant, weed the crops or generally tend to the farm. Gatjiek Mayen also loved farming and made a good use of us.

As young boys, however, our main activity was herding goats and cattle in the nearby bushes and forests. Every mid-morning, after breakfast, we would get together and drive large herds, comprised of cattle from different families, to the nearby forests for pasture.

On many occasions, cattle rustlers from the neighbouring Nyang clan of the Bul Nuer along the border gave us a hard time. Rival militias from the Nuer and Dinka clans living along the border usually raided each other in search of livestock.

Every time we were in the field, we would watch out both for wild animals and the militiamen. By sunset, after a successful herding day, we would drive the animals back home, tie them in their designated cowsheds (Luak) and start milking goats while the women milked the cows and cooked for us delicious food.

As I followed my grandmother's migration to Bonwiir fishing camp during the dry seasons, I learnt how to catch fish and row canoes. With time, I learnt rowing alone and could occasionally go out with the canoe to check our fishing lines and rods if they have caught some fish.

Whenever I returned home in the mornings with plenty of fish, my relatives would be happy since they knew they will eat fish - a delicacy amongst the Dinka people that day. During this time, Bonwiir was the only source of livelihood for the people of Akotong village during the summer season. But the situation would change as the cold season approached, when people would leave the fishing camps and move back to the village to prepare their lands for cultivation.

In 1979, I was enrolled in Ajak Kuac Primary School in Akotong, where the only mode of teaching was in Arabic language. My maternal aunt, Nyaduat Mayen Majak, escorted me to school on foot every morning from Akotong village to Ajak across a stream called Duor River a distance of half an hour. She would return home after dropping me in school every morning but come back for me in the evening to take me home.

This went on until January 1980, when my stepbrother Thunduk Rolnyang and cousin Wichar Ruathdheal came looking for me in Akotong village. They told my grandmother that they had come to take me back to Bul Nuer land. My maternal uncles and grandmother did not buy their idea, arguing I was too young to live there without the care of my mother.

However, my stepbrother and cousin insisted that they were implementing the wish of my father, who, while on his deathbed, had asked them to ensure that they should take good care of me and take me back to my Nuer people should my mother move with me to Dinka land upon his death.

The guests' insistence did not change my grandmother's position, leading them to report the matter to Chief Manydeng Nyinkuany. On receiving the report, the Chief summoned my grandmother and maternal uncles to appear before his elders.

Sitting under a big tree, Chief Nyinkuany called the meeting to order and my brother was summoned to explain why he had sought help from the local administration. Thunduk Rolnyang explained his mission to Chief and the elders, and how my maternal uncles had refused to let me go with him.

After listening to all the parties, Chief Nyinkuany finally ruled that I should be allowed to go with my stepbrother and cousin, since my mother was officially married in the Bul Nuer community and the two were my close blood relatives with whom I deserved to live with.

My grandmother and maternal uncles gave up their quest to have me continue living with them. They promised to respect the ruling and did not press their case further. We, therefore, went back home so as to start the journey back to the land of the Bul Nuer people, the land of my forefathers, the following day.

At dawn, the following morning, Thunduk Rolnyang and my cousin came back for me and we started our journey to Nuer land. The journey on foot across the savannah from the border of Bahr El Ghazal with Western Upper Nile to Mayom took nearly a full day.

When we arrived in the Bul Nuer territory, I was taken to the cattle camp to look after our family cattle, since they thought I was at the right age to herd cattle. I therefore stayed in the camp for a period of four months herding cattle.

While there, my stepbrothers, who had brought me back from Bahr El Ghazal, were fond of bullying me by assigning me heavy errands and tasks that could not well be done by a child of my age. I quit the camp life in January 1981 and went to live with one of my extended relatives called Gueh Tuoroah.

The bullying at the hands of my brothers made me feel lonely and miserable forcing me to keep remembering my maternal grandmother's strong resistance to let me come with them.

Later on, our cattle camp was relocated to a place called Kuiynam, near Wangkei town in search of greener pastures to take care of livestock. We camped at a village called Tharkuer Ciengjoak, where we easily crossed the river Nam to Wangkei market to sell milk with other boys and girls from our cattle camp.

One day, while on a trip to sell milk at Wangkei market, I met one of my maternal aunts, Mer Gatwech Reat, who lived in Wangkei. Mer Gatwech took me to her house and inquired on how I had got to the town. I told her that I had been living at Tharkuer cattle camp with my stepbrothers.

Looking concerned, she expressed her displeasure with what I was doing. She encouraged me to consider going back to school, and promised to help me join Wangkei Primary School. She openly disliked the idea of me staying at the cattle camp – a view that I shared.

After listening to her advice, I did not go back to the cattle camp. Instead, I stayed with her and spent that night at her house. The following day, she prepared breakfast for us and later on took me to Wangkei Primary School.

The school's Head Teacher, Mr Puok Bol Mot, welcomed us well and after making some inquiries from my aunt and myself, enrolled me in Primary Three. This was agreed bearing in mind that I did not complete my early primary school grades at Ajak Kuac Primary School when I was taken away by my brothers.

For the next one year, I dedicated myself to studies at Wangkei Primary School. Besides learning, I can say I also made friends with my fellow schoolmates such as Abraham Gum Makuac, Manydal Dau, and many others.

As fate would have it, when my brothers learnt that I had joined Wangkei Primary School, they came and hid next to a playground outside the school compound, where we played during break time. And as soon as my brothers spotted me, they grabbed me fast and sped away despite my crying loudly thinking someone would come and rescue me from them. They did not relent and moved with speed until we reached the cattle camp.

After the incident, my brothers kept monitoring my movement henceforth so that I would not be able to desert them again to Wangkei to continue with my schooling.

# Chapter 2
# Bul Nuer Spiritual leaders

The Bul Nuer people border the Dinka Twic in the West, Dinka Apuk (Gogrial) in the South West, Dinka Kongor, Luac and Lou (Tonj) in the South. They are Nilotic communities that live in the greater Upper Nile regions of South Sudan and speak the Nuer language. They have assimilated hundreds of Dinka ethnic community living along their borders.

As aforementioned, the larger Nuer is the second largest ethnic community in South Sudan. They keep livestock – something that has been their way of lifestyle since time immemorial. Cattle meat and milk constitute an important part of Bul Nuer diet. They also have a good share of cereals and fruits that grow in plenty in their motherland.

The Nuer communities receive facial markings (gaar) as part of their initiation into adulthood. The pattern of Nuer people's scarification varies within specific subgroups.

The most common initiation pattern among males consists of six parallel horizontal lines which are cut across the forehead with a small knife, often with a dip in the lines above the nose. The Bul Nuer People have dotted patterns, which are common in both males and females.

Among the Bul Nuer people, they used to have spiritual leaders that were popular and revered by all members of the community. The spiritual leaders included Tang Kuany Kunur Juear Thieh, Deng Kuoth Gatdeng, the three Deeys spiritual leaders and Gah -Gah Chung Loah plus other small fetishes.

### Tang Kuany Kunur

Tang Kuany Kunur Juear Thieh, a prominent elder among the Bul Nuer people, who used to occupy the present Mayom County in South Sudan, lived between 1895 and 1965.

Tang Kuany had powers to foretell phenomena that were going to happen in the community and would also predict good fortunes before they occurred within the community.

He was believed to have killed his own brother at the cattle camp at Padude Deng in Malou, Raar, around 1954, and consequently escaped to North Sudan through Kelek, Nuba Mountains. He finally managed to board a lorry from Nuba Mountains to Khartoum, capital of Sudan.

Tang Kuany converted to Islam and trained as a soldier by Abdal Rahman Al Mahdi while in the Sudan. He later joined the Mahdiyya revolution in Omdurman to fight against the British colony. The Mahdiyya revolution used to recruit youths from all over South Sudan to join the struggle against the Anglo – Egyptian condominium rule.

After spending three years with Mahdiyya, he was assigned to go back to Western Upper Nile to mobilize the youths to join the Mahdiyya revolution to help fight the foreigners that occupied Sudan.

According to elders, Kutey Nguore and Benjamin Bijany Tuor, who were among the youths recruited by Tang Kuany, he was an emissary, who was sent by Abdal Rahman Al Mahdi from Khartoum in 1955 with a message from Mahdiyya to recruit the youths to join the fight against the foreign occupation.

He was warmly welcomed by the Bul Nuer elders as a prophet and a person who possessed spirit due to the fulfilment of the events that he anticipated to take place, even though they were considered strange by the populations. The more he prophesied, the more they became convinced that he was possessed by spirits. Due to this strange character, people started giving him cattle and other gifts as part of appreciation to his prophecies.

The Bul Nuer elders eventually started building him a sacred place that came to be known as 'Thou Tang Kuany' that would later become synonymous with the present-day temples. Believing that Tang Kuany was a prophet or a god, the community would occasionally gather around him as they sang songs and conducted or incarnate sacrifices, hoping to please their new god, but Tang Kuany consistently denied that he was god.

In his free time, he told stories about the things he saw while he was staying in Khartoum, including how the northerners were a civilised people. Interestingly, at this time, people still believed that he was prophesizing an unthinkable world that they thought only existed in his imagination.

Tang Kuany eventually convinced them that he would take the youths with him to Khartoum to enable them see for themselves what he was telling the Bul Nuer people and confirmed to them that what he was talking about was real.

Knowing that the youths were not going to return sooner, he told the people that the youths were going to be enrolled in school to gain knowledge through education to become responsible people in future.

With his standing, the Bul Nuer people believed in him and willingly released their children to go with him in search of knowledge in Khartoum. Tang recruited over 500 youths, mostly boys who trekked to Khartoum to join the military as well as go to school. He pleaded with parents to donate at least two cows per home to feed the youths while on their long journey on foot to Khartoum. In December, 1955, Tang set off with the youths on foot for Khartoum through Nori-Kur, towards Kelek.

On his arrival in Kelek, he sent a telegram to Mahdiyya headquarters in Gizira Aba informing them about his arrival with the youths. Tang was told to proceed to El Obeid through Kadugli in the Nuba Mountains where they would be met by Mahdiyya revolutionaries to further arrange for their transport to Gizira Aba, the headquarters of Mahdiyya during the revolution.

Upon their arrival at the Mahdiyya headquarters, all the youths were converted to Islam and distributed to Islamic centres to study Holy Quran. After the training, some of the youths were enlisted in the army when Sudan attained independence on January 1, 1956.

However, some youths ended up living in the Sudan for good, while a few of them managed to return home, some sought refuge and became citizens in Omdurman, Sudan and never returned to Bul Nuer, South Sudan.

I was told that Tang returned to the Bul Nuer community for the second time in 1958 with the intention of recruiting more youths, but he was met with fierce resistance from the Bul Nuer politicians and Paramount Chief Monytuil Wicjang. Tang however, managed to take only a few youths from the Bul Nuer community and crossed with them to Leek and Jagei areas where he also tried in vain to lure the youths, so as to take them to Khartoum.

In Leek, area Chief Deng Jaak and Jagei, Nyaruac Kulang Ket, become Jagei prophetess after she was seized by the divinity of her father. After the death of her father Kulang Ket on June 24, 1925, the people resisted her moves.

Tang challenged Nyeruac and told her of his willingness to take her to the Mahdi in Khartoum, since her father's divinity was called Maani, meaning Mahdi. Kulang Ket borrowed the name from the Mahdi when he visited Mahdi and spent three years and only returned to Western Upper Nile when Omdurman fell to Kitchener's army of Anglo-Egyptian in September 2, 1898 -1901. Nyeruac Kulang Ket, however, ignored Tang's challenge.

The Bul Nuer Paramount Chief by then, Manytuil Wicjang, wrote a letter to Deng Jaak informing him that Tang came from Khartoum to Bul Nuer to traffic youths again for the second time. Tang unfortunately escaped arrest and went towards Kaljaak in the Leek area with a few Bul Nuer youths that he wanted to take to Khartoum.

Manytuil Wicjang told Deng Jaak to locate and arrest him and return the Bul

Nuer youths that went along with him to Kaljaak. Tang was attacked and shot on the thigh by Chief Deng Jaak's police officer at Kaljaak when he resisted an order from the Chief to release the boys whom he was taking to Khartoum.

Tang was not as famous in Leek and Jagei areas, as he was in the Bul Nuer community's dominated areas; hence he was unable to recruit youths from the two areas. Chief Manytuil conspired with Deng Jaak, Chief of Leek and Tang was arrested and sent to exile in Malakal where he served a life imprisonment until his death in 1965. His body was interred at Bam neighbourhood in Malakal.

To his close associates, including his cousin Rok Daang, Tang was not a prophet, but a very intelligent man. Rok Daang later on refused to offer sacrifices at Tang's sacred tree as others were doing.

Tang behaved like a prophet and attracted large crowd, whom he exhorted to confess their evil deeds. He suddenly took advantage of the fact that people could not understand what knowledge he acquired in Khartoum that made him to be worshipped as a spiritual leader and how he developed a plan to take their children to Khartoum. This was somehow sinister but still the Bul Nuer people believed that he was a great person whom they had no problem with trafficking youths to Khartoum – a move that was seen as successful since those who went to Khartoum later managed to educate their children and some of whom are currently working in the government of the Republic of South Sudan.

Tang's plan was to enroll the Bul Nuer youths in school while those who did not want to go to school were to be enlisted in the army and other formal employment. It is, therefore, important to remember Tang as a great and prominent person in the Bul Nuer community history since he was also the first person from the community who went to Dapany (däpäny) is a name given to the Mahdi tomb in Omdurman, where Tang Kuany discovered that Jagei prophet Kulang Ket was one of the pioneers who had also visited the Mahdi and joined the Mahdiyya revolution in 1898.

Upon his arrival in Jagei Nuer, Kulang Ket claimed that he was possessed by "Maani" which literally means Mahdi, the name he borrowed from Mahdiyya. Before his death, Tang cursed Chiefs Manytuil Wicjang and Deng Jaak and their families for mistreating him. According to people who were close to Tang, they believed that he cursed Chief Manytuil Wicjang, saying, "*Ci kuayku bi riang amäni cäng kel*," which literally means that none of his descendants would ever build a lasting wealth or riches in their lifetime.

Tang further said that Manytuil Wicjang descendants would be hated by the Bul Nuer people wherever they may be in the Bul Nuer communal land. For

Chief Deng Jaak, Tang cursed him saying, "Bi thil Kuay amäni ciang," which means in Leek land the Chief Deng Jaak would never have many descendants in the area.

The Bul Nuer people have a special sentimental connection with the people of North Sudan through the relationship that was established and cemented by Tang Kuany when he visited the Mahdiyya in 1954.

Tang is believed to have said, "my road to däpäny - Mahdi tomb, would never turn off, it would be traversed forever by the Bul Nuer generations to come, and will never come to an end". Today, Tang's Road is open from Mayom to the North of Sudan through the Nuba Mountains.

It is through this special connection he established that promoted armed groups from the Bul Nuer community to take up arms against the regime in South Sudan, a move that was highly welcomed by the successive governments in the North Sudan. It's worth noting that some of the youths that were taken to the North by Tang Kuany did not return. They have become citizens in sudan and their children are the ones working in the successive governments in the Republic of Sudan. The people from the Bul Nuer community who are residents in Sudan have been of assistance to their own brothers and sisters back in the Bul Nuer community in South Sudan.

A case in point is when Nuer rebel leader Paulino Matip rebelled against the SPLM/A in 1985. The government of Sudan gave him sophisticated weapons to use against his enemies. The northerners have also previously supported Peter Gatdet's group and Gen. Bapiny Monytuil by availing weapons to them to help them mount their offensive against the government of South Sudan. The government of Sudan gave Gen. Bapiny Monytuil 100 fighting vehicles mounted with different types of weapons.

The former President of the Republic of Sudan, Omar Hassan El Bashir, received blessings from the Bul Nuer elder Yap Tekjiek Dualdong in 1988, when El Bashir recaptured Mayom town from the SPLM/A. Yap Tekjiek Dualdong blessed him and wished him a bright future saying that he will one day rule Sudan. "My son you will be powerful and you will one day rule the Sudan."

He then handed him a great sacred spear and told him to keep it for the rest of his life as it will save him wherever he may be. El Bashir, who was a Brigadier General by then, accepted the gesture and he immediately went to Khartoum and seized power from the civilian government of Sadiq El Mahdi on June 30, 1989. This gesture according to most people is credited to the connection that existed between El Bashir and the Bul Nuer people.

In 1994, Bakuony Manytuil, the son of Paramount Chief Wicjang, at the time, approached elder Ruay Gatluak to call the Bul Nuer elders to take the children of Manytuil to the shrine or under the sacred tree of Tang Kuany known as Thar Thoah Tang Kuany to offer sacrifices for Tang to cleanse his curse off Manytuil's family.

Ruay Gatluak mobilized some Bul Nuer elders and moved to the sacred tree of Tang Kuany with Manytuil's sons and their families to offer sacrifices. As soon as they arrived and gathered around the sacred tree, elder Ruay Gatluak started invoking (Lam) in the name of Tang telling him to remove the curse from the Manytuil family. Strangely, before he could open his mouth to say a word, a swarm of bees appeared from nowhere and stung elder Ruay Gatluak's tongue. The bees also stung and dispersed the crowd who ran helter-skelter for safety, as they left behind everything they had carried, including the cows that were to be slaughtered as a sacrifice. Notwithstanding, that elder Ruay Gatluak did advise the Manytuil's sons before they left Mayom that Tang was not a spiritual leader or a god whose curse would have been cleansed through spiritual rituals.

Ruay Gatluak also explained to them that the late Tang cursed their family and that the family could have sought his consent to withdraw the curse when he was still alive.  His advice was however not listened to as the sons continued hoping that the ritual would have resolved their vexatious tragedy.

*Tang Kuany with stick in his hand in Kadungli around 1960s.*

***Thou Tang Kuany (Tree)***

**Deng Kuoth (Gatdeng)**

It is not really clear how Deng Kuoth came into being in the Bul Nuer community, but there are two conflicting versions from the elders. The first version holds that Deng Kuoth had fallen from the Sky long time ago, on a Dinka boy from Tonj in Warrap, Bahr El Ghazal region around 1886.

Deng literally means the name given to a god by Dinka people while Kuoth means (God) in Nuer, and altogether it is called Deng Kuoth which means a god called Deng, and the person seized by Deng is called Gatdeng which means son of Deng.

Therefore, the boy that was seized by Deng Kuoth wandered around in Toch between Warrap and Mayom, within the Bul Nuer community. He was found in the bush by Nyekuolä Luoy Dhuor Chuol, wife of Nhial Luom Duok who had gone to fetch firewood.

As the woman approached, the boy told her, "*Hen ci nyaŋwei*," in Dinka, which literally means "I was abandoned by my people." Unable to understand the language, she took the boy home to her husband Nhial Luom.

Even there, the boy, who could not speak the Nuer language, kept saying Nyangwei (I was abandoned). Nhial Luom and his wife concluded that his name must be Nyäwey, in Nuer iteration. They adopted the boy and called him Nyäwey Nhial Luom.

The boy grew up but had some strange behaviours that were not welcomed in the society. By the time Nhial Luom initiated him into the *nyaanä* age-set, at around 1907, his strange behaviours had begun to be seen by all following his alleged claims that he had been seized by a "god" called Deng.

He was taken home for a traditional prayer meeting to build a shrine for Deng at a place called Daŋe Lual. With time, Nyäwey started interacting with the Bul Nuer people and he became fluent in the Nuer language.

Nhial Luom gave cattle to Nyäwey to pay dowry, have his own home and establish his own family. He got married and had a son called Tutroah Nyääwiah, but unfortunately Nyäwey lacked good manners and respect amongst his peers. He abused his spiritual powers and started mistreating people because of his god. For example, he had a dispute with a man called Kuony Niap Där from (cieŋ) Dar Chung after exchanging Kuony Niëp's ox with a white heifer. Later, the white heifer became a big cow and sired calves one after the other, and Kuony Niäp Där had lots of milk.

On seeing this, Nyäwey became jealous and decided to take his cow back with all the offspring. Kuony Niëp was not happy with Nyäwey's decision and conspired with his clansmen to kill Nyäwey.

On the day they planned to do this, Tong Kuänywär went to see Nyäwey at the cattle camp and requested tobacco snuff and cow dung ash, in anticipation that he will be killed and he may not see him again.

Nyäwey gave him tobacco snuff, but already Kuony Niep had organized his men who were to ambush and kill him. Nyäwey was killed by Kuony Niep's men around 1920 at a place called Gamdhang in Mayenjur area and his body was taken and buried at Nyebitek, a high ground covered with more coconut trees in South of Ruäthnyibol.

The place was renamed Ruath Nyäweah which means Nyäwey's bush forest because he was buried there. Nyäwey was not taken to Daŋe Lual's shrine for burial because there were a lot of floods at that time of the year.

The second version of Nyahwey story holds that his mother was abducted as a little girl from the Dinka Tonj in Bahr El Ghazal region during the war between the Bul Nuer and Dinka Tonj communities on their common border at Toch.

The girl was adopted by Luoy Dhuor Chuol who named her Nyekuola Luoy

Dhuor. Luoy Dhuor later married the girl off to Nhial Luom and they gave birth to a boy who had one eye. When her mother saw that the child had one eye, she got scared and ran away to Bahr El Ghazal and Nhial Luom named the boy Nyangwei Nhial which means an abandoned person, but the name was later changed to Nyahwey Nhial.

Nyahwey Nhial grew up and was initiated into the Nyaana age set. A few years after the initiation, he began experiencing some spirits and he one day claimed that he had been seized by Deng Kuoth. He got into disagreements with his peers and they accused him of abusing his spiritual powers against his people.

He was later on killed by Kuony Niap Dar over a disagreement of a cow as explained in the first version. When Nyahwey Nhial died in 1920s, Deng divinity seized his son Tutroah Nyahweah, the same year. Tutroah fell sick and died in the 1960s and he was buried at Terkeah's shrine and the divinity seized his son Mut Tutroah Nyahweah the same year.

When Gatdeng Mut Tuoroah Nyahweah fell sick in 2018, he was taken to Juba, South Sudan and was later on transferred to Khartoum for further treatment. But when he knew that he was going to die, he told the people around him that his days were numbered and that he needed to be taken back home and be buried at Terkeah, besides his father's tomb.

Before he could be taken to Juba, the Bul elders who were close to him at the shrine advised that whenever Gatdeng was sick, he was not supposed to be taken for treatment in hospital, nor be flown in a plane.

They believed that whenever Gatdeng fell seriously ill, people should gather at the shrine to offer sacrifices, and he would heal. His aides, however, doubted his chances of survival since he was being taken to hospital against his spiritual wishes.

He later died on December 23, 2018 at Koatna, Gatdeng's shrine on his return from Khartoum and he was taken to Terkeah for burial as he had requested while still alive.

The first Gatdeng's shrine was at Danga Lual in Kuac area, but the shrine was abandoned when Northern Arab Missiriya kept attacking the Bul Nuer people in 1980s, and the shrine was moved to Terkeah where Tutroah Nyahweah was buried. From Terkeah it was moved to Koatna, the current place where it is located.

When Gatdeng (Mut Tuoroah) died, Deng seized his son Garang' Mut Tuoroah on February 22, 2019. Garang Mut is the current Gatdeng in Bul Kuac community. It is worth mentioning that Garang Mut was a Juba University student when he was seized by Deng Kuoth.

## Gatdeng spiritual powers

Deng was believed to have powers of healing the sick people, rain making, driving away cattle diseases and protecting people from being attacked by evil spirits or man-eaters. People with problems were only required to invoke his name and their problems would disappear.

He also blessed barren women with children as well as helping in settling disputes among the people. Even criminals ran to Gatdeng's shrine for repentance and forgiveness. He protected all of them and warned them against continuing with criminal activities. Gatdeng married 52 wives, 30 of which hailed from the Nuer community and 22 hailed from the Dinka community of Bahr El Ghazal.

Throughout his life, he refused any attack by his Bul Nuer people against the neighbouring Dinka, even at times when the Dinka were the first to attack. He often opted for a peaceful resolution of the issues that brought friction between the two communities. Amongst the Bul Nuer people, Gatdeng acted as the peace maker as he helped settle disputes, besides helping pay dowry for the poor people who could not afford cattle to pay dowry.

He assimilated many different people, such as the Dinka and other South Sudanese tribes to his family. Gatdeng was liked by the Bul Nuer people following his love for a peaceful neighbourliness with the neighbouring communities, especially the Dinka.

At the time of his death, he had 208 children and had accumulated a lot of wealth, mainly cattle that he was given as gifts at his shrine. His death is seen as a major blow to the Bul Nuer people and the neighbouring Dinka community as they will miss his wise counsel that kept the two communities together.

He will be remembered as a responsible, great and peace-loving spiritual leader in the Bul Nuer community.

***(Gatdeng) Mut Tuoroah in blue clothe flanked by his two wives.***

***In a pink shirt is the current Gatdeng, Garang' Mut Tuoroah before he was repossessed by Deng Kuoth.***

## The three Deeys Spiritual Leaders.

There are three Deeys in the Bul Nuer community namely Deey Dak, Deey Mayil Bangoang and Deey Gai Biey

## The 1st Deey.

The first Deey known as Deey Dak was a cuol wic, meaning a person who died in mysterious circumstances and his body could not be traced for burial. There are different forms of cuol wic deaths amongst the Bul Nuer people. These include someone who dies from a bolt of lightning and his body could not be found, or someone that was taken by a whirlwind into the sky. Amongst the Bul Nuer people, it is believed that the body of a cuol wic is taken by a god who comes as a spirit and seizes the person and later the person dies mysteriously.

The three Deeys were the three people called Deey since they died and became cuol wic or divinities in their respective areas using the names of their respective persons (Deey) who died from different mysterious causes.

The first Deey was a cuol wic from Nyang Gan Gaah. When he died, his spirit seized his longtime friend Deey Dak in Dejuul Goah around the 17th century. When Deey Dak died, the divinity seized his son Jut Deey.

When Jut Deey died, the divinity appeared and seized his brother Jany Deey. Jany Deey died, and the divinity seized Duoh Gatluak. When Duoh Gatluak died in 2010, the Deey divinity seized Bol Puok Gatluak in 2018. Deey now has become the god of Cieŋ Nyawar or Cieŋ Bol Kang in Gok area in Bul Nuer.

## The 1st Deey's Manifestation.

From time immemorial, the first Deey was believed to have been turning people into Kiil bird (marabou stork) or Kiel in Nuer language. It was believed that if a man slept with a lady during a ceremonial dance, the man would get stuck on the lady he was sleeping with. According to traditions, the man would be asked to pay dowry to the family of the lady and also offer sacrifices to Deey, so that he is freed by Deey.

## The 2nd Deey.

The second Deey known as Deey Mayil Bangoang is believed to have fallen from the sky a long time ago in Dejuul Goah and seized Bangoang Kuay around 17th century. When Bangoang Kuay died, Deey seized his son Gatkuoth Bangoang Kuay.

When Gatkuoth Bangoang Kuay died, the divinity went and seized his brother Mayil Bangoang and before Mayil Bangoang Kuay died in 2016, the divinity left Mayil and seized his brother's son Bol Gatkuoth Bangoang while Mayil was still alive and this caused a disagreement within the family of Bangoang.

Mayil Bangoang was not happy with this and called it a spiritual coup against him by his brother's son, but Bol Gatkuoth manipulated the divinity until Mayil died in 2016.

Like other Deeys, Deey Mayil Bangoang also had powers of healing the sick, driving away cattle diseases, plague, and was a rain and peace maker among his people.

**The 3rd Deey.**

The third Deey is known as Deey Gai Biey. It is believed by the Bul Nuer people that he too fell from the sky many years ago in Dejuul Goah in the Bul Nuer community, and seized Biih Ruea Geng around 18th century.

When Biih Ruea Geng died, the divinity seized his son Gai Biey in 1971, and when Gai Biey died in 2009, Deey is believed to have gone back to the sky and has not yet appeared and seized anyone up to the time I am writing this book.

Like other Deeys, Deey Gai Biey also had healing powers, power of exercising different kinds of cattle diseases including plague, rain-making and settling of disputes among his people.

Amongst the Bul Nuer, Deeys are given names of people they have seized in order to differentiate them since they are three in number and share the same name (Deey). This is why they are called Deey Mayil Bangoang, Deey Gai Biey and Deey Dak for easier identification.

**Gah- Gah Chung Loah.**

Gah- Gah Chuong Loah was a cuol wic who disappeared in the afternoon storm while collecting some dry cow dung to his byre (Luak). He seized Dador Gatdena Long around 1941, and when Dador Gatdena died in 2015, Gah -Gah Chuong Loah seized his grandson Gatluak Wey Dador, the same year.

It is said that Gah- Gah Chuong Loah seized Gatluak Wey Dador, even before Dador died, but Dador did not accept to let his divinity go to his grandson while he was still alive. The boy was chased away and he ran to his maternal uncle's home and only managed to come back after the death of his grandfather (Dador) to be in charge of the divinity.

Gah -Gah Chuong Loah or Gatkura, the nickname that was given to his god or his ox, has a lot of well-known manifestations.

## Gah -Gah Chuong Loah's Manifestations.

Whenever one defies or challenges Gah- Gah's spiritual powers, he often condemns people to the following spiritual punishments;

- He sends mosquitoes to bite someone, his/her family and cattle.
- He sends one lions and other beasts to eat or kill the victim's cattle and relatives.
- He sends one snakes wherever they will be.
- He sends a crocodile to kill one while crossing the river.
- He sends one cattle disease/plague to kill all the cattle plus other forms of punishments.

Like other gods, Gah-Gah heals people who are sick, protects cattle from different kinds of diseases, harbors and protects those who have run to his house for their crimes and settles their cases with the government authorities and warns them to stop their criminal activities.

As a rain maker, Gah- Gah ensured that his subjects received rain without thunder, made peace amongst his subjects and at times asked protagonists to drink his tobacco water to see who was the culprit or to send them to a tree full of bees to see if the bees would sting them or not.

Whoever was stung by the bees was damned as the culprit and the one who was spared was set free as an innocent person. Sometimes, he would order the two people to drink his tobacco water and whoever drank the water died immediately. If one knew that he/she was wrong, he refused to drink the tobacco water.

In most instances, people who knew that they were on the wrong, often surrendered before Gah -Gah for forgiveness. There are also other small clans and family divinities or fetishes (dayiemnä) in Bul Nuer which are not mentioned here.

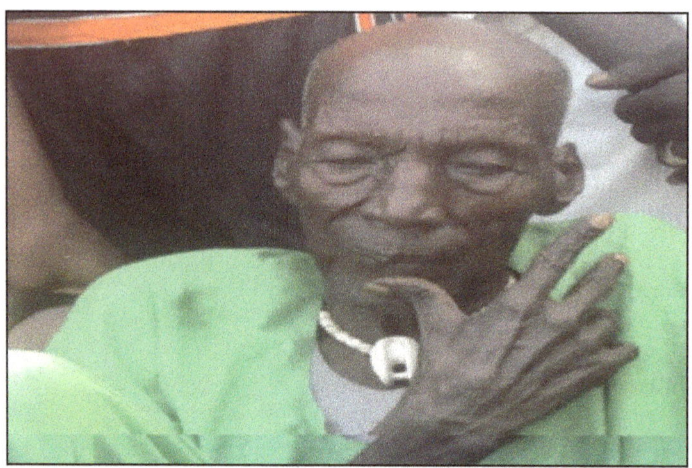

***Gah Gah Chung***

***Gah -Gah Junior, Gatluak Wey Dador, the grandson of Gatkura (2018).***

## The Wiu Nyang's Story of Conjuring Ritual

The Nyang elders believed that Wiu Nyang was brought to Nyang from Western Jikany Nuer many years ago by a man called Gaah Rem.

When Gaah became furious with his half-brother Barpuoh Rem over the castration of his bull, Barpuoh did not confess to having committed the offence.

When Gaah realized that his bull was castrated in the grazing field, he looked around for the culprit who had done that, but no one came out to own up or to volunteer information leading to finding the culprit.

Gaah was very annoyed by his people and decided to migrate to his maternal uncle's people in Jikany Nuer land. He lived in Jikany for sometimes until a man by the name Buom Dar Chuong whose son had testicle problems hinted that it could be Gaah who was behind his son's trouble since Gaah was not told who castrated his bull.

Buom Dar Chuong set off for Jikany to look for Gaah, he finally found him and pleaded with him to return to his original home and help rescue his sick son, and he promised to tell him who castrated his bull that made him migrate to his maternal uncle's place.

At first, Gaah refused to go back to his home with Buom Dar, but his maternal uncle advised him to go with him. As they were about to start their journey back to his people, Gaah was called aside by his maternal uncles ostensibly for further consultation. The uncle produced the Wiu sacred spear, broke its tip, blessed it and gave it to him and he was told to take the tip of the sacred spear to his people to protect them against any misfortune.

When Gaah arrived home with Buom Dar, a public meeting was convened and Buom Dar pointed at Barpuoh saying that he is the one who castrated Gaah's bull. Barpuoh admitted to having committed the offence before the elders and everybody was shocked since no one knew who castrated Gaah's bull. Gaah shot up and told his brother Barpuoh that he had forgiven him for what he had done to his bull but he will migrate with his family and live in a place away from Barpuoh's homestead.

On hearing this, Buom Dar gave Gaah part of his land in the current settlement of Nyang Gaat- Gaah called Bieh Nyang, leaving his brother Barpuoh in Nyang Maloah in Tam area.

The two brothers, especially Gaah, came up with a covenant between them to avoid further family conflicts in the future. Gaah told his brother Barpuoh that if one of their descendants live with both of them, he will not build the apex of his byre (Luak) high point, instead he will build a flat topped Luak called (buj) in the Nuer language.

He further added that if the two meets in the same cattle camp, a heap of cow dung (buth) will be placed in between their cattle camps to separate the camps.

This is the reason behind the division that exists between the two brothers. The two Nyang are divided into Nyang Gan-Gaah and Nyang Maloah, Nyang Gan-Gaah settles in Bieh -Nyang, while Nyang Barpuoh settles in Tam.

## Bul Nuer Age set

The Bul Nuer boys are initiated into the community when they reach ages 15-18, an age set that reveals that they are ripe to be warriors and capable of defending the community in times of invasions by the neighbouring communities. However, these days the initiation takes place at ages 13 to 15 like Lual and Thieeng. The interval between the opening and closing of the age sets vary from one age set to another.

The initiation amongst the Bul Nuer people was first carried out beginning with the Nyaana age set in 1901 and has continued to be carried out when the British started to put marks on the forehead of the Nilotic people in order to recognize them from other communities. Initially, it was not a tradition among the Nuer people to initiate their men by making such marks on their forehead. The past age set of Wandel, Ruobnä, Lielkang, Lielcuath and Kebkol were not initiated.

The British divided South Sudan into sub-colonies commanded by British administrative officers. They devised a strategy to enable them to know different communities since they found it difficult, given the similarities, to differentiate a Dinka from a Nuer. This is how they came up with various types of scarifications as a form of identity to different communities in South Sudan.

They decided to give the Nuer men at least six parallel marks across their foreheads and devise almost similar marks for some sub tribes of the Dinka in Bahr El Ghazal region, specifically in the modern-day Lake State. The Dinka Rek and Malual-Giernyang have their lines run across their head all the way to the back and instead of six marks they gave them eight cuts on the forehead.

Other District Commissioners came up with more but distinct marks for other sub tribes of the Dinka and their neighbouring communities. The table below indicates various age sets in the Bul, Leek and Jagei Nuer people who usually share the same age sets:

| S/N | Section | Age -set | Date of initiation |
|---|---|---|---|
| 1. | Bul, Leek, Jagei | Nyan (Nyaana) | 1901 |
| 2. | Bul, Leek, Jagei | Kuei (Kueth) | 1915 |
| 3. | Bul, Leek, Jagei | Chotnyala (Choatnyala) | 1926 |
| 4. | Bul, Leek, Jagei | Kur (Kuor) | 1935 |
| 5. | Bul, Leek, Jagei | Bilnyang (Bielnyangna) | 1949 |
| 6. | Bul, Leek, Jagei | Weah (Weahna) | 1963 |
| 7. | Bul, Leek, Jagei | Koy (Koayna) | 1972 |
| 8. | Bul, Leek, Jagei | Lith (Liethna) | 1986 |
| 9. | Bul, Leek, Jagei | Lual (Luaal) | 1997 |
| 10. | Bul, Leek, Jagei | Thiang (Thieeng) | 2010 |

***Note:*** Tang Kuany was a Kuëi age set. He took Kuor and Bielnyäŋnä to Khartoum. Bielnyäŋnä were still boys and were not initiated by then, but some of the boys got initiated when they came back from däpäny (Omdurman).

***A Nuer boy being initiated into manhood according to the community rites in 2017.***

# Chapter 3
# Bul Nuer Traditional Rulers (Chiefs)

It is not clear who was the first Paramount Chief of the Bul Nuer people during the time of Turko - Egyptian reign in 1840 - 1885. But some say, it was Guot Nhial Geah, while others say it was Pey Puor.

Pey Puor is well known amongst the Bul Nuer people since the time he met the white man at the bank of river Naam. It was at this time that the white man asked the people gathered to tell him the name of their Chief, but they kept quiet forcing Pey Puor to tell Bul people around him that why don't you just say we are Pey Puor's Bul Nuer, then the white man took his name and confirmed, Pey Puor as their Chief.

From that time, the myth has been that the Bul Nuer people are Bul Pey Puor but nobody confirmed him to be the chief, so it has remained that way in the Bul Nuer history as Bul Pey Puor.

Anthropologist Douglas Johnson did mention Kuom Tutdeal as the first Paramount Chief of the Bul Nuer people at the time of Turko – Egyptian reign. It is said that Guot Nhial Geah from Cieŋ Dieŋ clan was selected by the government to be the Chief of the Bul people, at the time, but his reign did not last since he relinquished his Chieftaincy in favor of his brother's son Tekjiek Dualdong Nen who went on to rule the Bul people for 19 years.

After ruling for 19 years, Tekjiek Dualdong became an old man who could not give fair judgement on civil cases against his subjects. The Chieftaincy was therefore given to Manytuil Wicjang Wuor in 1937 and he ruled the Bul Nuer people for 32 years.

In 1969, Manytuil Wicjang was defeated by Diu Koang Kueth in an election that was supervised by the government officials. Diu Koang became the Chief for the Bul Nuer people, but he ruled only for 4 years and was killed by a man called Nyamile in 1973, in a mysterious circumstance. Manytuil Wicjang was again installed as Paramount Chief of the Bul Nuer people the same year to replace Diu Koang.

In 1980, Manytuil Wicjang was again defeated by Luk Gatluak Thon, his court clerk in another election that was also supervised by government officials. After the second defeat, Chief Manytuil Wicjang retired to his rural home and he later died in 1985.

Luk Gatluak Thon became the first Chief of the Bul Nuer people who could read and write in both Arabic and English languages with ease. He was, however, killed by Paulino Matip's militia forces on October 18, 1987 in Kadugli, Nuba Mountains.

Since then, no one was elected to replace him as this was the time when the SPLM/A soldiers arrived in Western Upper Nile region. The table below shows a list of Paramount Chiefs who ruled the Bul Nuer people starting from the time of the Turko - Egyptian condominium, down to the coming of the SPM/A and subsequent independence of the Republic of South Sudan.

| S/N | Paramount Chief | Section or clan | From | To |
|---|---|---|---|---|
| 1. | Kuom Tutdeal | Cieŋ Chuol | 1901 | 1915 |
| 2. | Guot Nhial Geah | Cieŋ Dieng | 1915 | 1918 |
| 3. | Tekjiek Dualdong Nen | Cieŋ Dieng | 1918 | 1937 |
| 4. | Manytuil Wicjang Wuor | Nyang Barpuoh | 1937 | 1969 |
| 5. | Diu Koang Kueth | Cieŋ Reel | 1969 | 1973 |
| 6. | Machar Mayiel Thonok | Nyang Barpuoh | 1973 | 1979 |
| 7. | Manytuil Wicjang Wuor | Nyang Barpuoh | 1979 | 1980 |
| 8. | Luk Gatluak Thon | Cieŋ Nyaloah | 1980 | 1984 |

When the Bul Nuer people came under the control of the SPLM/A, in 1984, Bul was divided into two Chieftaincies or chiefdoms namely Kuac and Gok. The following Head Chiefs were either elected or appointed to rule;

- Patai Tut Nyal, head Chief for Gok area
- Kuol Nguon Kuer, head Chief for Kuac area

Gok Chieftaincy was later divided into two major sections and had chiefs appointed to manage the areas. These were as follows;

- Patai Tut Nyal, head Chief for Cieŋ Chuol
- Nyal Yaka Ruot, head Chief for Cieŋ Pareng

Further, Kuac Chieftaincy was also divided into two major sections with the following elected or appointed as administrators; Deng Choap Nyuot, head Chief for two Nyang (Nyang Gan-Gah and Nyang Barpuoh). Malual Turoah Nyahweah, head Chief for Gaat Buol. In 2001, The Bul Nuer was divided into 10 Chieftaincies as indicated in the tables below.

**Kuac chieftaincies**

| S/N | Head Chief | Section or clan | HQS |
|---|---|---|---|
| 1. | Madut Gatluak Kerekna | Nyang Gan - Gah | Bieh |
| 2. | Char Joak Limnyien | Cieŋ Dar | Kueryiek |
| 3. | Malith Guol Nor | Cieŋ Duoh | Ruathnyibol |
| 4. | Wecnyang Puoc Lok | Nyang Barpuoh | Tam |
| 5. | Gatduel Wuor Jal | Chambuol | Ngop |

## The Kuac Subsections

## Clan (cieŋ) Nyang Gan-Gaah Rem Sub-sections

| S/N | Subsection | Settlement (locality) | Lineage |
|---|---|---|---|
| 1. | Jääh | Jiey Muk | Cieŋ Juoma |
| 2. | Cieŋ Gëëh | Tuoc loka | Cieŋ Juoma |
| 3. | Cieŋ Toang | Machar | Cieŋ Kuot |
| 4. | Cieŋ Guul | Jiathchuol | Cieŋ Kuot |
| 5. | Cieŋ Bidit | Jualding | Cieŋ Kuot |
| 6. | Cieŋ Juol | Nor Chuor | Cieŋ Kuot |
| 7. | Cieŋ Degool | Nor Gai | Cieŋ Kuot |
| 8. | Cieŋ Kuoy | Tong Tuol | Cieŋ Kuot |
| 9. | Cieŋ Thon | | Cieŋ Kuot |

**Note**: - The above are the two families of Juom Gakä and Kuot Gakä (sons of Rëm).

## Clan (Cieŋ) Dar Chuong Buol Sub sections

| SS/N | Sub -section | Settlement (locality) | HQS |
|---|---|---|---|
| 1. | Cieŋ Lil | Nyediet | |
| 2. | Cieŋ Naam | Nor Thiep | |
| 3. | Cieŋ Chung Nyal | Kuel | |
| 4. | Cieŋ Chuom | Kueryiek | |
| 5. | Cieŋ Deang | Wath Chakuen | |
| 6. | Cieŋ Gieh | Wancieh Cieh | |
| 7. | Cieŋ Niep | Lel Cieng Dar | |
| 8. | Cieŋ Dhien | Kuoy | |

## Clan (Cieŋ) Duoh Chuong Buol Sub sections

| SS/N | Sub -section | Settlement (locality) |
|---|---|---|
| 1. | Cieŋ Lam | Koaang |
| 2. | Cieŋ Duoh | Ruathnyibol |
| 3. | Cieŋ Chuol | Nyoat |
| 4. | Cieŋ Jurbeak | Ruathdong |

## Clan (Cieŋ) Nyang Barpuoh Rem sub sections

| SS/N | Sub -section | Settlement (locality) | HQS |
|---|---|---|---|
| 1. | Cieŋ Geng Geeng | Rupliethna | |
| 2. | Cieŋ Dien | Lony | |
| 3. | Cieŋ Mandiing | Keay | |
| 4. | Cieŋ Puol | Tuoc Bora | |
| 5. | Cieŋ Ker | Kai Kang | |
| 6. | Cieŋ Yikoah | Nora Kur | |
| 7. | Cieŋ Nyakiech | Nora Kur | |
| 8. | Cieŋ Wuor | Nora Kur | |
| 9. | Cieŋ Mathou | Mabil | |
| 10. | Cieŋ Weat | | |
| 11. | Cieŋ Thieh | Nyoat/Nyiker | |
| 12 | Cieŋ Buah | Pul-Puob | |

## Clan (Cieŋ) Cham Buol Sub sections

| SS/N | Sub -section | Settlement (locality) | HQS |
|---|---|---|---|
| 1. | Cieŋ Teny | Juom | |
| 2. | Cieŋ Nyakoh | Chotjiok | |
| 3. | Cieŋ Diing | Rubguey | |
| 4. | Cieŋ Kaang | Mangaar | |

## Gok Chieftaincies

| SS/N | Head Chief | Section | HQS |
|---|---|---|---|
| 1. | Patai Tut Nyal | Cieŋ Nyawar | Mankien |
| 2. | Nyal Yaka Ruot | Cieŋ Dieng | Wangkei |
| 3. | Kamwini Gatduel Teny | Cieŋ Pareng | Thargena |
| 4. | Gagah Thiey Thong | Cieŋ Nyaloah | Riaak |
| 5. | Toang Ruea wic | Cieŋ Chuol | Wangbuor |

## The Gok sub sections
## Clan (Cieŋ) Nyawar sub sections

| SS/N | Sub section | Settlement (locality) | HQS |
|---|---|---|---|
| 1. | Cieŋ Bol Kang | Yidit | |
| 2. | Cieŋ Buor Kang | Puor | |
| 3. | Cieŋ Yok Kang | Wicthiep | |
| 4. | Cieŋ Guah Kang | Geat Jaah | |
| 5. | Cieŋ Nyejal Yang | Deng Bou | |

## Clan (Cieŋ) Ding sub sections

| S/N | Subsection | Settlement (locality) | HQS |
|---|---|---|---|
| 1. | Gaat Ken | Dhulek | |
| 2. | Cieŋ Biliu (Yuot) | Paluang | |
| 3. | Cieŋ Nhial Geah | Burjik | |
| 4. | Cieŋ Chol | Kuerbona | |
| 5. | Cieŋ Nyediang Wuut | Buor Buor | |

## Cieng (Clan) Pareng Sub sections

| S/N | Subsection | Settlement | HQS |
|---|---|---|---|
| 1. | Cieŋ Gai | Wicruob | Cieŋ Ruea Deng |
| 2. | Cieŋ Kuciang | Thargena | |
| 3. | Cieŋ Kuoy | Nyingar | |
| 4. | Cieŋ Duoth | Koc Puow | |
| 5. | Cieŋ Mok | Matni Bul | |

## Clan (Cieŋ) Nyaloah Sub sections

| S/N | Subsection | Settlement (locality) | HQS |
|---|---|---|---|
| 1. | Cieŋ Nyewaar | Lingiera | |
| 2. | Cieŋ Kuoth | Kualkuony | |
| 3. | Cieŋ Dhuong | Chotchara | |
| 4. | Cieŋ Roah | Ngoany | |

## Clan (Cieŋ) Chuol Sub sections

| S/N | Subsection | Settlement (locality) | HQS |
|---|---|---|---|
| 1. | Cieŋ Juear | Thar Thou | Gatkuany |
| 2. | Cieŋ Lam | Nor Riah | |
| 3. | Cieŋ Nyin Yaar | Chuothdiir | |
| 4. | Cieŋ Cien | Keay cienglian | |
| 5. | Luaal | Kuergan Gaah | |
| 6. | Cieŋ Chambeal | Thar Ruath Ter | |

## Marriage amongst Bul Nuer

Whenever a young man wanted to marry amongst the Bul Nuer community, they were expected to give 30 to 35 herds of cattle as bride price in appreciating the parents and family of the would-be wife.

However, traditionally, one may even pay less than that, depending on the negotiations leading to the official engagement, especially those negotiating on behalf of the man marrying.

In the recent times, the bride price has drastically increased based on individual's interest. This habit has become a common trend more so after the SPLM/A began to establish its administration in the areas under its control and subsequent independence of the Republic of South Sudan in 2011.

It is a known fact that the Bul Nuer people's traditional marriage has been commercialized in recent times, especially by people who have amassed wealth after stealing livestock from innocent people.

They steal the cattle and rush to pay dowry and get married so as to avoid being caught by the livestock owners. This weird trend is attributed to the abrupt increase of the bride price in the Bul Nuer people and South Sudan in general.

In the Nuer marriage, a dowry of a bride is divided among all the family, relatives and friends by shares as explained in the tables below:

## Paying dowry to in-laws

### Pëk Gualëën Guande (share to the side of a bride's paternal step-uncle)

| S/N | Description of cows | Number of cows | Remarks |
|---|---|---|---|
| 1. | Yaŋ Gualëën guande kene dowde | 02 | |
| 2. | Thäk Gualëën guande | 01 | |
| 3. | Bäär Thuom | 01 | |
| 4. | Dooŋ | 01 | |
| 5. | Waay | 01 | |
| 6. | Waŋnëën guande kene Chopde | 02 | Sometimes |
| 7. | Grand Total | 08 | |

### Pëk Gualëën Mande (share to the side of a bride's paternal uncle)

| S/N | Description of cows | Number of cows | Remarks |
|---|---|---|---|
| 1. | Puaŋ kene Thäkde | 02 | |
| 2. | Gualëën mande kene dowde | 02 | |
| 3. | Waŋnën mande kene Chopde | 02 | sometimes |
| 4. | Grand Total | 06 | |

### Pëk Guan Nyaal (Share to the side of a bride's father)

| S/N | Description of cows | Number of cows | Remarks |
|---|---|---|---|
| 1. | Yaŋ guande kene dowde | 02 | |
| 2. | Yaŋ Kuoth guande | 01 | |
| 3. | Thäk guande | 01 | |
| 4. | Yaŋ Jiey | 01 | |
| 5. | Yaŋ Mäthä | 01 | |
| 6. | Yaŋ Bilä | 01 | |
| 7. | Yaŋ Tuyä hok | 01 | newly created |
| 8. | Hok Galaam (pen cows) | 05 | newly created |
| 9. | **Grand Total** | **13** | |

## Pëk Man Nyaal (share to the side of a bride's mother)

| S/N | Description of cows | Number of cows | Remarks |
|---|---|---|---|
| 1. | Yaŋ mande kene dowde | 02 | |
| 2. | Yaŋ Kuoth mande | 01 | |
| 3. | Yaŋ ditä | 01 | |
| 4. | Thäk daman Nyaal | 01 | |
| 5. | Yaŋ Kuoth Doar | 01 | |
| 6. | Yaŋ bokä | 01 | Newly created |
| 7. | **Grand Total** | **07** | |

## Pëk Näärä

## Näär Guande (share to the side of a bride's maternal step-uncle)

| S/N | Description of cows | Number of cows | Remarks |
|---|---|---|---|
| 1. | Näär guande kene dowde | 02 | |
| 2. | Waŋnën guande kene chopde | 02 | Sometimes |
| 3. | Dooŋ | 01 | |
| 4. | **Grand Total** | **05** | |

## Näär Mande (Share to the side of a bride's maternal uncle)

| S/N | Description of cows | Number of cows | Remarks |
|---|---|---|---|
| 1. | Puaŋ kene Thäkde | 02 | |
| 2. | Näär mande kene dowde | 02 | |
| 3. | Waŋnën mande kene chopde | 02 | Sometimes |
| 4. | **Grand Total** | **06** | |

## Summary of the bride price

| S/N | Pëk (Share) | Number of cows | Remarks |
|---|---|---|---|
| 1. | Gualëën guande | 08 | |
| 2. | Gualëën mande | 06 | |
| 3. | Guan nyaal | 13 | |
| 4. | Man nyaal | 07 | |
| 5. | Näär nyaal | 11 | |
| 6. | **Grand Total** | **45** | |

1

*Pek (Side or share), Guan (Father), Man (Mother), Gualen (Paternal uncle), Nyal or Kaw (girl or bride), Naar (Maternal uncle). Gualen Guande (Paternal step -uncle), Gualen Mande (Paternal Uncle), Guan Nyaal (Father of the Girl or Bride), Man Nyaal (Mother of the girl or Bride), Naar Guande (Maternal step -uncle), Naar Mande (Maternal Uncle).*

# Chapter 4

## Bul Nuer Political and military leaders

**Charles Kuot Chatiem**

Charles Kuot Chatiem was a prominent politician from Bul Nuer, Nyang-Gan-Gaah. He worked as the Minister of Decentralization in South Sudan regional government in 1981, and was elected as Member of Parliament in Juba regional government. He was appointed District Commissioner of Bentiu in 1984 when Bentiu was promoted to the level of the district.

He was captured by the SPLM/A forces under the direct command of Capt. Bateah Wagah in December 1984, at Tong village. Charles Kuot was taken to Bilpam by order of the SPLM/A chairman Dr John Garang' De-Mabor. He was assigned to work with the humanitarian relief organizations and transferred to Yirol, in Bahr El Ghazal, where he was killed in 1991, during the split of the SPLM/A.

*Luis Keah Maduot, Minister of Physical infrastructure and urban development.*

## Luis Keah Maduot

Luis Keah Maduot was a prominent politician from Bul – Nuer, Nyang-Gan-Gah. He worked in several institutions in the old Sudan as government official. He worked for the Sudan Council of Churches (SCC), he was appointed to the Sudan national assembly during Khartoum Peace Agreement in 1997. He was appointed as Minister of Physical Infrasture and Urban Development in Unity State under the governmorship of Taban Deng Gai, by the time he was killed on 11, July, 1999, by militia forces of Gen. Paulino Matip Nhial in Bentiu town on political dubious.

*Col. Martin Machot Deng died while still serving as the SPLM Chief Whip at the Unity State Legislative Assembly.*

## Col. Martin Machot Deng

Col. Martin Machot Deng is from Bul – Nuer (Nyang-Barpuoh), he was born around 1968, at Nyiker in Malou - Mayom County, Unity State. He obtained his Sudan Secondary School Certificate in (1990–1992), at Imatong Secondary School. He was given a partial scholarship to study law in India, but, unfortunately, he did not manage to get the required fees for his travel to India. Then, he enrolled at Juba University in first year in 2012, to study political science, but was interrupted by the crisis of 2013. He joined the SPLM/A in 1984, but later he defected along with Gen. Paulino Matip when Matip broke away from the SPLM/A in 1985, and formed his own Anya Nya II armed group. He was trained as radio operator in Paulino Matip group in 1992.

He served as field officer with the Sudan Relief Rehabilitation Commission (SRRC) based in Lokichogio – Kenya (popularly known as Loki in South Sudan) in (1997–1999). He defected with Gen. Peter Gatdet Yaka from the South Sudan United movement/Army (SSUM/A) back to the SPLM/A in 1999, where he served three times as commissioner of Mayom County from (2000–2003), (2005–2008), and (2011–2012) respectively. He had also served briefly as minister of social welfare in former Unity State from (2010 - 2011). He was serving as the SPLM chief whip in the Unity State legislative assembly until his ultimate demise. Col. Machot's car was ambushed and killed in mysterious circumstances at Biel in Rubkotna County on December 20, 2013, and he was later buried in Nhialdiu town even though investigation leading to his death were not complete yet. People say, the Governor of Unity State, honorable Dr Joseph Manytuil was behind his death.

*Tut Keaw Gatluak, Presidential advisor.*

## Tut Keaw Gatluak

Tut Keaw Gatluak is from Bul - Nuer, Cieng Lian section. He was a young boy in Mayom town in 1985, from there he was taken by Brig. Omar Hassan El Bashir the former President of the Republic of the Sudan, when Omar was the Mayom area commander of the Sudan armed forces fighting the SPLM/A. Tut became friend with Omar El Bashir, who later asked him to work for him in the Sudanese armed Forces Barrack in Mayom where he worked for two years.

When Mayom was captured by the SPLA in 1987, Tut Keaw went with El Bashir to North Sudan (Khartoum) and continued to work for him there until El Bashir took power on June 30, 1989 and assigned Tut Keaw to be the translator for Paulino Matip as well as monitoring activities of Paulino Matip and report them directly to him. El Bashir later ensured that Tut Keaw got converted to

Islam. In the referendum that gave birth to the independence of South Sudan, Tut did not vote for the separation. He was against the separation of the South Sudan from the rest of the Sudan because he believed in a united Sudan. Tut Keaw did not go to school at his young age because he was engaged by El Bashir and therefore had no time for formal learning.

**Dr Joseph Nguen Monytuil**

Dr Joseph Nguen Monytuil Wicjang comes from Bul-Nuer, Nyang- Bar-puoh section, his father Manytuil Wicjang was the Paramount Chief of Bul –Nuer from 1937 – 1969 and again from 1979 – 1980. Dr Joseph Monytuil is not a medical doctor by profession, but he is a medical assistant.

*Dr Joseph Nguen Manytuil Governor of North Liech State.*

He was taken to the National Service by Sudan Armed Forces so that after training, he could upgrade his diploma in order to be a medical doctor, but unfortunately, he did not achieve that because when Paulino Matip was diagnosed with diabetes and hypertension, he was assigned to look after Paulino Matip as his personal medical assistant in order to take care of his medical needs and to inject Paulino Matip all the time as prescribed by the doctor.

So, Joseph Nguen did not make it to Juba where he was set to fight the rebels along with all the students conscripted that year to be in the field for three years, after which they should go to university to pursue their further studies. Dr Joseph Nguen Manytuil became Paulino Matip's Personal medical personnel and at the same time he was promoted to the rank of a commander in Paulino Matip Militia command. This was how Joseph Monytuil found his way to be with Paulino Matip militia command.

In 2003, he was appointed Governor of Unity State. When Paulino Matip decided to join the government of South Sudan in 2007, Tut Keaw refused to come with Paulino Matip, only Dr Joseph Monytuil came to Juba with Paulino Matip. Joseph Monytuil was appointed as minister of health in the government of the South Sudan and was removed later and assigned as presidential advisor and finally appointed as the Governor of former Unity State.

Tut Keaw and Gen. Bapiny Monytuil the brother of Joseph Nguen Monytuil joined the government of South Sudan in 2013, and Tut was appointed as Presidential National Security Advisor. Tut and Joseph Nguen Monytuil fell out with Gen. Bapiny Monytuil in 2016, and Bapiny fled the country and formed his own movement called South Sudan Liberation Movement/Army (SSLM/A). They accused Gen. Bapiny of rejecting the creation of controversial 28 states that were decreed by the President of the Republic of South Sudan, Salva Kiir Mayardit. Gen. Bapiny Monytuil along with other rebel groups signed the revitalized peace agreement on September 12, 2019, and came to Juba, and reconciled with Tut Keaw and Joseph Nguen in Khartoum.

*James Liyliy Kuol*

**James Liyliy Kuol**

James Liyly Kuol hails from Bul –Nuer in Cieng Pareng section. He worked as an official in the old Sudan in the regional government's institutions. He joined the SPLM/A in 1983. He was commissioned as a Lieutenant in the SPLM/A, and commanded a Battalion in western Upper Nile in 1988. He was appointed commissioner of Mayom County in (2003 –2005. James Liyliy Kuol has been elected as chairman of Bul community, the position he is holding to date.

*Sultan Kong-Kong Bol*

## Sultan Kong-Kong Bol

Sultan Kong-Kong Bol, was deputy head chief to Chief Luk Gatluak. Sultan Kong-Kong was appointed as a commissioner of Mayom County in 1994 and later on as a Minister of Gender and Social Welfare in Unity State in 1997.

In 2000, he was appointed as Minister of Finance in Unity State under the governorship of John Dor Majok. In 2003, he was appointed Advisor for political affairs in Unity State under the governorship of Dr Joseph Nguen Monytuil.

In 2005, he was appointed Minister of Gender and Social Welfare and at the same time appointed as Deputy Governor of Unity State under the Governorship of Taban Deng Gai. In 2010 he was appointed commissioner of Mayom County for the second time and in the same year he was appointed Presidential Advisor for peace and border demarcation. In 2011, Sultan Kong-Kong Bol was appointed as a member of the council of states based in Juba, a position he is currently holding as I write this book.

*Gen. Paulino Matip Nhial SPLA Deputy Commander – in- Chief*

## Gen. Paulino Matip Nhial

Gen. Paulino Matip Nhial is from Bul- Nuer Cieng Reel section. He was a community Police man in the court of Chief Francis Nyir Gatluak in the old Sudan. He joined the Anya-Nya-II at Bilpam in 1975 under the command of Gordon Koang Chuol. He was promoted to the rank of 1st Lt in the Anya Nya II command in 1978.

When the Anya Nya II was defeated in Bilpam battle by the SPLM/A in 1983, the Anya Nya II moved to the South Sudan country side under the command of Commander Akuot Atem, deputized by Gai Tut Yang. When Akuot Atem and Gai Tut were killed in 1984, William Abdallah Chuol took over the command of the Anya Nya II. Paulino Matip was arrested by William Abdallah Chuol Deng. He was accused of persuading Bentiu sons to desert with him to Bentiu. He escaped from jail with David Gatluak Domai and Michael Kel Gatwech and on their way to Bentiu, they met with the deserters of Tiger and Tumsah battalions in Laak area under command of Sergeant Gatbel Rolnyang Kai. The deserters of Tiger and Tumsah appointed Paulino Matip as their commander and proceeded to western Upper Nile with Paulino Matip.

When they arrived in Western Upper Nile (Bentiu), they were welcomed by the Anya Nya II forces that were already operating in western Upper Nile, at the time under the command of Paul Thong Ruac deputized by Robert Ruay Kuol Jal. Paulino Matip Nhial was selected by the Anya Nya II camps to be their leader.

When Major Paul Dor Lampuar came to Western Upper Nile in 1985, he integrated Paulino Matip and his Anya Nya II forces into the SPLM/A with the rank of a Captain and assigned Paulino Matip as his deputy and commander of Petrol Battalion at the same time.

Paulino Matip fell out with Paul Dor Lampuar and formed his own Anya Nya II command in Western Upper Nile in 1985 and he reported his defection to William Abdallah Chuol. In 1988, Paulino Matip became the leader of the whole Anya-Nya -II command in Western and Eastern Upper Nile when Gordon Koang Chuol joined the SPLM/A, on January 25,988.

Gen. Paulino Matip was appointed Chief of Staff of SSDF by Riek Machar during Khartoum Peace Agreement that was signed in 1997. He joined the government of South Sudan in 2007, and appointed Deputy Commander in Chief of the SPLA, the position he held until he died on August 22, 2012 in Karen, Hospital, Kenya after a short illness with diabetes complication.

*Gen. Peter Gatdet Yaka, Chairman and commander - in - chief of SSUM/A, and chairman of (SSOA).*

## Gen. Peter Gatdet Yaka

Gen. Peter Gatdet Yaka, was first trained in the old Sudan in what was called Civil Defense Police. He was taken to war in Iraq in 1982, when Sudan was supporting Iraq in the war against Syria. When he returned from Iraq in 1983, he worked briefly as the bodyguard of Bentiu District Commissioner, Charles Kuot Chatiem. He joined the SPLM/A in 1984 and he was deployed at the headquarters of the chairman and Commander - in - Chief of the SPLM/A, John Garang' De-Mabior.

In 1991, when SPLM/A had split into two factions of (Nasir and Torit), Peter Gatdet was arrested in Kapoeta and accused of attempting to defect to Nasir faction, and in 1992, he escaped from jail in Kapoeta and reported himself to Nasir faction in Waat area where he met Riek Machar and got arrested too with charges of being sent from Torit faction to assassinate Riek Machar, but he was released later and redeployed to command a task force that was sent to Eastern Equatoria to liberate it from the SPLM/A Torit faction.

In 1998, he defected from the South Sudan Independent Movement/Army (SSIM/A), a new name created for (SPLM/A Nasir faction) and he joined the South Sudan United Movement/Army (SSUM/A), the movement formed by Gen. Paulino Matip Nhial when he fell out with Riek Machar in 1998. On September 5, 1999, Gatdet defected from the SSUM/A to the SPLM/A with a large force leaving Gen. Paulino Matip with a small force in Bentiu town. It was a big blow to Gen. Paulino Matip. In 2002, Gatdet fell out with subordinate commanders and defected from the SPLM/A back to SSUM/A under Gen. Paulino Matip. He was welcomed back by Gen. Paulino Matip and appointed him as operations officer for the SSUM/A. In 2003, Gatdet broke away from SSUM/A, and formed his own armed group stationed at Wangkei alongside the Sudan Armed Forces Garrison. In 2004, He briefly abandoned his armed group and joined the SPLM/A, and in 2005, he defected again from the SPLM/A to SSUM/A under Gen. Paulino Matip, he was also welcomed back to the SSUM/A.

In 2006, he joined the government of South Sudan under Juba declaration with Gen. Paulino Matip. He was tasked to integrate the forces of SSUM/A into the SPLA and in 2008, he was deployed as Deputy Commander of the SPLA 7th Infantry division based in Shilluk Kingdom.

In 2009, he was redeployed as Commander of the SPLA Air defence unit and in 2010, he was redeployed as Deputy Commander of the SPLA 3rd Infantry division, Peter Gatdet defected in the same year from the government of South Sudan to Khartoum and formed his own armed group under the same name of SSUM/A, the faction abandoned by Gen. Paulino Matip when Gen. Paulino Matip joined the government of South Sudan. He was joined by Gen. Bapiny Manytuil and Gen. James Gai Yoay and he became their leader in SSUM/A.

In 2011, Gatdet defected from SSUM/A, back to the government of South Sudan. He was deployed as the commander of Jonglei disarmament forces fighting Yau-Yau militias, and after disarmament he was redeployed as the commander of the SPLA 8th Infantry division in former Jonglei State. On December 15, 2013, when war broke out in Juba between forces loyal to President Salva Kiir

Mayardit and Riek Machar Teny, Gatdet declared his allegiance to Riek Machar and captured division 8th HQS and Bor town. In 2015, Gatdet defected from the SPLM/A- IO, and formed his own armed group under the same name of his previous movement (SSUM/A). In 2018, Gatdet signed the revitalized peace agreement with the government of South Sudan under the umbrella of South Sudan Opposition Alliance (SSOA) along with other opposition groups including the SPLM/A-IO. Gen. Peter Gatdet elected as the chairman of the SSOA in an election held by SSOA groups after every 6 months. Gatdet became the chairman of the SSOA, until his demise on April 15, 2019. His position has been retained by his deputy his brother-in-law Gen. Diney Chagor.

**Gen. James Gatduel Gatluak**

## Gen. James Gatduel Gatluak

Gen. James Gatduel Gatluak comes from Bul Nuer (Cieng-Chol), he joined the Anya Nya II at Bilpam in 1975, and left Bilpam for Western Upper Nile in 1982, and captured Mankien Police Station on May 30, 1982. He joined camp with Sudan army X- soldiers who mutinied from Sudan Army Garrisons of Wangkei, Abiemnom, Bentiu and Mayom and together formed the Anya Nya II of Western Upper Nile on March 15, 1983, under the leadership of Paul Thong Ruac and Robert Ruac Kuol Jal. James Gatduel joined the SPLM/A in 1985, when Major Paul Dor Lampuar came to Western Upper Nile. He commanded several units during the SPLA in the bush time. After the comprehensive peace agreement, he was deployed as Commander of the SPLA 5th Infantry division from 2008 – 2009 and redeployed to the SPLA 4th Infantry division from 2010 – 2013.

He was transferred to the reserve list in 2013, and shortly reinstated in the SPLA active list during the crisis of 2013. Gen. Gatduel was transferred from the SPLA active list to the South Sudan National Police Service and assigned as the Assistant Inspector General of Police (IGP) for Social Welfare, a position he is holding to date.

***Gen. Bapiny Manytuil Wicjang Chairman and commander -in -Chief of the SSLM/A***

## Gen. Bapiny Manytuil Wicjang

Wicjang comes from Bul- Nuer in Nyang Barpuoh section. He joined the SPLM/A in 1983, and trained as artillery gunner. He formed his own militia group called South Sudan Liberation Movement/Army (SSLM/A) in 2003. He joined the government of South Sudan in 2013 and defected again in 2016 and formed his own militia group again under the same name. He signed the revitalised peace agreement with the government of South Sudan under the umbrella of other armed groups known as South Sudan Opposition Alliance (SSOA).

*Gen. Michael Chiangjiek Gey*

## Gen. Michael Chiangjiek Gey

Gen. Michael Chiangjiek Gey hails from Bul Nuer Cieng Pareng section or clan. He joined the SPLM/A in 1984, and trained with the SPLA Muormuor division, Tuek-Tuek Battalion. He specialized in artillery unit. After his graduation, he was deployed in Akobo operations. He was recalled thereafter to attend shield - 4 Cadet in 1986, and on his graduation, he was deployed to Nuba mountains with Volcano battalion in 1987.

Michael Chiangjiek held several positions and served in many fronts during the SPLA liberation struggles. When the Comprehensive Peace Agreement (CPA) was signed, Michael Chiangjiek was deployed in Khartoum as National Security Officer and then, transferred to Juba as head of National Security for Central Equatoria in 2010 - 2011. Gen. Michael Chiangjiek served in Unity State as security advisor, then as deputy Governor of Unity State in 2011 - 2013,

The position he held until crisis of South Sudan in 2013, when he joined the SPLM/A – IO, and he was assigned as deputy Chief of Staff for Logistics in the SPLM/A –IO. In 2015, when peace agreement was signed between the government of South Sudan and the SPLM/A – IO, Dr Riek Machar was re - installed as the first Vice President of the Republic of South Sudan, but the peace agreement did not hold as the forces loyal to President Kiir and first Vice President Riek Machar clashed at J-1. Riek was dislodged out of Juba and fled to Congo border – where he was picked up by the UN helicopters on humanitarian grounds.

Gen. Taban Deng and Gen. Michael Chiangjiek remained behind saving the country from going back to war. Taban was appointed to replace Riek Machar as first Vice President and Gen. Michael Chiangjiek was appointed as Minister of Interior. When Revitalized Peace Agreement was signed in 2018, Dr Riek returned to his position as the first Vice President in Juba, while Gen. Taban Deng was appointed Vice President in the government of Revitalized Transitional Government of National Unity (RTGONU). Gen. Michael Chiangjiek has been appointed as Minister of Land and Housing – a position he was holding at the time I was writing this book.

# Part II: Liberation Struggle and Post -Independence

## Chapter 5:
## The Sudan's first civil war

*The brief history of the Anya Nya I*

The Anya Nya, was a guerrilla name from a Madi word which means a snake poison (venom), which kills human being slowly. Monani Alison Magaya says that the Anya Nya I war was the first civil war in the Sudan, which was sparked by an order from the Sudan government to transfer all Southern soldiers of the Equatoria corps from the South to the North Sudan and be replaced by the northern forces, and the rumors that the southern forces would be disarmed by force before they could be moved to the north.

Another situation was caused by the shooting of the demonstrators of the textile workers of Nzara in Yambio, which also angered the southern soldiers that were deployed in the area. The situation remained tense between the northern and southern forces, until August 18, 1955, the mutiny broke out in Torit garrison, the headquarters of the Equatoria corps, and spread to all other Southern regions. Even though it was not properly coordinated, southern mutineers in Torit started killing the northern officers, administrators, merchants and their families. They also killed some southerners who were accused of being the collaborators who were cooperating with the northerners against the southerners. The remaining northern survivors ran and took refuge with the missionaries in the churches.

The Southern mutineers and their families moved to the Uganda - Sudan border to settle their families in the refugee camps and would come back to fight the northern soldiers. The attempts by the British and Sudan governments to restore order in Torit and other parts of South Sudan failed. The mutineers who were arrested by the northerners were summarily executed in Torit. The army carried out revenge killings or retaliations on innocent civilians around the area, and this urged more southerners to join the rebellion.

On January 1, 1956, the British government granted formal independence to Sudan, after Southern Politicians were persuaded by the British government to go with the northerners with the assurance that a federal constitution would be given serious consideration thereafter. The Sudan became independent with more issues not resolved at all, and to that extent, the parliament dissolved the constitution in 1958, instead of allowing it to take a decision for the federalism. The referendum for the South Sudan that was supposed to take place was cancelled in 1982, instead, the people of South Sudan to register their opposition to subdivision of Southern region. There was disagreement over the drafting of the permanent constitution of the Sudan by British experts on the question whether the Sudan would be a federal or a unitary state or should have a secular or an Islamic constitution. Southern politicians supported federalism in order to save South Sudan from being controlled by the dominated northern central government, while northerners feared that, and they further said that this federalism may lead to the separation of South Sudan from the rest of the Sudan in the near future.

Southerners did not want to be Islamized and Arabized and the policy of this Islamization and Arabization was the main cause of armed struggle in the South Sudan during Ibrahim Abboud tenure. Many Southerners were encouraged to be converted to Islam especially the students.

In 1964, the Christian missionaries were blocked and expelled from the South Sudan and military campaign was stepped up to hunt down the Anya Nya soldiers who kept hiding in the bushes because they did not have the capacity and support to fight. The army resorted to burning villages and accused the villagers of harbouring rebels. Such repressive campaigns targeted Southern officials and this encouraged many educated Southerners to remain opposing the government. Many civilians were arrested and tortured and this sparked more defections of senior southern political figures to join the rebellion namely; Fr. Saturnino Lohure, Aggrey Jadden, Joseph Oduho, and William Deng Nhial. They went and formed the core of a guerrilla movement in exile and called it the Sudan African Nationalist union (SANU). The Anya Nya guerrilla lacked external military support. They depended only on what they captured from the enemy during the time of laying ambushes to army patrols across the Equatoria region.

In October 1964, Gen. Ibrahim Abboud stepped down after a series of demonstrations in Khartoum. He was replaced by a care taker civilian government. The Anya Nya leaders were invited to attend a round table conference offered by the new civilian rule in order to legalized the formation of the political parties. Those of Clement Mboro formed a political party called the Southern Front (SF) in Khartoum under Clement Mboro. Clement himself was appointed Minister of Interior in the new caretaker government. When the new civilian caretaker government invited the Southern politicians to participate in the round table conference, there was a split within the SANU. The invitation centred on discussions around the problem of South Sudan. William Deng Nhial accepted to attend the conference and became the leader of the SANU inside Sudan, advocating for a federal solution. Those of Aggrey Jadden and Joseph Oduho returned to Uganda as leaders of SANU, outside Sudan, advocating for the separation of South Sudan from the rest of the Sudan.

In 1967, Fr. Saturnino Lohure who was commanding Anya Nya forces that mutinied from Torit, was killed by Ugandan forces while crossing the border to Uganda, and after the death of Fr. Saturnino, the two army officers, Emilio Tefang and 2nd Lt Joseph Lagu, were at odds with each other, and by that time they were joined by Dinka leaders such as Gordon Muortat Mayen and Akuot Atem.

In 1968, Joseph Lagu formed his own movement called the South Sudan Liberation Movement (SSLM). It is this movement that regrouped all the different camps of the Anya Nya I from other parts of the Southern regions, and in 1969, the Anya Nya I rebels established contact with Israel to supply them with arms through Ethiopia and Uganda, and to train the Anya Nya I recruits. Also, the Anya Nya leadership managed to buy weapons from the Simba, a Congolese rebel group.

On May 25, 1969, Jaafar Nimeiri took power in Khartoum and declared that the problem of South Sudan would be solved through political and not military option.

During that time of the Anya Nya I, the prominent officers from the Equatoria region included:

1. Fr. Saturnino Lohure
2. Aggrey Jadden
3. Joseph Oduho
4. Gen. Emilio Tefang
5. Galerio Modi
6. Latada
7. Philip Angutwa
8. David Jada
9. James Loro
10. Joseph Lagu

The prominent officers from Bhar El Ghazal region included:

1. Gordon Muortat Mayen
2. Emanuel Abur Matuong
3. Agasio Akol Akol
4. Edward Nyial
5. Thomas Dhoal

The prominent officers from Upper Nile region included:

1. Akuot Atem De Mayen
2. Samuel Gai Tut
3. Paul Nyingoru
4. Joseph Akon
5. Paul Awel
6. Mathew Pagan
7. Amos Agok
8. Peter Mabil
9. Jacob Adier
10. William Abdalla Chuol Deng

***Note***: The names mentioned here are just examples.

The first Anya Nya I officer that was killed in Upper Nile was Paul Nyingoru from Anyuak tribe. Joseph Akon took over the command of the Anya Nya I Upper Nile command, and when Joseph Akon was killed, Paul Awel took over the leadership of the Anya Nya I in Upper Nile.

On February 27, 1972, South Sudan Liberation Movement negotiated peace with the Sudan government under Nimeiri in Addis Ababa, Ethiopia. The South Sudan Liberation Movement (SSLM), accepted the proposed regional autonomy that was proposed and agreed to the integration of the guerrilla forces of the Anya Nya I into the national army and other organized forces.

The agreement granted the Southern regional government powers to raise revenues from the local taxation, added to the revenues from the central government. In the negotiations also, the Southern Sudan Liberation Movement proposed that the Southern soldiers would be deployed in the Southern Sudan for the protection of civilians from the Northern army. The Addis Ababa agreement was incorporated in the permanent constitution of 1973.

In May 1983, Nimeiri subdivided the South Sudan into three regions of Bhar El Ghazal, Equatoria and Upper Nile regions.

Here is the Anya Nya I hierarchy;

1. Aggrey Jadden from 1967 - 1969
2. Gordon Muortat from 1969 - 1971
3. Joseph Lagu from 1971 - 1972

As a result of the Anya Nya I war, two million people died of war, famine and diseases and about 4 million people displaced to refugee camps.

### The Anya Nya II movement

The name Anya Nya II was created by the holdout groups or ex–Anya Nya I soldiers who expressed discontent with the terms of the Addis Ababa agreement. These ex-Anya Nya I veterans remained in the bush in their own camps on the Ethiopian–Sudan border, but they were not active until they were joined by various mutineers in 1976, led by 2nd Lt. Vincent Kuany Latjor and Corporal Bol Kur from the Sudanese army garrison of Akobo.

The Ethiopian authorities used these Anya Nya II soldiers on their border to threaten Sudan government to stop supplying weapons to its Eritrean rebels who were based in the Sudan fighting the Ethiopian government. The Ethiopian government promised to give full support to the Anya Nya II remnants on Ethiopian border who refused to accept the Addis Ababa peace agreement.

Nimeiri did not stop supplying the Eritrean rebels with ammunitions and weapons as requested by the Ethiopian government, as a result, the Ethiopians continued to support the Any Nya II by arming and training them fully and, at the same time, Libya also started to supply the Any Nya II with arms and other military support through Ethiopia.

The Anya Nya II remained insignificant in Ethiopia until 1980 and 1981, when they gained more support from Southern soldiers and civilians. In 1982, the Any Nya II managed to establish bases in Nasir, Bentiu and Fangak districts and established contact with the local Southern police and soldiers persuading them to join the rebellion.

By that time, Akuot Atem De Mayen and other Southern politicians who refused to accept the Addis Ababa agreement were in Ethiopia seeking for political and military support to fight the government of Sudan and liberate South

Sudan.

Akuot Atem was from Dinka Bor, he was then appointed as Minister of Interior in the Anya Nya I government.

Samuel Gai Tut who is from Lou Nuer was appointed as Minister in the interim Southern Sudan regional government with William Abdalla Chuol from Fangak Nuer. Samuel Gai Tut and William Abdalla Chuol were in contact with Akuot Atem and they were smuggling arms and ammunitions to the forces of Akuot Atem on the Ethiopian - Sudan border.

Samuel Gai Tut was caught and charged with supplying the rebels with arms and ammunitions. (Douglas Johnson, 2003). Samuel Gai Tut and William Abdalla Chuol defected and joined Akuot Atem on the Ethiopian border and formed their movement, the United South Sudan Liberation Movement (USSLM), with the objective for separation of South Sudan from the rest of Sudan or to liberate South Sudan.

By that time, there were two Anya Nya II camps on Ethiopian border, the political wing of USSLM based at Iteng headed by Akuot Atem De Mayen, Joseph Oduho, Samuel Gai Tut, William Abdalla Chuol Deng, while the military wing was based at Bilpam under the command of Gordon Koang Chuol, the overall commander of the Anya Nya II forces at Bilpam.

Later, they were joined by 2nd Lt. Vincent Kuany Latjor and his group who defected from Akobo Sudan army Garrison in 1976. The Anya Nya II forces at Bilpam were redundant, they were not active or operational. They just used to come down from Ethiopian border to Sudan to forcefully snatch cattle and other valuable things from the innocent civilians and take them to Bilpam where they used the cattle and other materials in paying their dowry.

With this process, they had accumulated a lot of wealth and build big grass - thatched houses and made Bilpam their permanent home and forgot about the liberation struggle that took them to Bilpam. They did not challenge any single Sudan Army Garrison until they were joined by the SPLM/A in 1983.

---

# Chapter 6:
# Sudan's Second Civil war

*Brief history of the SPLM/A*

On May 16, 1983, the SAF army Battalion 105 of 1st Infantry Division mutinied in Bor in Jonglei region and a fight ensued at Malual Chaat Army Garrison between the mutineers (rebels) and loyal Sudanese troops. During this battle, a total of 78 soldiers were killed from both sides, including one Major and seven Non - Commissioned Officers (NCOs) and other ranked soldiers.

The mutiny that was sparked by an order directing the transfer of Battalion 105 from Bor in South Sudan to the Sudan (North) was led by Maj. Kerubino Kuanyin Bol. Col. John Garang' De-Mabior was sent by President Nimeiri as a Dinka to convince his fellow tribesmen in Bor town to lay down their arms. But because Col. Garang' himself was in secret contact with Maj. Kerubino Kuanyin Bol, he arrived in Bor on May 14, 1983 and joined the mutineers.

Col. Garang' instructed the mutineers to collect and carry the weapons, food, and medicine and move to the jungle towards the border of Sudan with Ethiopia. The mutineers moved to the border of Ethiopia and set up their base there under his command.

They established contact with the soldiers in Akobo, Pochalla, Pibor, Kapoeta, Rumbek and Aweil garrisons, urging them to join the rebellion. After a few months, the soldiers, other organised forces and government officials from these regions defected and joined the rebellion. It is worth noting that the bulk of the forces that formed the first SPLA Battalions were from the Nuer. The combination of the attack on Bor and the subsequent abolition of the South Sudan region created further rebellions and desertions from various garrisons across South Sudan.

In July 1983, about 3,000 soldiers defected and joined the new guerrilla base which had been established on the Ethiopia border. A further 1,000 soldiers defected from Bahr El Ghazal's various army garrisons and established their bases in the countryside in the rural villages and their leaders went to meet with Col. Garang' on the Ethiopia border. When Col. Garang' and his group arrived on the Ethiopian border, they were received and welcomed by the ill-equipped Anya Nya II forces that were already at Bilpam and Iteng areas.

The fact that Anya Nya II soldiers had already fought these mutineers before they joined the rebellion, made it difficult to unite them. Anya Nya II officers claim was that they were senior to the officers who had just joined them on the Ethiopia border from Bor.

In July 1983, Col. Garang' held a meeting with the USSLM leaders and the Anya Nya II commanders on the possibility of unifying the movements to fight one common enemy that was the Sudan government. All the commanders agreed in principle to unify the movement, but they failed to agree on the name of the new movement and its leadership structure. (M.H. Kanyane, JH Mai, D.A. Kuol, 2009).

The Anya Nya II commanders proposed South Sudan Liberation Movement/ Army (SSLM/A) to be the name of one united movement to help liberate South Sudan from the Arab rule, while Col. Garang's group proposed South Sudan Peoples' Liberation Movement/Army (SPLM/A).

When the Ethiopian authorities were informed that there was a disagreement among the two factions, the leaders of the SSLM/A and SPLM/A were invited to Addis Ababa to meet the Ethiopian senior officials. Col. Garang', Akuot Atem, Joseph Oduho, Samuel Gai Tut, and Salva Kiir Mayardit were airlifted from Mangok area to Addis Ababa by a helicopter courtesy of the Ethiopian Government. When they arrived at the meeting, they were asked by the Ethiopian authorities to present their respective movement's manifestos that explain the objectives and goals of their different movements. The Col. Garang's faction had recommended that the movement should keep on fighting for the unity of the Sudan.

Garang' also seems to have known regional politics well. The Ethiopian Government was all along supporting a united Sudan and intended to overthrow President Nimeiri from power due to his open support to the Eritrean rebels who were fighting for the separation of Eritrea, and further to form their own government from the Ethiopian Government.

If Col. Garang' would have adopted the ideology of the Anya Nya II that called for the separation of the South Sudan from the rest of the Sudan, the Ethiopian Government officials at the time would not have supported them since it would look like the Ethiopians were endorsing the separation of the Eritrean rebels from the rest of the Ethiopia.

Col. Garang' and his rebel faction from Bor were still at odds with the old Anya Nya II faction of Akuot Atem, Samuel Gai Tut, William Abdalla Chuol Deng, and Joseph Oduho. This team of Anya Nya II veterans did not buy Garang's overall strategy. They were keen on fighting for the liberation and independence of South Sudan.

In addition, the Anya Nya II faction wanted to retain their seniority over the Bor mutineers. They preferred the separation of the military from the political wing of the movement as was in the Anya Nya I, where the political wing was separated from the military wing. (M.H. Kanyane, J.H. Mai, D.A. Kuol, 2009).

Samuel Gai Tut and the other members of USSLM proposed that Akuot Atem should be the leader of the newly created political wing (SPLM) movement, and that he be deputized by Joseph Oduho. They further proposed that Samuel Gai Tut become the leader of the newly created military wing - the SPLA and that Col. Garang' become his deputy. These suggestions were rejected by Kerubino Kuanyin Bol and William Nyuon Bany who viewed Samuel Gai Tut and the faction as their enemies before they joined the rebellion. The two wanted Col. Garang' to be their leader, while the old Anya Nya II veterans also claimed that they were senior to Col. Garang' and his team insisted that it was wrong for Col. Garang' to be named as their leader.

After listening to their presentations and a careful scrutiny, the Ethiopian authorities chose the one that was presented by SPLM/A and asked Akuot Atem group to abandon their movement ideology and join Col. Garang's faction. The Ethiopians officials further admired Col. Garang' because of his education and his youthfulness compared to Anya Nya II veterans who had little education and were older.

Akuot Atem, Samuel Gai Tut and Anya Nya II senior officials agreed in principle and adopted the new name (SPLM/A), but further raised concern on the leadership, ideology, and policy of the movement. From then on, it became clear that Col. Garang' was the new leader of the movement endorsed by the Ethiopian authorities.

To date, nearly all observers of South Sudan's history have noted that Col. Garang' brought into the movement a level of sophistication the other leaders had lacked. It was for that reason that it quickly became known that he was being supported by many prominent South Sudanese politicians who were in exile.

Samuel Gai Tut and Akuot Atem went to their camp at Iteng separate from those of Col. Garang's camp and the faction was secretly getting weapons and ammunitions as well as receiving trainings from the Ethiopian authorities. The USSLM camp in Iteng noticed this and withdrew to South Sudan with their supporters on September 3, 1983 and operated independently, for fear of being attacked and arrested by the Ethiopian forces.

The USSLM forces established bases in Waat and Kongor areas, the respective home areas of Samuel Gai Tut and Akuot Atem. Politicians from the areas had told the Anya Nya II commanders at Bilpam not to recognize the SPLM/A under Col. Garang' and his faction.

In October 1983, the Ethiopian Government and Bor mutineers, mainly from SPLM/A launched an attack on the Anya Nya II camp at Bilpam and dislodged, dispersed and disorganised them. The SPLA scattered the Anya Nya II militias and incorporated some of them into the SPLA structure.

Commander Duay Taitai Badeng from the Bul Nuer was killed in the attack on the Anya Nya II side as Vincent Kuany Latjor with his supporters surrendered to the SPLM/A. Gordon Koang Chuol went with the bulk of the Anya Nya II forces and joined those of Samuel Gai Tut faction.

The two factions were unified under the name Anya Nya II under the command and leadership of Akuot Atem De Mayen. After some time, a serious split emerged again within the newly unified Anya Nya II faction.

Unfortunately, both Samuel Gai Tut and Akuot Atem De Mayen were mysteriously killed by the end of 1983. Commander William Abdallah Chuol took over the leadership of the Anya Nya II and Gordon Koang Chuol was named his deputy. Now, the Anya Nya II new leadership that was mainly made up of Nuer sons established contact with the Sudan government and they started receiving military supplies from Khartoum. It is worth noting that the differences between the Anya Nya II veterans and the SPLM/A were based on ideology and personal differences, and not tribal ones, since Col. Garang' and Akuot Atem were both Dinka from Twic Bor clan in Kongor District, and other commanders from both Nuer and Dinka were supporting either side.

The Sudan government, beset by wrangling among the Arab elites, found in the Southern insurgency a perfect outlet to rally Northern populations and bolster their standing. Sentimentally, they revelled in the notion of the North being prosperous while the South was in turmoil. Still, they loathed the idea of SPLA fighting for better governance of Sudan, and championed those fighting for secession, which they projected as being funded by foreign enemies of Sudan, in particular Israel and the United States.

The government created several militias as friendly forces against the SPLA, especially amongst the Toposa, Murle, and Mundari communities. It also intended to nurture a Nuer army to fight the SPLA which they saw as a faction that was dominated mainly by the Dinka people.

The Anya Nya II drew its support from the Bul Nuer people in Western Upper Nile under the command of Paulino Matip, Laak Nuer, in Fangak under William Abdallah Chuol Deng, and from Lou and Jikany Nuer. The Anya Nya II forces occasionally attacked and dispersed the SPLA recruits and refugees that crossed from Bahr El Ghazal, Western Upper Nile and Fangak under the SPLA escort to Ethiopia's border. They cut the SPLA supply line from Ethiopia to Fangak, Western Upper, and Bahr El Ghazal areas.

The fighting between the Anya Nya II and the SPLM/A continued for five good years until Gordon Koang Chuol joined the SPLM/A in 1988, along with the bulk of the Anya Nya II forces.

# Chapter 7

## The Anya Nya II in Western Upper Nile

*The Sudan's 2nd civil war starts at Wangkei not in Bor*

On March 15, 1983, the Southern Soldiers of Battalion 105, that were deployed in Western Upper Nile (WUN) were mainly made up of Bentiu sons, who defected from the Sudanese army garrisons of Bentiu, Mayom, Abiemnom, Wangkei and Parieng respectively. They regrouped and called themselves the Anya Nya II in Western Upper Nile, the name they used after the Anya Nya I. These are the soldiers of Battalion 105, that were deployed in Western Upper Nile and their headquarters was in Bor town under Maj. Kerubino Kuanyin Bol.

The defection was caused by the order from the Sudan Army General headquarters to transfer the forces belonging to the Battalion 105 from the South to the North Sudan. The transfer would start first with the outposts of Battalion 105 deployed in Western Upper Nile towns of Wangkei, Abiemnom, Mayom, Bentiu and Parieng. These soldiers refused to be transferred to the Northern Sudan and mutinied against their command on March 15, 1983, before even the attack on Bor on May 16, 1983 could start.

They killed their platoon commander 2nd Lieutenant Mohamed Ahmed at Wangkei SAF's garrison and they crossed River Wangkei to the countryside where they were warmly received and welcomed by the local population. It is important to note that the mutiny by the SPLM/A started at Wangkei town in Mayom area, in Unity State, not in Bor town as is believed. The attribution to Bor might have come about because the Battalion headquarters under the command of Maj. Kerubino Kuanyin Bol was in Bor but Wangkei was the historical town at the time.

This was narrated to me by Gen. Robert Ruay Kuol Jal in 2018, who was the second in command of the Anya Nya II in Western Upper Nile. He told me that after they killed their commanding officer, they withdrew to the countryside of Western Upper Nile where they established camps and promoted themselves to different ranks, and called themselves Anya Nya II in Western Upper Nile.

The Western Upper Nile mutineers who promoted themselves were Lieutenant Col. Paul Thong Ruac, Lieutenant Col. Robert Ruay Kuol, Lieutenant-Col. James Liah Diu Deang, Maj. Khalifa Toc, Maj. Bol Nyawan, Maj. Bishar Ket Dirbang, Maj. Gona Duop among others. They were later joined by Anya Nya

II officers namely Lieutenant Col. James Gatduel Gatluak, Lieutenant Col. Michael Char Makuei, Maj. Malek Rolnyang Kai among others who were scattered and dispersed from Bilpam as a result of the SPLM/A attack on Bilpam in October 1983.

When Bilpam was attacked and dispersed by the SPLM/A in October 1983, sons of Bentiu from the Anya Nya II Bilpam namely James Gatduel Gatluak and Michael Char Makuei among others crossed to Western Upper Nile and joined the Any Nya II groups who defected from the government garrisons of Wangkei, Mayom, Abiemnom, Bentiu and Parieng and established Any Nya II camps in Western Upper Nile countryside.

It is important to note here that James Gatduel Gatluak and Nuai-Nuai used to shuttle between Bilpam and Western Upper Nile in 1982 to mobilize the Southerners to join the rebellion, even before mutineers of Battalion 105 in Western Nuer garrisons rioted. James Gatduel and Nuai-Nuai captured Mankien using axes on May 30, 1982.

There were some serious clashes between the Anya Nya II in Western Upper Nile and those who came from Bilpam because of power and leadership struggle, and often time, they did not understand each other. They never listened to one another and they kept attacking each other's camp as part of their power struggle. Lt. Col. James Gatduel Gatluak joined camp with Lt. Col. Paul Thong Ruac, and Lt. Col. Paul Thong became their camp leader. Michael Char Makuei refused to join their camp and they together fought Michael Char Makuei several times until Michael Char withdrew to Mayen Abun in Bahr El Ghazal region, where he sought alliance with Anya Nya II of Bhar Ghazal under Maj. Gen. Paul Malong Awan in Aweil and Maj. Gen. Miakol Deng Kuol of Anya Nya II in Abyei area. These Anya Nya II of Bhar El Ghazal supported Michael Char Makuei with ammunition to fight back against the other camps in Western Upper Nile.

The Anya Nya II camps in Western Upper Nile had no clear direction and vision as they were operating without a headquarters to report to as the Anya Nya II Headquarters at Bilpam was attacked and dispersed by the SPLM/A in October 1983. All Anya Nya II units operating in remote areas were cut off from their headquarters and could not have direct contact with their leaders. The Anya Nya II in Western Upper Nile were fighting among themselves because of power struggle and the resources such as cattle and goats that they snatched from civilian populations in pretext that they intended to buy ammunition to fight the Arabs and Sudan government. In fact, they managed to neutralize and deter the Arab Missiriya who used to displace Bul Nuer and Leek Nuer from their old and original respective settlements at Malou Raar and old Leek when these communities were settling around Kelek and Nyama bordering Nuba Mountains. The armed Arab Missiriya nomads displaced the whole Bul and Leek population from their original settlements and resettled across the rivers Cuolpi and Nam.

The Anya Nya II played a very crucial role in defeating the Arab Nomads and prevented further displacement of Leek and Bul people that were caused by the Arab Missiriya nomads.

### Arrival of Paulino Matip Nhial in Western Upper Nile

Paulino Matip Nhial, who joined the Anya Nya II in 1975 at Bilpam with Gordon Koang Chuol and others, was commissioned as an officer in the Anya Nya II movement. He later withdrew with the Anya Nya II fighters when Bilpam base was attacked and captured by the SPLM/A in October 1983. However, he was later arrested and charged by William Abdallah Chuol Deng who had taken up the leadership of Anya Nya II after the death of Akuot Atem and Samuel Gai Tut.

Paulino Matip was arrested after being accused of mobilizing, instigating and agitating the soldiers from Bentiu region to desert with him to Bentiu to establish his own camp in Western Upper Nile. He later managed to escape from jail together with James Gatluak Domai and Michael Kel Gatwech who were arrested along with him. On their way from Eastern Upper Nile to Bentiu, they met with some nearly 100 deserters from the SPLA Tiger and Tumsah battalions who deserted from Pochalla operations in Jonglei area heading to Bentiu. The deserting soldiers were led by senior NCOs, including Gatbel Rolnyang Kai, Dor Bidoang, and Makuar Gatluak Wupieu.

Since these deserters had no officers to command and lead them, they asked Paulino Matip to be their commander on their way to Bentiu, an offer he readily accepted with his two hands and immediately, they proceeded to Western Upper Nile. By the end of December 1983, Paulino Matip arrived in Bentiu along with 100 deserters from the SPLA Tiger and Tumsah battalions. They were warmly welcomed by the Anya Nya II factions who were already operating in Western Upper Nile under Lieutenant Col. Paul Thong Ruac as their unified leader.

In November 1984, the Anya Nya II officers in Western Upper Nile proposed Paulino Matip to be their leader, and he was to be deputized by Robert Ruay

Kuol and followed by Paul Thong Ruac and James Gatduel Gatluak. This was, based on their seniority in the Anya Nya II hierarchy, but Paul Thong Ruac, who was the leader of the Anya Nya II before the arrival of Paulino Matip refused to surrender his position to Paulino Matip. He was later convinced by his colleagues to relinquish his position to Paulino Matip for the unity of purpose among the sons of Western Upper Nile to fight a common enemy. Paulino Matip was also assigned to convince Capt. Michael Char Makuei who had been fighting with them to come back and rejoin the group.

Paulino Matip now assumed the leadership of the Anya Nya II in Western Upper Nile and he managed to convince Capt. Michael Char Makuei who was fighting the rest of the Anya Nya II camps to join him, and from there, Paulino Matip promoted himself to the rank of a Col. in the Anya Nya II of Western Upper Nile command.

Paulino Matip, operated in Western Upper Nile without a headquarter to report to, since he deserted from the Anya Nya II in Eastern Upper Nile under William Abdalla Chuol. He had no contact with William Abdalla Chuol. Paulino Matip decided to operate as an independent commander without reporting to any commander.

In Western Upper Nile, there were other SPLA deserters operating in Leek Nuer area apart from the Tiger and Tumsah deserters who came with Paulino Matip from Eastern Upper Nile. These deserters were from Jamus Battalion under Bateah Wagah Kueat. They deserted from Malakal operations and crossed to Western Upper Nile and set up their own camp at Nyieng Gatdet Dhuor in Leek countryside parallel to the Anya Nya II camps in Western Upper Nile. Bateah Wagah promoted himself to the rank of a Captain and maintained his own camp without joining the Anya Nya II camp in Western Upper Nile.

On November 12, 1984, Capt. Bateah Wagah lured Bentiu District Commissioner Charles Kuot Chatiem for a meeting at Tong area, two kilometres from Bentiu town, ostensibly to surrender to the Sudan Government. The Commissioner came with other government officials to meet the rebels at Tong. Capt. Bateah Wagah captured him together with his officials among them, Puok Bol Mot, who is currently a Member of the South Sudan Parliament; Chuol Rambang (an Executive), Thijin Mamun (Inspector), Luis Lambah, Francis Gey Majok among others. Bateah Wagah took Charles Kuot Chatiem and officials captured with him to Buoytong in Leek countryside under detention and were later taken to the SPLM/A headquarters in Bilpam for further interrogation. Five lorry-loads of different food items and one Land Rover were seized by

Capt. Bateah Wagah.

It is important to note here that, despite being an SPLA deserter, Capt. Bateah Wagah was operating in Western Upper Nile in the name of the SPLM/A, while the Anya Nya II, camps were operating in the name of the Anya Nya II.

### Arrival of Major Paul Dor Lampuar in Western Upper Nile

On November 18, 1984, Maj. Paul Dor Lampuar arrived in Western Upper Nile, (Bentiu) with the SPLA forces comprising of two Battalions of Tiger and Tumsah plus elements of Jamus Battalion who deserted their units around Malakal and were found on their way to Western Upper Nile. Soldiers under Maj. Dor were mainly made up of sons of the Nuer and Panaru tribesmen who were mainly from Bentiu.

Maj. Paul Dor was accompanied by SPLA officers namely, Capt. Hakim Gabriel Aloung (his Deputy), Second Lieutenant Wilson Deng Kuicrot (Adjutant), and Second Lieutenant Taban Deng Gai (political commissar), plus other junior officers who were commanding the units.

On their arrival in Western Upper Nile, Lt. Col. Paul Thong and Kot Thian of the Anya Nya II, who were opposed to the leadership of Paulino Matip rushed to receive Paul Dor and accused Paulino Matip of wanting to join the Anya Nya II of Eastern Upper Nile under William Abdalla Chuol. They asked Paul Dor to join camp with them.

Maj. Paul Dor was sent to Western Upper Nile by the SPLM/A headquarters to regroup, organize and command all the scattered SPLA soldiers who deserted to Western Upper Nile from the SPLA various fronts. This group included the government soldiers who defected from the army garrisons in Western Nuer and who formed Anya Nya II camps in Western Nuer and the Anya Nya II soldiers who deserted from Bilpam during Bilpam attack and crossed to Western Nuer.

Major Paul Dor established his headquarter at Dhorkan and called Anya Nya II Col. Paulino Matip and his group for a meeting at Dhorkan in Leek area, Rubkona County. When Paulino Matip came with his Anya Nya II officers, Maj. Dor told them that he was sent from the SPLA headquarters to regroup, organize and command the SPLA forces in Western Upper Nile who deserted from their different units and to integrate the Anya Nya II forces that were operating in Western Upper Nile into one supreme command. He asked Paulino Matip and his team to abandon the Anya Nya II group's ideology and join the SPLM/A.

While most of the Anya Nya II members agreed to join SPLM/A, Paulino

Matip was sceptical because he wanted to be the leader in Western Upper Nile. He was equally unhappy with Lt. Col. Paul Thong for reporting that he had wanted to join the Anya Nya II of Abdallah Chuol Deng.

Maj. Dor ignored issues that were raised by Paulino Matip and he went ahead to recommend the names of the Anya Nya II officers in Western Upper Nile to the SPLA headquarters for quick integration into the SPLA. The SPLA headquarters confirmed the integration of the Anya Nya II officers into the SPLA with the following ranks, namely: Capt. Paulino Matip Nhial, Capt. Robert Ruai Kuol, Capt. Paul Thong Ruac, Capt. James Gatduel Gatluak, Capt. Bol Nyawan and Capt. Char Makuei Ruea, and Other junior officers were made 1st and 2nd Lieutenants.

The forces of Anya Nya II and SPLA in Western Upper Nile were reorganized into five Battalions as follows;

1. Petrol Battalion, led by Capt. Paulino Matip Nhial
2. Jamus Battalion, led by Capt. Bateah Wagah Kueat
3. Tiger Battalion, led by Capt. Tito Biel Chuor
4. Tumsah battalion, led by Capt. Juol Banak
5. Koryom battalion, led by Capt. Joseph Mathok Thiep.

Capt. Paulino Matip was deployed as commander of the Petrol Battalion and as deputy to Maj. Dor as well. The rest of former Anya Nya II officers were deployed as Company and Platoon Commanders.

The Anya Nya II forces in Western Upper Nile were completely re-organized and re-named Petrol Battalion in the SPLA. Capt. Paulino Matip was, however, not happy with this move, but Maj. Dor kept ignoring his complaints. However, Capt. Matip did not like the integration of the forces he used to command into the SPLA in Western Upper Nile.

He felt that with the integration, he no longer had direct authority over the forces and civil population in Western Upper Nile as he used to before the arrival of Maj. Dor in Western Upper Nile. In his thoughts, he still wanted Maj. Dor to be his deputy because he, Capt. Matip had gone ahead and promoted himself to the rank of a Col. that was a grade higher than that of Maj. Dor.

Capt. Matip ostensibly asked Maj. Dor to grant him a few days leave to go to his home village for some traditional ceremonies, and then come back to take over the command of the new battalion assigned to him.

Maj. Dor accepted his request and allowed him to visit his home, which was situated around the Bul Nuer area. Strangely, Capt. Matip informed his loyal soldiers secretly that they should desert after him to Bul Nuer area, and that he was not going to come back to work under Maj. Dor. He gave them the rendezvous in Bul land but unfortunately his plan leaked out before he could leave for Bul Nuer area.

Thus, on March 10, 1985, around 10 a. m, we were ordered to assemble at a parade in Nyeromna village, but before our officers could come to the parade, a fight broke out between the forces of Maj. Dor and soldiers loyal to Capt. Matip that were led by Maliny Kawaye Goh.

At that time, I was among the forces loyal to Capt. Matip and we were outnumbered and dislodged from the parade ground by the bulk of the SPLA forces that were loyal to Maj. Dor and we were pushed towards Bul Nuer area across the Naam river. Many soldiers were killed on both sides and we fled to Bul Nuer the same day across the Nam River.

On April 15, 1985, Capt. Matip announced his defection from the SPLA, declaring that he joined the Anya Nya II faction that was under Abdalla Chuol Deng, based in Eastern Upper Nile near the Ethiopian territory.

The announcement intensified the fighting between the Anya Nya II forces of Capt. Matip and the SPLA under the command of Maj. Dor. Seeing an opportunity to tilt the scales, the Sudan government started to supply the Anya Nya II soldiers under Capt. Matip in Bentiu and Abdalla Chuol in Eastern Nuer with military supplies to fight against the SPLM/A since they viewed them as friendly forces.

Beside the loss of lives, civilians were severely hit as their properties and livestock were looted, their houses destroyed and a lot of atrocities committed, including rape and other forms of gender-based violence. The two sides had no laws protecting civilians and their properties.

On May 13, 1985 Capt. Michael Char Makuei defected from Capt. Matip's Anya Nya II to the SPLA along with other junior officers. This saw a massive reduction in Capt. Matip's forces, forcing him to retreat to Mayom town where he joined the SAF to fight against the SPLA.

On August 3, 1985 Abdalla Chuol Deng was killed by the SPLA. Gordon Koang Chuol took over the leadership of the Anya Nya II and was deputized by Capt. Matip from the Western Nuer Anya Nya II command.

I had wanted to further my education and I had placed a request towards this wish. Fortunately, in December 1985, I was released by Capt. Matip to pursue my studies in Khartoum. I joined Omdurman Comboni Primary School to study English and later on joined Intermediate school in Nadi El Umaal in Khartoum Bahri. I later on got admission at St. Augustine's Seminary, a Catholic institution with an ambition to become a priest, which I later discontinued and re -joined my life career of being a soldier and liberator.

**The arrival of Maj. Riek Machar Teny Dhur-gon in Western Upper Nile.** On January 1, 1986, Maj. Riek Machar Teny Dhur-gon was deployed to Western Upper Nile by the SPLA headquarters to replace Maj. Paul Dor. He was the commander of the SPLA Wolf battalion, also known as Gol Battalion, and as assigned to regroup, organize and command the scattered SPLA forces in Western Upper Nile and to make peace with Paulino Matip who had been fighting Paul Dor Lampuar.

Maj. Riek Machar came to Bentiu to take over as was the procedure but Maj. Dor refused to hand over to him, claiming that he was senior to him. This disagreement was communicated to the SPLA headquarters, and it was confirmed that Maj. Riek Machar was senior to Maj. Dor by virtue of being a member of the SPLM/A Alternate Political Military High Command (APMHC) while Maj. Dor was not a member of APMHC, even though the two were both in the same rank of a Major.

Not pleased with the decision, Maj. Paul Dor still refused to hand over the command. A standoff ensued and Maj. Riek Machar ordered for his arrest and sent him to the SPLA headquarters under the escort. Maj. Machar thereafter wrote a letter to Capt. Matip, the leader of the Anya Nya II in Western Upper Nile who had earlier refused to join forces with Maj. Paul Dor, asking for reconciliation so that Capt. Matip would join forces with the SPLA to reinforce war against the government of Sudan.

Maj. Riek Machar's letter was misinterpreted to Capt. Matip by his adjutant, Gek Liem, that Maj. Riek Machar was insulting him and threatening to fight him whenever he crossed to the Bul Nuer land.

Capt. Matip got annoyed and instructed his forces to remain vigilant and to be ready to fight Dr Riek Machar whenever he set foot in Bul Nuer land. When Maj. Riek Machar tried to cross the river Naam to Bul Nuer area to approach Capt. Matip with the aim of making peace, his forces were attacked by forces loyal to Capt. Matip, an action that led to the outbreak of the war between the SPLA under Riek Machar and Capt. Matip's Anya Nya II forces that continued for many years.

On April 16, 1986, Col. Maliny Kawaye Goh was killed in the frontline by the SPLA forces in one of the fierce battles where his head was cut off and taken to Tharkuer Ciengjoak, the headquarters of Maj. Riek Machar, and hanged on a pole on the road side for the public to see. Such barbaric killing annoyed and instigated the Bul Nuer to hate Riek Machar forever and supported and stood in solidarity with Paulino Matip.

On July 7, 1987, Maj. Riek Machar forces became stronger and advanced to capture Mayom, and the Anya Nya II forces withdrew to Heglig oil fields together with the forces of the Sudan Armed Forces (SAF) under Capt. Ahmed Kabacha, but Mayom was later recaptured the same year by a combined forces of SAF and the Anya Nya II under the overall command of Brig. Omar Hassan El Bashir, who was the overall operation commander for the government forces in Western Nuer with the support of the Anya Nya II of Western Upper Nile under the leadership of Capt. Matip. The SPLA lost lots of weapons including SPG-9, after, the SAF and the Anya Nya II recaptured Mayom the same year.

As the loss dealt a big blow to SPLA, Capt. Michael Char Makuei, the SPLA commander in Mayom, was immediately arrested by Maj. Riek Machar for not putting up a fierce fight to save Mayom from falling to the enemy. While being taken to the SPLA headquarters after being arrested, Capt. Char Makuei jumped into the river Nile from the boat that was ferrying him and drowned instantly.

After the capture of Mayom by the SPLA in 1987, Maj. Riek Machar ordered the relocation of Bul Nuer people from Bul mainland and settled them across the Naam river at a place called Kuiynam or Bul II since he had accused the Bul Nuer people of supporting Anya Nya II faction of Capt. Matip.

The Bul Nuer people were not happy with this move and to make it worse, many of their livestock died from disease outbreak and people faced famine when they reached the new settlement site.

In the year 1988, many people died of hunger and the survivors resorted to eating plant called "Nyakuojuok" which was unfit for human consumption but the Bul Nuer people ate it for survival and they named that year (Ruon-Nyakuojuok) because they left their houses and lived under hardships without shelter and food to eat.

# Chapter 8

## Differences within the leadership of the SPLM/A

In 1987, Dr John Garang' De-Mabior had confrontations with various senior members of the SPLM/A Political and Military High Command (PMHC), especially Kerubino Kuanyin Bol and Arok Thon Arok.

Dr Garang' accused the two senior officers for attempting to overthrow him, an accusation that led to the arrest of the two senior officers. On their part, they accused Dr Garang' of running the movement as his own private property and blamed him for failing to convene a meeting for members of the PMHC since the inception of the movement.

Arok Thon Arok, who was senior to current President Salva Kiir Mayardit when they were in SAF, doubted Dr Garang's ability of leading the movement based on his dictatorial tendencies.

In 1988, Gordon Koang Chuol and most of the Anya Nya II forces in Eastern Nuer territory negotiated with the SPLM/A fraternity and they joined the SPLM/A. The two Stephen Duol Chuol and Gordon Koang Chuol were integrated into the SPLA as Commanders, and further, Gordon Koang was appointed as alternate member of the PMHC of the SPLM/A.

General Paulino Matip became the leader of the Anya Nya II both in Western Upper Nile and in Eastern Upper Nile. Abraham Bol Nyathony, who was the leader of the Eastern Upper Nile, was appointed as his Deputy.

In the same year, 1988, Brig. James Koang Ruac, the right-hand man of General Paulino Matip defected to the SPLM/A with Brig. Thoare Gatkuer and a large number of soldiers, causing a big blow to the leadership of General Paulino Matip. Consequently, Brig. Koang and Thoare Gatkuer were integrated into the SPLM/A as alternate commanders.

James Koang was deployed as the commander of SPLA in Bul Nuer area in Western Upper Nile, while Thoare Gatkuer was transferred to the SPLA headquarters along with many former Anya Nya II officers mainly from Bul Nuer community.

In 1989, with the blessing of elder Yap Tekjiek, a Bul Nuer elder who gave a spear to Brig. Omar Hassan El Bashir and blessed him to rule Sudan, El Bashir asked General Paulino Matip to provide him with the forces to overthrow the government of Sadiq El Mahdi. El Bashir had earlier become a close friend to

General Paulino Matip during their field operations days that led to the recapturing of Mayom town from the SPLA in 1987. General Paulino Matip provided Brig. Omar Hassan El Bashir with forces and he went and took power on June 30, 1989.

Brig. El Bashir pledged that his government will support General Paulino Matip with military support that he required to fight and crush the SPLM/A in a proxy war. This would intensify the wars even further. Unfortunately for Thoare Gatkuer, he was killed in 1991, in a battle with SAF in Equatoria region at mile 40 at a bridge along Yei–Juba Road, also known as Kubri Arba'een.

In December 1993, James Koang Ruac was again killed by the forces of General Paulino Matip after he escaped from Nhialdiu Prison in an attempt to defect to Bentiu town to form his own movement.

## The major split within the ranks and files of the SPLM/A

On August 28, 1991, Dr Machar, Lam Akol, and Gordon Koang Chuol sent a radio message to all SPLA units announcing the overthrow of Dr Garang' as the leader of SPLA. Later that evening, they made the same announcement over the British Broadcasting Corporation (BBC) World Service.

They accused Dr Garang' of his dictatorial tendencies that included running the movement like a briefcase business. The leaders called for democratic traits in running the movement affairs. They pledged to promote and advocate for human rights within the movement and to put an end to the recruitment of child soldiers as part of the movement's army.

The group also ordered for the release of all political prisoners in the SPLA controlled areas that were detained during the leadership of Dr Garang'. Further, they committed that the main objective of the SPLM/A was to fight for the independence of South Sudan.

The ouster of Dr Garang' was quickly supported by Nuer militias that were fighting alongside the SAF against the SPLM/A, especially the Bul Nuer and Lou Nuer militia units operating in Mayom and Doleib Hill. The two SPLA factions were referred to as SPLA Nasir and SPLA Torit or SPLA mainstream.

No side was willing to cede ground, leading to regular confrontation of forces in Upper Nile, Bhar El Ghazal and Equatoria regions. Some of the deadly clashes took place in areas around Waat, Ayod, Sobat, Bor, and Bahr El Ghazal.

A split among the Shilluk soldiers, many of whom refused to join Lam Akol while Maban soldiers that were under the command of Lam Akol also refused to join him and withdrew to the areas controlled by Dr Garang' supporters.

Dr Garang' ordered William Nyuon to attack Ayod, Adok, and Leer, but the Nasir faction forces in Ayod were reinforced by the Anya Nya II forces from Fangak and Bentiu and repulsed an SPLA attack on Ayod commanded by William Nyuon Bany.

In November 1991, Dr Riek Machar sent a combined force of the Anya Nya II and Nasir faction supported by Nuer armed civilians known as "white army" to attack Kongor and Bor, the home area of Dr Garang'. As a result, the people of Bor who were innocent were massacred and when Dr Machar was informed of the killings in Bor, he ordered immediate withdrawal of his forces from Bor to Ayod, Duk, and Yuai areas.

As the fighting was continuing, the SPLA Nasir faction was receiving military supplies from the Sudan government. Taban Deng Gai was sent to Khartoum to coordinate support for Dr Machar's movement, and he established a liaison office there.

He managed to meet President Omar Hassan El Bashir and El Turabi, and other senior army officers who pledged to support their faction. The army gave a green light for the use of Antonov cargo planes to transport military supplies to areas controlled by the SPLA Nasir faction, and started dropping military supplies from the air to Leer and Duar in Western Upper Nile and other areas in Eastern Upper Nile and Jonglei.

In 1992, militia forces of Paulino Matip, mainly made up of men from the Bul Nuer, were integrated into the SPLA Nasir faction and Paulino Matip was integrated with the rank of commander along with his senior officers namely Peter Ruot Chuol, Stephen Chap Majuan, and John Kuachuor Chung. Paulino Matip was appointed as a member of Dr Machar's high command council and overall commander of Western Upper Nile zonal command.

During the integration of the forces, I was integrated along with Paulino Matip officers with the rank of 1st Lt in the SPLA Nasir faction and shortly I was promoted to the rank of Captain and assigned as a radio operator at the headquarter of Paulino Matip in Western Upper Nile zonal command.

On August 15, 1992, I was transferred from the Western Upper Nile zonal command to Eastern Upper Nile to the headquarters of Dr Machar as signal officer.

In 1992, the Sudan government, with support from the SPLA Nasir faction under the command of Dr Machar recaptured more territories in Jonglei and Eastern Equatoria regions. William Nyuon released political prisoners, including Joseph Oduho, Kerubino Kuanyin Bol, and Arok Thon Arok. Interestingly

William Nyuon defected from the SPLA mainstream to the Nasir faction in September 1992.

On November 14, 1992, the Nasir faction attacked Malakal town in order to capture it so that Dr Machar will gain support from regional and international community and win over forces of Torit faction to join him by justifying his plans of making democratic reforms in the movement and also to be seen to be fighting for the liberation of South Sudan, contrary to Dr Garang's vision. Dr Machar's move was supported by the Anya Nya II elements as this was their original objective in fighting the SPLM/A.

On December 6, 1992, I was transferred from Dr Machar's headquarters as officer in charge of signals to Maiwut on the Ethiopian border to be trained as a military intelligence officer. After one year, I was appointed as General Intelligence Service (GIS) officer in Maiwut, to work with Commander Kwong Danhier Gatluak who was the area commander by then and Chief of Military Intelligence in the SPLA Nasir faction.

In 1993, Dr Machar, Kerubino Kuanyin Bol, William Nyuon Bany, Joseph Oduho, Arok Thon Arok, Kuac Kang, and other senior members of the Nasir faction high command were attacked by SPLA Torit faction at Panyagoor. Joseph Oduho and Commander Kuac Kang were killed in the attack and Dr Machar was defeated and withdrew to Waat area.

In 1993, I was attacked at Maiwut by Gajaak armed civilians whose intention was to kill Dinka soldiers who were with me in Maiwut in retaliation for Commander Kuac Kang who was killed in Panyagoor attack by the SPLA Torit faction. But I managed to inform all Dinka soldiers in the camp under 1st Lt. Chol Mabil Deng to move from Maiwut to Nasir to report to the headquarters of Kerubino Kuanyin Bol that was based at Nasir town. Kerubino Kuanyin Bol was the deputy chairman and commander in chief of the Nasir faction at that time. About 75 officers, NCOs and men from Bahr El Ghazal moved from Maiwut to Nasir on foot for their safety from a planned attack by Gajaak armed youths.

In 1994, Kerubino Kuanyin Bol moved from Western Upper Nile to Bahr El Ghazal with his own forces that were mainly composed of men from the Dinka of Bahr El Ghazal, but he was defeated by the SPLM/A forces in Northern Bahr El Ghazal forcing him to withdrew to Abyei government army garrison, where he established his headquarters and continued to operate and recruit soldiers from sons and daughters of Bhar El Ghazal region. Luckily for him, he was however reinforced by the forces of Paulino Matip from Bul Nuer militias. Dr Machar later dismissed Kerubino Kuanyin Bol, William Nyuon, and Arok Thon

Arok from his movement for collaborating with the Sudan government to overthrow him.

On March 13, 1994, the forces of the SPLA Nasir faction in Lafon captured a government convoy that was passing through their area and afterwards they persuaded William Nyuon to rejoin the SPLM/A. So, on April 27, 1994, Dr Garang' and William Nyuon signed what they called the Lafon Declaration that paved the way for Nyuon's rejoining the SPLM/A Torit faction which marked the reunification of the movement.

When Dr Machar heard this declaration, he rejected it and his reaction annoyed Nyuon who later announced that he has dismissed Dr Machar from the SPLA Nasir faction and that the movement has reunified with the SPLM/A Torit faction. Nyuon formed a new Executive Council and he was supported by the SPLM/A Torit faction in a joint successful offensive against the government and the SPLM/A Nasir faction where he fell into an ambush and was killed in January 1996. Riek Machar later renamed his Nasir Faction as South Sudan independence Movement/Army (SSIM/A).

In May 1996, I was promoted to the rank of Alternate Commander (A/Cdr) in the - would be South Sudan Defense Force (SSDF) under the leadership of Dr Machar who would later become President of the Southern Sudan Coordinating Council.

# Chapter 9

## Khartoum Peace Agreement

When Dr Riek Machar failed to secure military support from the international community to fight the government of Sudan as well as SPLM/A mainstream, he opted to sign peace deal with the Sudan government.

On April 21, 1997, Dr Machar signed a peace agreement with the Sudan government and he was appointed President of Southern Sudan states Coordinating Council.

He was also made Commander-in-Chief of the South Sudan Defense Forces (SSDF) by other South Sudanese armed groups that were fighting alongside the Sudanese government against SPLM/A under the umbrella of the political wing of the United Democratic Salvation Front (UDSF).

The agreement defined a four-year interim period to enable the Southern states recover from the civil war, and also formed a coordinating council of the Southern states to oversee the transition government.

Under the agreement, a referendum was to be held after four years to enable South Sudanese choose to remain in a unified Sudan government or separate and form their own South Sudan government in accordance with the boundaries that were drawn in 1956.

The agreement, however, bestowed the control of the armed forces and other security apparatus in the hands of the central government, while the government of the Southern states was allowed minimal control over economic development only. The latter was, clearly, non-existent.

The president of the coordination council was appointed by the President of the Republic, while the president of the southern coordinating council appointed the Cabinet Ministers and Governors of the Southern states through final approval by the President of the Republic. Unfortunately, this agreement was not implemented in letter and spirit as had been agreed earlier.

### General Paulino Matip Defects from Dr Machar

In September 1997, a misunderstanding erupted between the forces of Dr Machar and those of Gen. Paulino Matip over the appointment of the Governor of Unity State. Dr Machar wanted Taban Deng Gai to be the Governor, while Gen. Paulino Matip was in favour of Ustaz Paul Liyliy Mathoat.

Following this disagreement that led to a fight, Gen. Paulino Matip defected from the SSDF and formed his own movement and named it the South Sudan United Movement and the South Sudan United Army (SSUM/SSUA). I was among the committee that was formed to draft and suggest the name SSUM/SSUA for Gen. Paulino Matip's faction. Our goal and mission were to unite all militias fighting alongside the government under one supreme command and to enter into agreement with the SPLM/A. Thereafter, I was promoted to the rank of commander and was assigned as the commander of the SSUM/SSUA's Signal Unit. The Sudan government under Brig. Omar Hassan El Bashir continued to supply both Gen. Paulino Matip and Riek Machar with ammunition and guns to fight each other forces in the battlefield which, generally, were rapidly dwindling in numbers and commitment.

In January 1998, Kerubino Kuanyin Bol re-defected from Dr Machar's faction to the SPLM/A mainstream faction. His forces attacked Wau army garrison in an attempt to capture it and gain credit from the SPLM/A mainstream, but he was repulsed and the SAF inflicted a lot of casualties on his forces.

Peace Delegation to Bahr El Ghazal.

On July 18, 1998, Commander William Manyang Mayak and I, accompanied by junior officers, were delegated by Gen. Paulino Matip to go to Bahr El Ghazal to make peace with the SPLM/A forces in Bhar El Ghazal.

We sent Capt. William Bajuoy Makuet ahead of us on July 15, 1998 to inform the authorities on the border side at Bahr El Ghazal that we shall be crossing the border for a meeting. We went and were warmly welcomed by James Yuol Kuol and Ajing Path, the Commissioners of Twic and Abyei Counties respectively. On July 20, 1998, we signed a peace agreement with the Commissioner of Twic Yuol Kuol and Commissioner of Abyei Ajing Path.

The agreement was a memorandum of understanding to pave the way for the unification of the leadership of the SPLM/A and SSUM/A. It was meant to;

1. Foster understanding at the leadership level of both sides in order to work out on how to unify the two forces.
2. Allow free movement of civilians and cattle across the border.
3. End cattle raids across the border.
4. Guarantee free trade across the border, among others.

## Defection from SSUM/A to SPLM/A.

On my return from Bahr El Ghazal after signing the peace deal, I was summoned by commanders the late Gen. Peter Gatdet Yaka, Thayip Gatluak Taitai,

Samuel Gai Yirchak and Francis Nyir Gatluak who wanted to know who sent me and the kind of peace deal that we discussed with the Dinka at Bahr El Ghazal.

I told them that it was Gen. Paulino Matip who delegated me to make peace with the people of Bahr El Ghazal. They then told me to go to the radio room to ask Gen. Paulino Matip who was in Khartoum, Sudan to confirm whether what I am saying is true.

We went to the radio hut to ask Gen. Paulino Matip, but strangely, and unfortunately for me, Gen. Paulino Matip did not come out openly to say that he approved and delegated me to go to Bahr El Ghazal for the peace talks.

Instead, he told the Commanders to forgive me since he could not recollect very well if he approved my going for the meeting, Matip was afraid to say that he had given me a green light to make peace with the people of Bhar El Ghazal because he could be overthrown by these commanders. The Commanders met and decided that I should be detained at Wangkei main prison till Gen. Paulino Matip comes down from Khartoum.

I was much disoriented and disappointed by this action by the Commanders as this to me was a betrayal by my colleagues.

On August 10, 1998, I decided to defect and rejoined the SPLM/A. I moved from Mankien to Bahr El Ghazal border and from there I established contact with my supporters to join me at the border. Many people did not want to go with me to Bahr El Ghazal for fear of being targeted by the Dinka soldiers since many Nuer and Dinka people had died on both sides during the 1991, coup that was staged by Dr Machar.

The two tribes earlier resorted to targeting each other on tribal lines, but this time I managed to mobilize about 300 officers, NCOS and men from Bul Nuer and Dinka militias who had been supporting Gen. Paulino Matip under command of Commander Anyar Mayol.

I was warmly welcomed in Bahr El Ghazal by the civilian authorities at the border and they immediately informed their leaders on my arrival in the area. Comrade Salva Kiir Mayardit, the current President of South Sudan was the overall commander of the SPLA 3rd front, in Bahr El Ghazal region by the time.

I established my camp on the border side of Twic, Bahr El Ghazal region with Western Upper Nile and established contact with Commanders Philip Bipean Machar, Anyar Mayol, and William Manyang Mayak whom I had left behind in Nuer land to join me later in Bahr El Ghazal.

But the three commanders could not make the move, they were accused of planning to follow me by joining the SPLM/A. On November 30, 1998, they were attacked and dislodged from Ruathnyibol by Commander Samuel Gai Yirchak.

Left with no ammunition, they crossed the border and established their camp at Mayenjur on Bahr El Ghazal side of the border. Together, we were integrated into the SPLA as commanders with effect from October 1, 1998.

I was then deployed as Chief of Operations on the border of Bahr El Ghazal with Western Upper Nile where I served for one year, and then I was again transferred to Thiet, Yiethkuel third front headquarters that was commanded by President Salva Kiir Mayardit who was the overall commander of Bahr El Ghazal region.

## Death of Kerubino Bol

Kerubino Kuanyin Bol fell out with Dr Garang' again and fled from Nairobi to Mayom, Mankien in Western Upper Nile to stay with his son in law, Gen. Paulino Matip who married his daughter. He was later killed in a mysterious circumstance in Mankien by forces of Peter Gatdet Yaka on September 10, 1999, who by this time had defected from Gen. Paulino Matip's movement (SSUM/A) to the SPLM/A mainstream.

In 1999, Dr Machar left Khartoum for Nairobi to regroup his followers who were scattered and some of them had already rejoined the SPLM/A mainstream, Torit faction leaving him with fewer followers and without a proper movement. Dr Riek Machar resigned in 2000, from the Sudan government as president of Southern coordinating council, and formed his own faction under the name of Sudan Peoples' Democratic Front (SPDF) and established his base at Maiwut near the Ethiopian border.

In 2002, he rejoined forces with the SPLM/A and became number three in ranking after President Salva Kiir Mayardit in the hierarchy of the SPLM/A. In the year 2000, I was assigned as Chief of Logistics in the third Front by Commander Salva Kiir Mayardit, and thereafter I was selected to go on a central mission with Commander Pieng Deng Kuol to attack and capture Raja town in Western Bahr El Ghazal.

In 2001, I was nominated to attend a military course at the SPLA Institute of Strategic Studies at Laso, South of Yei town, near the border with the Democratic Republic of Congo (DRC), for one year.

Upon my return, I went to Western Upper Nile to assist Commander Peter Gatdet in establishing and streamlining administration in Western Upper Nile, but strangely Peter Gatdet became furious with me and claimed that I was sent by Commander Salva Kiir Mayardit to take over his command, a move that led Peter Gatdet to defect and joined Paulino Matip again.

### The Riah incident.

In 2002, senior officers under Peter Gatdet, namely Commander John Jok Nhial and Commander Samuel Gai Yirchak, supported by civil servants that were working in Mayom County, conspired against Peter Gatdet and wrote a letter to Dr Garang' that they do not want Peter Gatdet to be their commander. They further insinuated that Peter Gatdet be replaced forthwith with Commander John Jok Nhial and Commander Samuel Gai be appointed as his Deputy.

The information reached Dr Garang' who supported the idea, but he did not discuss this matter with Gatdet. Instead, he summoned Peter Gatdet to his headquarters and he told him to go to school and leave the command to the next senior officer in command.

Peter Gatdet would hear none of this. He refused to go to college as advised by Dr Garang' and insisted that he wanted to continue working at his base. Unfortunately for him, this decision could not be changed as there was no plan for his return to Western Upper Nile.

This conspiracy to replace Peter Gatdet from his command base was plotted and supported by John Madeng Gatduel, Karlo Kuol Ruac, Martin Machot Deng and Michael Chiangjiek Gey.

### Conspiracy Meeting at Riaak.

One day, Commanders John Jok Nhial and Samuel Gai Yirchak convened a meeting at Riaak village at 6 pm in the evening and they invited me as an observer since I was based in Bahr El Ghazal and just came to Western Upper Nile on permission.

During the meeting, Commander John Jok Nhial and Commander Samuel Gai Yirchak told us that they had taken over the command of Peter Gatdet's forces and threatened to deal with Peter Gatdet if he set foot in the area again. The pronouncement was followed by a moment of silence in the room as some of us present looked down in amusement and others looked sideways.

At this point, I raised my hand and told the two commanders that what they were doing was not in order in line with the military procedures. "It is better you raise your complaints to the SPLM/A leadership and wait for further directive from the Commander-in-Chief," I told them.

Instead, they wished me away saying that I should stop interfering with their internal affairs adding that I had just come from Bahr El Ghazal and therefore I am a stranger with no right to talk about their command affairs. The two Commanders further accused me of indirectly supporting Peter Gatdet. I decided to keep quiet until the meeting ended and thereafter, I went back to where I was living.

The same night, the information regarding the meeting reached Peter Gatdet's supporters, including Commander Tito Biel Wic who was at the frontline at Wangbieth area.

Tito Biel Wic was a commander based at Peter Gatdet's headquarters but he was not informed about this meeting, and he became very furious when he heard what had happened.

The following morning, Commander Tito Biel Wic came to Riaak with a sizable battalion, and on seeing him, all the commanders in Riaak ran for their lives helter-skelter. As others took off, I remained behind, met and asked Tito Biel Wic, why he had come with such a big number of forces to Riaak all the way from his base.

Instead, Tito Biel ordered his forces to kill me. I got angry and I ordered my bodyguards to get ready to fight Tito Biel Wic in self-defense, but the officers who came with Tito Biel, including 1st Lt. William Bajuoy Makuet, intervened and stopped the commotion.

I then ordered Tito Biel Wic and his officers to sit under a tree for a meeting to listen to their grievance since in my knowledge I had no problem with him and his team. Tito Biel and his team agreed and while in the meeting, I explained to them exactly what transpired at the meeting that was held and blamed them for overreacting based on false information.

Tito Biel Wic told me that he had come to arrest the commanders who wanted to overthrow Peter Gatdet plus "you Stephen Buoy because you were also in the same meeting," he said.

He said that 1st Lt. William Bajuoy Makuet, a relative of Peter Gatdet, had sent him a message the previous night and informed him wrongly that all Commanders in Riaak had been asked to report to SPLA headquarters, but they refused to go and instead they wanted to overthrow Peter Gatdet.

Commander Tito Biel Wic was then told to come to Riaak and arrest the conveners of the meeting if indeed he was not part of the group who were out to oust Peter Gatdet. "If indeed you are not part of this conspiracy, come and arrest the commanders who have convened the meeting," he was told by the officers of Gatdet's headquarters at Riaak.

I told him that I attended the said meeting, but I was not part of the conspiracy against Peter Gatdet. I told him further that I was in the meeting to help arbitrate based on the issues that were raised.

By this time, as we were meeting under the tree, all the commanders who ran away were rounded-up in the bush and were brought back handcuffed. I ordered that they should be set free and escorted to their respective homes awaiting a further action on the matter the following morning.

I immediately established contact with Gen. Bior Ajang Duot to send a plane to evacuate these commanders to the headquarters at New-Site, Kapoeta area before information could reach Peter Gatdet, otherwise, all of us would be killed, as he wouldn't believe even my neutrality in this matter. I proceeded and jammed all radio communication lines that were directed to Peter Gatdet to ensure that no one talked to him in regard to this matter.

The next day, Gen. Bior Ajang sent a plane early in the morning and I boarded the plane together with John Jok Nhial, Samuel Gai Yirchak, John Puoljor Wicyoak, James Nhial Wathkak, Karlo Kuol Ruac, and Philip Bipean Machar heading to New-Site headquarters where the Commander-in-Chief of the SPLA Dr John Garang' de Mabior was based.

Philip Bipean Machar was not found when the commanders were arrested. He ran up to Mayenjur the same day, but we had to pick him from Mayenjur the same day on our way to New Site.

### Gatdet Defects to General Paulino Matip's faction

When we arrived at New Site, Peter Gatdet was summoned by the Commander-in-Chief to come to New Site to help resolve the stalemate between him and the commanders under him. He, however, refused to come, since he was misinformed that he would be arrested if he availed himself.

The Commander-in-Chief told Peter Gatdet, that I want Stephen Buoy to go back to Western Upper Nile to act in his place in his absence as a neutral person until the case between him and the commanders was resolved.

Peter Gatdet became furious and refused to hand over and made claims that Stephen Buoy was the cause of this conspiracy since he was assigned by Commander Salva Kiir to cause the tension so that the Commander, Salva Kiir, could launch a coup against Dr Garang'.

Then, the Commander-in-Chief asked Peter Gatdet, "whom do you think can act in your absence till your case is over and resolved with your commanders?" Peter Gatdet refused to answer the question forcing Dr Garang' to suggest another name of Commander Stephen Duol Chuol to serve in his absence until the case between him and other commanders was resolved.

Peter Gatdet, on hearing the change of name, agreed with the Commander-in-Chief and immediately Commander Stephen Duol Chuol was rushed to the area to control and command the forces of Western Upper Nile in acting capacity. He was warmly received by A/Cdrs Mathew Puljang Top, Tito Biel Wic and Michael Kolchara Nyang.

Peter Gatdet instead decided to report to Sudan Embassy in Kenya when he failed to establish contact with his forces on the ground to arrange for him a plane to take him to Riaah. He made this arrangement since he was misinformed that Stephen Buoy was already in charge of the command and he would be killed if he goes there.

Due to this confusion, Peter Gatdet decided to defect and rejoined Gen. Paulino Matip in Khartoum who welcomed him back and appointed him as Chief of Operations for his forces. On hearing news of Peter Gatdet's defection, the Commander-in-Chief convened an urgent meeting with commanders that had worked under Peter Gatdet and he asked Taban Deng to attend the meeting too. Strangely, I was not even invited to attend the meeting.

Unknown to me, Taban Deng had conspired with the commanders to accuse me before the Commander-in-Chief that I am Salva Kiir Mayardit's and Peter Gatdet's man and that I should not be allowed to go back to Western Upper Nile with them.

After the meeting the Commander-in-Chief Dr Garang' made the following deployment: -

1. Commander Stephen Duol Chuol was appointed Commander of the Western Upper Nile.
2. Commander Philip Bipean Machar was deployed to Western Upper Nile, headquarters.
3. Commander Stephen Buoy Rolnyang was deployed as Chief Relief Coordinator for Upper Nile to base in Lokichogio.
4. Commander John Jok Nhial was deployed to Western Upper Nile headquarters.
5. Commander Samuel Gai Yirchak was deployed as Commander of Mayom Operations.
6. Commander Karlo Kuol Ruac was deployed as commander of Bentiu Operations.
7. Commander Michael Chiangjiek was deployed as chief of Military Intel-

ligence in Western Upper Nile
8. Commander John Puoljor Wicyoak was deployed to Western Upper Nile headquarters.
9. Commander James Nhial Wathkak was deployed to Western Upper Nile headquarters.

We were invited to attend a short meeting where the Commander-in-Chief informed us of our new assignment with specified roles and duties. The commanders were very happy to hear that we were given a new assignment and, more so that I was transferred to Lokichogio in the Kenyan border to work as a relief worker.

In their earlier meeting, that I did not attend, the Commander-in-Chief told them that Peter Gatdet had defected and there was no need to keep them here in Newsite. He told them to go back to Western Upper Nile to control the forces.

In Lokichogio, Kenya, I established contact with A/Cdrs Mathew Puljang Top, Tito Biel Wic, and Michael Kolchara Nyang and told them not to embrace the commanders who had been deployed to their areas from New Site since they were going to take over their role and command responsibilities.

When the commanders arrived in Western Upper Nile from New Site, there was high tension and they were initially not allowed to disembark from the plane, but later they were allowed and were detained at Riaak by forces loyal to A/Cdrs Mathew Puljang Top. Stephen Duol Chuol pleaded with those of Mathew Puljang Top to release the commanders. His plea was accepted by Mathew Puljang Top, Tito Biel Wic and Michael Kolchara Nyang, who released the Commanders, but on condition that the Commanders should report to their respective homes and not to give any directives in any command activity in Western Upper Nile.

After this tension, Stephen Duol Chuol recommended the three A/Cdrs Mathew Puljang Top, Tito Biel Wic, and Michael Kolchara to be promoted to the rank of Commander. Dr Garang' promoted the three A/Commanders to full commanders and maintained their command status quo and base.

### Lokichogio, Kenya

I went to Lokichogio, Kenya to start working at my new station as Chief Relief Coordinator for Upper Nile region – well aware that my deployment was instigated by Taban Deng because he wanted to command Bentiu through Stephen Duol Chuol to gain support on the ground.

I did not stay long in Lokichogio as I wanted to visit my family whom I had not seen for some time. I requested Commander Salva Kiir Mayardit, the Deputy Chairman and Commander-in-Chief of the SPLM/A to allow me to go to Bahr El Ghazal to visit my family. He granted me the permission and I flew to Lietnhom, where my family was, and spent one month there on holiday, ostensibly to catch up with my family members after a long absence.

While still on holiday, I heard that Dr. Machar and Taban Deng Gai were going to Western Upper Nile on a tour. I asked for permission from Commander Kiir to meet with them, and he agreed. I walked on foot together with my bodyguards to Western Upper Nile, and met Dr. Machar and Taban Deng Gai at Lare area, and together we moved to Mayenjur. While at Mayenjur, Dr Machar ordered for the creation of Abiemnom as a separate county from greater Mayom.

We proceeded back to Lare and from there, we went to Riaak where Dr. Machar called all commanders in the Bul Nuer area for a meeting. There, Dr Machar asked commanders Mathew Puljang and Tito Biel Wic to choose between Commanders Philip Bipean Machar and Stephen Buoy Rolnyang who to remain with them in Bul Nuer area and whom they recommend to serve as their overall Commander. All commanders said that they preferred me to become their overall commander.

Thereafter, Dr Machar and Taban Deng Gai left me in Riaak with Commanders Mathew Puljang and Tito Biel Wic as they proceeded further to Leer. He then sent a message to all units to appoint me as the commissioner of Mayom County as well as John Jok Nhial, whom he also appointed as the Commissioner of Rubkona County.

I felt cheated when I received the message, because I had not expressed interest to be the commissioner. Secondly, Dr Machar had no authority to appoint any SPLA senior officer to a position that was reserved for a civilian without the knowledge of the Chairman and Commander-in-Chief of the SPLM/A.

I wrote back and informed Dr. Machar that I was not willing to take up the new appointment as a Commissioner for Mayom county. After considerations, I was assigned as Chief of Operations for Western Upper Nile under the direct command of Commander Stephen Duol Chuol.

When Commander James Hoth Mai was appointed as overall commander of Upper Nile in 2003, he appointed me as commander of Western Upper Nile, and I was deputized by Commander John Jok Nhial.

Further changes were made in the command of Western Upper Nile after a conference that was held in Upper Nile in Panyagoor in 2003, that was chaired by Dr. Garang'. Commander Peter Bol Kong was deployed as commander of

Western Upper Nile and I was appointed his deputy.

I worked with Commander Peter Bol Kong for one year, before he was transferred from Western Upper Nile to the Lou Nuer area. After his departure, I was appointed for the second time, as commander of Western Upper Nile till 2006.

## The Comprehensive Peace Agreement (CPA)

On January 9, 2005, the SPLM and the government of Sudan, the National Congress Party (NCP) signed a Comprehensive Peace Agreement (CPA) that granted the two protagonists' power of sharing wealth from the South Sudan.

The peace agreement was signed following pressure from the international community that wanted to see that human rights abuses, especially on the South Sudanese, were stopped.

Under the CPA, a referendum was to be conducted to enable the South Sudanese people to make one last decision whether to remain in a united Sudan or go separate ways and form the government of South Sudan that was to be ruled by South Sudanese themselves.

It was also agreed that the two standing armies form a joint integrated unit to be drawn from both parties for a six-year period, after which a referendum was to be held for the people of South Sudan to decide their fate. The idea of having a referendum was mooted to enable them remain in Sudan as a country or allow them to break away and go as a separate sovereign state.

On July 8, 2005, Dr. Garang', the leader of the SPLM/A, set foot in Khartoum for the first time in more than two decades following the civil war that was mainly fought in the bushes of South Sudan.

He was sworn in as the First Vice President of the Republic of the Sudan and at the same time as the President of the Government of South Sudan (GOSS). Salva Kiir Mayardit became his Deputy in the government of South Sudan.

The agreement that included a permanent ceasefire, wealth and power sharing amongst others, paved the way for Dr Garang' who set foot in Khartoum on July 8, 2005 for the first time after spending decades in the bush fighting successive governments in Sudan.

Unfortunately, Dr. Garang' did not enjoy the dividends of the long struggle and the peace he signed with the Sudanese government after decades of misunderstanding that led to war. He died in a helicopter crash after boarded a Ugandan plane on July 30, 2005 as he was returning to his base at New Site, following a meeting in Kampala with Ugandan President Yoweri Museveni.

Upon this sad development, the SPLM leadership met at New Site, the headquarters of Dr Garang', and nominated his Deputy Salva Kiir Mayardit to replace him as the First Vice President of the Republic of Sudan and the President of the Government of South Sudan in accordance to the political and military protocol of the SPLM/A. Dr Machar was selected as the 1st Vice President of the government of South Sudan (GOSS) and James Wani Igga as the 2nd Vice President of the (GOSS).

After all these confirmations, on August 11, 2005, and after the burial of Dr. Garang, Salva Kiir went to Khartoum, Sudan where he was sworn in as the 1st Vice President of the Republic of Sudan and the President of the government of South Sudan.

President Kiir held negotiations aimed at bringing all other armed groups that were fighting the SPLM/A alongside the Sudan armed forces on board and managed to convince Gen. Paulino Matip Nhial to join the government of South Sudan.

In 2007, Gen. Paulino Matip Nhial and his group joined the government of South Sudan under what was so-called the Juba Declaration Agreement. The forces of SSDF were integrated into the SPLA, and Gen. Paulino Matip Nhial was appointed as deputy Commander-in-Chief of the SPLA, a position that was not in existence before, but was created to accommodate him.

In 2005, I was transferred to Kapoeta area to command the SPLA mobile force Infantry brigade that was deployed in eastern Equatoria. I commanded the mobile forces in Kapoeta for one year after which I was transferred to the SPLA headquarters in Juba, where I was deployed to establish the command of the SPLA Military Police for the first time after the CPA as there was no military police unit in South Sudan at the time.

I later successfully structured and established the Military Police Unit along with the SPLA commando elite unit, making the two units Special Forces in the SPLA.

# Chapter 10

## The establishment of the SPLA Military Police Unit

In 2007, the SPLA Chief of Gen. Staff, Oyai Deng Ajak, ordered for the redeployment of the troops from Kapoeta to Western Upper Nile to supplement the number of the SPLA forces in Bentiu.

In Kapoeta I was in charge of SPLA Mobile Force Infantry brigade that was deployed in the area after the Comprehensive Peace Agreement (CPA) in 2005.

Following the transfers, Brig. Gen. Kongor Reech Gak took over the command from me and I reported to the SPLA headquarters in Juba to be in charge of the Military Police unit, a position that was created for the first time in the Republic of South Sudan. I assumed the command on December 5, 2007 and went ahead to establish the SPLA Military Police in the same year as I was directed.

The Military Police was assigned to protect the lives of people and their properties, protect army installations, enforce military laws, regulations and to maintain discipline within the SPLA units. It was also charged with the responsibility of controlling traffic within Juba City, preventing crime and responding to all emergencies within the city. The Military Police were also responsible for supporting the Police in managing civil disturbances when called upon by the police authorities to intervene.

Under my tenure, the Military Police made many achievements in Juba city, including preventing and neutralizing crimes in the city. I made sure that criminals who commonly operated at night, looting people's properties and killing innocent people, were neutralised. We disciplined members of the SPLA that were loitering in the town and public places while in uniform and also controlled the unnecessary movement of the SPLA vehicles after closing hours.

### Special Forces

In addition to establishing the Military Police Unit, I also established in 2007 other two important units namely the SPLA Commando and SPLA Special Forces. The commando nucleus was formed with my bodyguards and the bodyguards of other senior officers in the SPLA headquarters, including the bodyguards of the former SPLA Chief of Gen. Staff (COGS) Gen. Oyai Deng Ajak and Gen. Pieng Deng Kuol who was by then the Director of Operations at the SPLA headquarters.

The commandos were sent to Ethiopia to undergo a one-year intensive training and they later came back to Juba after completing their course. The Special Forces were drawn from various SPLA units in 2006, and then sent to New Kush General Training Centre for a three years training by the British special instructors led by Retired Col. Richard. I accompanied them back from their training camp in New Kush to New Site in Juba in 2008 after their graduation and they were later deployed under my direct command.

I used the three units namely Military Police, Commando and Special Forces to enforce laws and regulations and protect the lives of civilians by preventing crimes in Juba city.

The two units, Commando and Special Forces were later integrated into one unit called Commando and were separated from the military police.

The difference between the Commando Unit and other SPLA units is that commando is a small elite force that is trained for making quick raids against the enemy forces, while the others are large in number and highly organised force concerned mainly with ground rather than air or naval operations.

In 2008, I was transferred to Lanya to lead the commando unit while Brig. Simon Madit Ngor was assigned as the commander of Military Police and remained in Juba. I stayed there for almost a year on a special mission of tracking the Uganda-based Lord's Resistance Army (LRA) that was led by Joseph Kony with the aim of keeping him off our territory where they often run to after attacking the Ugandan bases and innocent civilians in Northern Uganda. Kony had lodged a hide and seek war against Uganda's President Yoweri Museveni with the aim of toppling him. He was taking refuge in the dense forest of South Sudan. The LRA was operating on the border of South Sudan with Uganda, and sometimes with the DRC border where they committed crime around the border and at times would move to Uganda, commit raids and other crimes against humanity, and run back to the forest.

I pursued Kony from Uganda - South Sudan border up to the Garamba Park on DRC border with South Sudan, where he disappeared and melted into Darfur, Sudan region and he has never been heard of again till now.

In 2009, Gen. James Hoth Mai was appointed as SPLA Chief of Gen. Staff (COGS) and he redeployed me back to Juba to command the Military Police Unit for the second time. Maj. Gen. Mangar Buong Alueng was deployed as the new commander of the SPLA Commando. In 2010, the anticipated general elections were held and El Bashir and President Kiir won. President Kiir was sworn in as the first Vice President of Sudan and the President of the government of South Sudan.

However, the outcome of the elections was challenged by Lam Akol of the SPLM Democratic Change (SPLM-DC) on grounds that the process of elections had been rigged in favour of El Bashir and Kiir by the SPLM.

In April 2010, President Salva Kiir was elected President of the Republic of South Sudan with 93 percent of the votes, marking a positive step towards the separation of South Sudan from the Republic of Sudan. Thereafter he was re-appointed as the 1st Vice President of the Republic of Sudan according to the interim constitution of Sudan.

## Independence and Reconstruction.

The long-awaited referendum was held in 2011 and it gave the South Sudanese an opportunity to decide whether they preferred to remain united with the Sudan or stay separate from the Sudan.

It was announced on January 9, 2011 that 99 percent of South Sudanese voted to secede from the Sudan and on July 9, 2011, the independence of the Republic of South Sudan was proclaimed at the Dr Garang's Mausoleum ground in Juba. Thereafter, populations and the government officials hit the ground running as they started nation building in earnest.

The long-awaited struggle for self-determination that had looked far-fetched to opponents of the South Sudan and in the process to attainment had costed millions of lives and destruction of properties was at last becoming a reality to the surviving Anya Nya war veterans and dedicated civilian collaborators. The date for the referendum was set for January 9, 2011 and in earnest preparations began early for the day whose dream started way back with the formation of Anya Nya - I veterans who launched massive fights from the bush, some of whom were unlucky to participate in the day.

The South Sudanese populations woke up early in the morning to vote in this historic event that most of them were taking part in honour of their departed kinsmen who put up a strong fight to ensure that they one day become self-rule.

After the counting of the votes, about 98.83 percent of the population voted in favor of separation from the Sudan and independence of South Sudan as a sovereign state.

South Sudan became independent officially from Sudan on July 9, 2011, but some of the disputed areas such as Abyei, Heglig in Bentiu, Joda in Renk, mile 40 in Aweil and Kafia Kenygi in Raja regions had their cases pending following disagreements on these locations.

On July 14, 2011, the Republic of South Sudan flag was raised at the headquarters of the United Nations (UN) in New York as a welcoming ceremony of the 193rd member of the UN.

On July 27, 2011, the flag of the Republic of South Sudan was again raised at the headquarters of the African Union in Addis Ababa, as the 54th member state. In early March 2012, the SPLA forces clashed with Sudan armed forces over the Heglig dispute and the SPLA soldier's emerged victorious after capturing Heglig oil fields from SAF.

Heglig is a disputed oil field between South Sudan and the Sudan, but the SPLA withdrew from Heglig on March 20, 2012 due to pressure from the international community, especially from the then UN Secretary Gen., Ban Ki Moon.

### Heglig battle.

On March 12, 2012 a war broke out between South Sudan and Sudan over the disputed oil rich Heglig area. Additional troops were required to go to Bentiu to reinforce forces of 4th Infantry division. I sent one full battalion of Military Police to Bentiu to participate in Heglig operations. During this operation, the SPLA forces captured Heglig and advanced to Karasana, North of Heglig, but they were ordered to withdraw to South Sudan border due to pressure from the UN and other international organisations.

On June 6, 2012, I went to visit the 4th Infantry division SPLA forces that participated in the Heglig war at their headquarters. I went further to Lalob area to meet commando forces, then to Tomor and Mayom town to meet forces of Military Police and the Republican Guards that were deployed there to deter movement and activities of militias.

In my assessment, our forces had very high morale, even though they lacked the following;

1. In most instances, if they got food, it was not enough and was only maize grain. They sometimes resorted to killing animals in the nearby bushes for survival.
2. Most of our forces wore only one pair of uniform since the fighting erupted and some did not have boots as all their luggage remained at Heglig. I noted that our forces had left their luggage behind when they were instructed to attack Kilo 23. Unfortunately, when they went back to pick them, they found out that the forces that remained at Heglig had left the

place. Their luggage got messed up and some were taken by the forces they left behind and were already not at the base.

3. The boots that were given to them were of low quality and got spoiled so fast.
4. They had no sleeping bags and cooking utensils.
5. They had neither houses nor tents and occasionally were exposed to rain. The most affected were the Commando forces that were at Lalob, where there were no huts.
6. They suffered malaria and dysentery attacks.
7. They had no standby fuel for emergency cases including transporting sick soldiers to Bentiu State and Teaching Hospital for treatment.

**Frontline Forces at Heglig.**

More than 1,000 vehicles that were captured by our soldiers in Heglig disappeared in the hands of individuals who turned them to private use. The same people also took military vehicles that were captured from the enemy, and they went ahead and changed their colours before converting them to their personal use.

Hundreds of trucks, including Ural - big military vehicles and damp trucks that are useful for military operations, were taken to Wau and Rumbek, and had their colour changed and were converted into private business trucks. Even bulldozers and excavators that are useful in transporting tanks were used for private business purposes.

Low-beds that were meant for soldiers were also taken by these people for their own personal use in their residence. The Soldiers at the camps were surprised to see the vehicles they captured from Heglig passing by and carrying goods, headed to the market, same vehicles now owned by some of their colleagues.

The pickups that were supposed to be used to mount the machine guns were used as family vehicles while many of our guns were placed on the ground due to lack of vehicles to mount them on.

These vehicles were supposed to be distributed to the military units that fought at Heglig to improve their operations, but some senior officers did the contrary by converting them to their private use. Strangely, even all food and non-food items, including cattle that were willingly contributed by the civilian populations and States did not reach frontline forces in the battlefields.

The action demoralised the forces that were aware that the contributions were made for their assistance as the announcement was made through the media.

Such actions, even though deserve thorough investigations, none of which has been conducted to date.

### The 4th Infantry Division Command.

The actions and lack of support from commanders disoriented forces of 4th Infantry division, majority of who were demoralized. During this time, each infantry brigade that was supposed to have a good number of soldiers was unable to raise two complete battalions and to make it worse, each battalion could not raise two full companies (Coys).

This happened because the soldiers were scattered in the villages and only few were in the front line alongside the reinforcement forces that came from the SPLA General Headquarters (GHQS).

### Soldiers Oversight.

Some soldiers from the reinforcement forces of the SPLA headquarters, especially the Military Police and Republican Guards, were fond of deserting duty and going for leisure in the town at a time when they were supposed to be working.

They were uncomfortable living under unbearable conditions that included lack of proper food, basic items and sustained health service. Occasionally some soldiers were engaged in random shooting into the air to cause panic that led to desertion and others getting engaged in weird activities that only spoiled the name of disciplined forces.

The soldiers had a tendency of going to the villages and nearby towns armed with guns. Often, they got involved in looting from populations, a trend that led to absenteeism and disorder in the camps when they returned.

These actions brought soldiers in regular direct contact with businessmen and civilians and paved the way for smugglers, especially civilian businesswomen, who dealt in selling alcohol into the frontline bases.

### Heglig Battle Miscalculations.

Failure to plan, coordinate and direct the Heglig war properly was to blame for our loss at the hands of our opponents. Despite the fact that our infantry forces had all it takes to win the battle, but they lacked a coordinated command in the front line. Our forces were defeated from Karasana by the Sudan armed forces and withdrew in disarray. Even when President Salva Kiir ordered for the withdrawal from Heglig, already our forces got dislodged and withdrew headlong without any control.

From onset, there was no physical briefing to the soldiers before the battle began as it was only the subordinate commanders that were briefed and directed on phone. The fighting was fought randomly since the reinforcements from the SPLA headquarters were instructed to attack and withdrew after attacking as they wanted while other forces were watching.

During this battle, there was no communication equipment used and no sand model (a sand table model used to show the areas where battle will be fought and how to fight it) was used to enable every unit to know their mission. Our tanks, artillery and air defence units were not used effectively since most of the gunners and drivers of the tanks were not from the SPLA proper soldiers who had participated in previous wars of liberation.

It was noted that some tank drivers most of the time abandoned the tanks due to disagreements and misunderstanding between them and their commanders, hence lower morale of foot soldiers on the ground who expected support from the tanks.

The forces that were fighting at the Heglig had high chances of winning but they lacked cohesion due to total command failures that were exhibited by the ground commanders.

If our forces could have advanced together based on plans that were drawn earlier up to Karasana, our enemy could not have eventually made it to Heglig again to launch a massive battle with us.

# Chapter 11

## The 2013, SPLM Political Crisis

On December 15, 2013, a political power struggle within the top leadership of the SPLM ruling party broke out between forces loyal to President Kiir and his Deputy Dr Machar. This is after Kiir accused Dr Machar and his group of attempting to oust him – a move which plunged the country into a civil war. The notorious recruited Dinka paramilitary known as Maithiang – Aynor and other non–civilized armed Dinka civilians in Juba took the law into their own hands, hunted down ethnic Nuer and targeted them in the capital Juba.

The fight spread fast across the country causing serious destruction in the country with civilians of either ethnic Dinka or Nuer being targeted on ethnic basis. Launching a full scale civil war in the country that resulted in the death of nearly 400,000, and displacement of more than 2 million people. Ugandan President, Yoweri Museveni, sent troops to Juba to fight alongside the SPLA and to protect the seat of government since the SPLA had split along tribal lines. Some Ugandan soldiers were deployed in Bor town to defend it and protect the civilians and their properties.

The conflict spread in many towns in Upper Nile where people's properties were set on fire and razed to the ground. When Dr Machar's faction failed to seize power, his military wing took the new name as the Sudan People Liberation Movement/Army in the Opposition (SPLM/A-IO).

Several ceasefires were signed and subsequently got violated by both sides during this period, until a final peace agreement was signed in Addis Ababa under the auspices of the Inter-Governmental Authority on Development (IGAD) following intense pressure and threats of enforcing sanctions against the two protagonists by the United Nations.

After the agreement had been signed, Dr Machar was installed as the 1st Vice President of the Republic of South Sudan and he returned to the capital Juba in 2016 to take oath of office.

However, before the ink of the agreement dried, intensive fight erupted again between the factions in Juba Palace -1 (J-1). Known the J-I dogfight. Dr Machar was forced to flee the country again and he crossed over to the DR Congo with his forces. Taban Deng Gai was however appointed 1st Vice President, replacing him and representing SPLM/A –IO.

### SPLA 1st Infantry division

By the time the conflict erupted, I was already deployed to the SPLA 1st Infantry division in Upper Nile as Deputy Division Commander to Maj. Gen. Angelo Jongkuc Jool. The division, code named "Jamus" is one of the SPLA Infantry divisions formed in 2005, after the signing of the CPA.

Jamus Infantry division has been deployed in the Upper Nile region on the border of Sudan along the White Nile, Blue Nile and Sennar states in the Northern part, and Ethiopia in the Eastern part of Upper Nile region.

During the crisis of 2013, Maj. Gen. Angelo Jongkuc was transferred to SPLA headquarters and I was appointed to succeed him as the commander of 1st Infantry division.

## Rebel SPLA-IO Activities

The rebels were recruiting civilians in the areas under their control and inside the Sudan by promising them promotion then take them for a two-week crash training in Buoth, Sudan Army Garrison. The Sudanese army was expected to equip them with different types of weapons and direct them to attack strategic locations of their interest in South Sudan territory.

The rebels had three camps namely Kilo-4 near Joda in White Nile State and Tibun and Buoth in Blue Nile State in the Sudan from where they were launching their attacks.

They set up these bases with the hope to capture Renk and the oil fields of Adaar and Paloch, use the bases as their supply routes to lower areas of Gajaak, Jikany and Lou Nuer respectively and as training centres for their new recruits.

Sudan pushed the rebels, SPLA-IO, to reject peace and continue fighting, with the promise that they would provide them with military equipment such as artillery, war tanks, and other equipment to topple the Government of South Sudan.

When our forces attacked a rebel base in Tibun in which two rebel mounted vehicles were destroyed and one mounted with anti-tank 82 MM recoil model captured, we discovered that the drivers of these artillery and tanks were Sudanese, meaning the rebels did not know how to operate them.

During the operation, our soldiers saw the rebel tanks running after their soldiers who were scattered all over but we ordered our forces to withdraw to our side of the border.

The agreement between the rebels and the Sudan Government was to take over the management of the oil fields of Upper Nile and Unity states and finally to share the oil revenues equally. Upon succeeding, the Sudanese government wanted the rebels to declare the region an autonomous region like that of Somaliland in Somalia to loot natural resources in the region and continue to support them until the government of South Sudan collapses.

They also had plans to work in shift near the supply routes along the border of Sudan with South Sudan to protect oil fields that were expected to be their main source of income.

The rebels were further in agreement with SAF on conducting joint operations against the SPLM - North and Government of South Sudan in return to receiving additional weapons.

The Sudan Government resorted to the use of what is so called "Rapid Support Forces" along the border of Sudan around Blue Nile, Sennar and White Nile states to reinforce the rebel's activities.

The Sudan provided Guest Houses to the senior rebel commanders and their families in Khartoum and equipped their coordination offices for recruitment and mobilization, and allowed them to arrest any South Sudanese citizen supporting the government of South Sudan.

The Government of Sudan also supplied the rebels with food and uniform, in addition to ammunitions, guns, vehicles and tanks, equipment that sustained their stay in the bush and made them stay in the fight.

The rebels were directed by SAF to arrest and confiscate any property belonging to the Sudanese traders who were smuggling goods and commodities to South Sudan.

Many traders as a result, lost their lives as some also lost their properties in the hands of the rebels along the Sudan White Nile, Sennar, and Blue Nile states borders with the South Sudan.

The SAF assigned members of the SPLA-IO along the border checkpoints to arrest and kill any South Sudanese seen crossing towards South Sudan, and as a result, many civilians from South Sudan also lost their lives at the border.

## Impact of 2013 Crisis

The military disturbances of 2013 caused a huge crisis within Jamus Infantry division. Over ten percent of Jamus forces, mainly made up of Nuer soldiers, defected from the Jamus 3rd Infantry brigade that was deployed in Malakal, Dolieb Hill, Ulang, Nasir, Longochuk, Maiwut and Pagak in the Southern and Eastern part of the Upper Nile state, and joined the rebellion.

Despite the fact that Jamus division stood the 2013, crisis, 20 percent of the soldiers either deserted, killed, wounded, disabled or went missing. Only a few soldiers deserted from the 1st and 2nd Infantry brigades of Jamus division. The division remained a united force that was inclusive of all tribes from South Sudan that stood and defended the country against the insurgency. The following are the details of the battles fought with the rebels (SPLM/A-IO) in Upper Nile region:

On April 23, 2014, the SPLM/A-IO attacked Renk town, the base of Jamus Division. The rebels were repulsed. Casualties on both sides were as below:

| S/N | Faction | Number of casualties | | |
|---|---|---|---|---|
| 1. | N/A | Killed in action | Wounded in action | POW |
| 2. | 1st infantry Division | 05 | 06 | 0 |
| 3. | SPLA-IO | 15 | 0 | 01 |

Several weapons captured from the rebels

On May 4, 2014, the SPLM/A-IO attacked Giziria and Khorneem, North of Renk, and they were repulsed without any casualties reported on both sides.

On June 9, 2014, the SPLM/A-IO attacked Gizira North of Renk for the second time and were repulsed, and the following were the casualties on both sides:

| S/N | Faction | Number of casualties | | |
|---|---|---|---|---|
| 1. | N/A | Killed in action | Wounded in action | POW |
| 2. | 1st Infantry division | 5 | 11 | 0 |
| 3. | SPLA-IO | 30 | 0 | 0 |

**Different types of small Arms were captured from the rebels**

On September 16, 2014 the SPLM/A-IO conducted an intensive shelling on Renk town and our forces responded with heavy artillery and silenced or suppressed their shelling. However, there were no casualties reported on both sides.

On September 21, 2014, our special forces, Jamus Battalion 107 attacked and destroyed the SPLMA-IO mobile forces that were coming from a mission in Pagak. The SPLM/A-IO headquarters attacked Renk town at a place called Gospami, with the following casualties recorded:

| S/N | Faction | Number of casualties | | |
|---|---|---|---|---|
| 1. | N/A | Killed in action | Wounded in action | POW |
| 2. | 1st Infantry division | 5 | 45 | 0 |
| 3. | SPLA-IO | 150 | 0 | 0 |

During this attack, our soldiers defeated the opponents forcing them to run in different directions. We also captured different types of weapons and equipment from them. On the same day, the SPLM/A-IO in Wedekona, Manyo County crossed River Nile and attacked Majak village in the South of Renk town, but they were repulsed with the following casualties:

| S/N | Faction | Number of casualties | | |
|---|---|---|---|---|
| 1. | N/A | Killed in action | Wounded in action | POW |
| 2. | 1st Infantry division | 3 | 15 | 0 |
| 3, | SPLA-IO | 3 | 0 | 0 |

On November 10, 2014, the SPLM/A-IO forces based at Tibun in the Sudan, attacked our location at Duk-duk Garrison, with the aim of capturing the Garrison, but they were repulsed and the following were the causalities:

| S/N | Faction | Number of casualties | | |
|---|---|---|---|---|
| 1. | N/A | Killed in action | Wounded in action | POW |
| 2. | 1st Infantry division | 05 | 21 | 0 |
| 3. | SPLA-IO | 34 | 0 | 0 |

**Different types of Weapons and equipment were captured.**

On November 13, 2014, the SPLM/A-IO that was based at Tibun in the Sudan attacked our location at Duk-duk for the second time, but our soldiers repulsed them and no casualty was reported on both sides.

On January 12, 2015, the SPLM/A-IO soldiers who were travelling from Buoth Sudan army Garrison with military supplies on their way to Pagak, attacked our location at Jamam with an intention to cause damages, but our soldiers repulsed them and the following casualties were recorded;

| S/N | Faction | Number of casualties | | |
|---|---|---|---|---|
| 1. | N/A | Killed in action | Wounded in action | POW |
| 2. | 1st Infantry division | 18 | 26 | 0 |
| 3. | SPLA-IO | 26 | 0 | 0 |

***Note:*** During this attack, 12 civilians, including women and 6 children, were killed in Jamam on government side and different types of weapons and ammunitions were captured from the rebels.

On January 18, 2015, the SPLM/A-IO forces based at Tibun attacked our location at Amdholwic but our forces repulsed them and the following casualties were reported:

| S/N | Faction | Number of casualties | | |
|---|---|---|---|---|
| 1. | N/A | Killed in action | Wounded in action | POW |
| 2. | 1st Infantry division | 4 | 15 | 0 |
| 3. | SPLA-IO | 24 | 0 | 0 |

We captured one mounted pick up with 82 MM recoil and different types of weapons and ammunitions from the rebels during the war.

On March 17, 2015, our joint operation forces of 1st and 7th Infantry divisions and Olony Aguelek division attacked and captured Wedekona, the SPLM/A-IO base, inflicting heavy casualties on their side and the following casualties were recorded:

| S/N | Faction | Number of casualties | | |
|---|---|---|---|---|
| 1. | N/A | Killed in action | Wounded in action | POW |
| 2. | SPLA joint forces | 7 | 19 | 0 |
| 3. | SPLA-IO | 300 | 0 | 10 |

Our Soldiers captured 3 T-55, 2 mounted pickups with 12.7 mm and different types of weapons and ammunitions from the rebels.

On May 1, 2015, our Jamus Special Forces of Battalions 105 and 107 attacked and captured the SPLA-IO base at Tibun near Sudan army Garrison where they were based to launch attacks on our locations at Duk-duk and Amdholwic and the following casualties were recorded on both sides;

| S/N | Faction | Number of casualties | | |
|---|---|---|---|---|
| 1. | N/A | Killed in action | Wounded in action | POW |
| 2. | 1st Infantry division | 3 | 10 | 0 |
| 3. | SPLA-IO | 15 | 0 | 1 |

**Different types of weapons, ammunitions and equipment captured**

On May 22, 2015, renegade Johnson Olony defected and joined the SPLM/A-IO and they attacked and captured Melut, using barges and steamers on the river Nile. I trekked with the SPLA's Jamus Battalion 107 Special Forces from Renk and attacked Johnson Olony and his SPLM/A-IO forces that captured Malakal and Melut. We destroyed the barges and recaptured Melut but incurred the following casualties on both sides:

| S/N | Faction | Number of casualties | | |
|---|---|---|---|---|
| 1. | N/A | Killed in action | Wounded in action | POW |
| 2. | 1st Infantry division | 5 | 28 | 0 |

All the attacking barges belonging to the SPLM/A-IO and Johnson Olony side were destroyed and hundreds of their soldiers died inside the barges and many drowned in river Nile. The following heavy weapons were captured in the barges;

1. 5 pieces of 14.5 mm high purpose machine guns (HPMG)
2. 10 pieces of 120 mm mortar
3. 30 pieces of 81/82 mm mortar
4. 3 pieces of Zu-23 plus different types of light weapons and am munitions.

On June 6, 2015, our combined forces of 1st and 7th Infantry divisions and forces of Ayuok Ugot destroyed SPLA-IO convoy that was advancing from Kaka towards Daba area with an intention of capturing Wedekona. Our soldiers repulsed them and the casualties were high as shown below:

| S/N | Faction | Number of casualties | | |
|---|---|---|---|---|
| 1. | N/A | Killed in action | Wounded in action | POW |
| 2. | Joint OPS forces | 0 | 0 | 0 |
| 3. | SPLA-IO | 30 | 0 | 0 |

We captured the following equipment from them;

1. 2 APCS
2. 2 mounted pick ups
3. 1 big truck loaded with different types of food items. The convoy was annihilated completely and we did not have any casualties on our side.

On June 17, 2015, our joint operation forces comprising of 1st and 7th and Ayuok Ugot forces attacked at SPLM/A-IO camp at Kaka with an intention to capture it but our forces were repulsed and recorded the following casualties;

| S/N | Faction | Number of casualties | | |
|---|---|---|---|---|
| 1. | N/A | Killed in action | Wounded in action | POW |
| 2. | 1st Infantry division | 5 | 18 | 0 |
| 3. | 7th Infantry division | 9 | 28 | 8 |
| 4. | Ayuok Ugot forces | 45 | 5 | N/A |

**One APC was captured by the rebels from our forces**

On July 6, 2015, our forces from battalion 108, supported by Abushok Baliet armed civilians, under Col. Majur Arok and overall command of Lt. Gen. James Ajongo Mawut, the then Deputy Chief of Gen. Staff for Operations (D/COGS), went to recapture Malakal from the rebels who had earlier overrun our soldiers and took control of it.

Unfortunately, during this operation, 6 soldiers, including Maj. Marko Lodich, were killed and 15 other soldiers were wounded. Casualties inflicted on the rebels were not reported to me since the mission was under the SPLA headquarters.

**On September 25, 2015,** the SPLM/A-IO on their way from Pagak to Buoth, Sudan Army Garrison, attacked our camp at Banachowa outpost, but our soldiers repulsed them and the following casualties were recorded on both sides;

| **S/N** | **Faction** | **Number of casualties** | | |
|---|---|---|---|---|
| | N/A | Killed in action | Wounded in action | POW |
| 1. | 1st Infantry division | 1 | 2 | 0 |
| 2. | SPLA-IO | 27 | 1 | 16 |

We captured one long range communication radio and different types of weapons and ammunitions from the rebels. Our soldiers also captured eight women who were later released to seek further refuge at the refugee camp of Jebelien in the Sudan.

On October 29, 2015, the SPLM/A-IO Shilluk ally Maj. Gen. Yuanis Ukic, the militia operation officer of Gen. Ayuok Ugot who were based in Wedekona, rebelled against the government and joined the SPLM/A-IO, on claims that their Shilluk land was given to the Dinka people in Malakal during the creation of 28 states by a Presidential decree. Their movements were monitored very closely by our forces and they were flushed out of Wedekona before they could attack our forces. The following casualties were reported on both sides.

| S/N | Faction | Number of casualties | | |
|---|---|---|---|---|
| 1. | N/A | Killed in action | Wounded in action | POW |
| 2. | 1st Infantry Division | 1 | 29 | 0 |
| 3. | Yuanis Ukic Side | 33 | 0 | 0 |

After they were defeated, they left behind the following equipment;

- 2 APCs in good condition
- 4 mounted pickups with different weapons and different types of guns.

On October 30, 2015, the SPLM/A-IO forces that were moving towards Sudan Army Garrison to reinforce Gen. Yuanis Ukic, fell into an ambush laid by our forces at Gabat, inflicting heavy casualties on the rebels with the following casualties;

| S/N | Faction | Number of casualties | | |
|---|---|---|---|---|
| 1. | N/A | Killed in action | Wounded in action | POW |
| 2. | 1st Infantry division | 2 | 3 | - |
| 3. | SPLA -IO | 13 | - | - |

We captured 2 APCs and different types of weapons and ammunitions from the rebels.

**SPLA 1st Infantry division successes**

After the above military operations, SPLA 1st Infantry division that was under my command made the following achievements;

1. Maintained law and order in Upper Nile region
2. Neutralized rebel activities in Upper Nile Region
3. Continued recruiting and training soldiers of 1st Infantry division
4. Discouraged and fought tribalism within the units.
5. Established a permanent defensive position in areas under the1st Infantry

division.

6. We gave all 1st Infantry division soldiers personal numbers to help identify them during parades.
7. We produced a special badge worn by our forces to distinguish between our forces from those who defected from 1st Infantry division.
8. We destroyed barges used by renegade Johnson Olony on the River Nile to capture Malakal and Melut.
9. We established English classes that were taught in the afternoon to empower our soldiers within the units.
10. We established a good working relationship with the civil authorities in the state.
11. We established what is called payroll system to help control parades so that the number of soldiers could not be increased by the subordinate commanders.
12. We acquired three boats, of which one was used for carrying light vehicles across the River Nile, another for reconnaissance on the river, while the third was used to ferry soldiers across the river within a capacity of 500.

The following is the general summary of all the casualties on both sides from 2014 - 2015 in Upper Nile State.

| **S/N** | **Faction** | **Number of casualties** | | |
|---|---|---|---|---|
| 1. | N/A | Killed in action | Wounded in action | POW |
| 2. | 1st Infantry Division | 93 | 278 | 8 |
| 3. | SPLA -IO | 690 | 0 | 27 |

During the fights, 12 civilians were killed on government garrison of Jamam.

# Chapter 12

## The SPLA 4th and 5th Infantry divisions

In 2015, I was transferred from the SPLA 1st Infantry Division to command the SPLA 4th Infantry Division in Western Upper Nile, Unity State.

The division is one of those that were formed in 2005, after the Comprehensive Peace Agreement (CPA) with the Sudan Government. Following the outbreak of the disturbances of 2013, the division was left in disarray since the bulk of its troops joined the rebellion with Commander Maj. Gen. James Koang Chuol Ranley – save for a few soldiers that remained loyal to the government.

The few soldiers from the 4th Infantry division that fought the rebelling soldiers remained in Jaw and Pariang areas while a few others who re-joined us were settled at the division's HQS at Rubkona. The troops at Jaw and Pariang were commanded by Maj. Gen. Thayip Gatluak Taitai.

The Division relied mainly on reinforcement forces from the 3rd and 5th SPLA Infantry Divisions which have been deployed in Western Upper Nile during the rebellion, when some soldiers in the 4th Infantry Division supported the rebellion. When the fight broke out in Juba, forces of militia leader, Gen. Bapiny Manytuil, known as South Sudan Liberation Movement and Army (SSLM/A) were already on the ground. The time they joined the government coincided with the 2013 rebellion.

This militia forces were mainly composed of soldiers from Bul Nuer and were stationed in Mayom after they came back from the Sudan. These militias played a significant role while fighting alongside the SPLA against the rebels. They were integrated into the SPLA but they refused to be redeployed to other government areas.

They insisted on remaining in Bul Nuer Mayom area and also refused to join the 4th Infantry Division in order to form one formidable command, yet this was contrary to the SPLA organisation and deployment policy.

When I took over as the Commander of the SPLA 4th Infantry Division from Maj. Gen. Thayip Gatluak Taitai, I reorganised and unified troops that were in Jaw, Pariang and the division's HQS into a new command in line with the SPLA organisation structure.

I also integrated the two battalions of the South Sudan Liberation Army (SSLA) under the command of Maj. Gen. Joseph Manyuat Manydhol that came to Bentiu from Mayom to give reinforcement to remnant forces of 4th infantry Division.

The rest of the forces of SSLA remained in a separate command in Mayom Bul Nuer area under the command of Maj. Gen. Mathew Puljang Top.

After taking over the command of 4th Infantry Division from Maj. Gen. Thayip Gatluak, I found a huge parade that included ghost names, disabled, elderly persons and under aged and female soldiers.

The parade was formed to pay salaries and not a combat one since half of the members were non-combat force. Once I discovered this malpractice, I reported to the SPLA General headquarters to avoid being blamed for having half of non-combatants in future in case we are defeated by the rebels.

**Parade**

| S/N | Unit | Officers | Other ranks | Total |
|---|---|---|---|---|
| 1. | 1st Infantry Brigade | 70 | 1,697 | 1,767 |
| 2. | 2nd Infantry Brigade | 100 | 1,717 | 1,817 |
| 3. | 3rd Infantry Brigade | 114 | 1,225 | 1,339 |
| 4. | Specialised units | 36 | 500 | 536 |
| 5. | Juba attaché | 44 | 1,019 | 1,063 |
| 6. | Non-combat | 50 | 3,812 | 3,862 |
| 7. | Division Headquarter | 144 | 1,072 | 1,216 |
| 8. | G/total | 558 | 11,043 | 11,600 |

## Infantry Brigades Deployment

The 4th Infantry Division's 1st Infantry Brigade was deployed in the North of Western Upper Nile along Bentiu - Panakuac - Heglig main road, the 2nd Infantry Brigade was also deployed in the areas of Jaw and Pariang and the 3rd Infantry brigade was deployed in the Southern Western Upper Nile areas of Guit, Nhialdiu, Tharjiath, Koch and Leer.

There were other reinforcement forces from 3rd and 5th Infantry Division that were deployed in Western Upper Nile alongside the forces from the 4th Infantry Division to supplement the low number since 4th Infantry Division was completely devastated by the civil war.

The forces of 4th Infantry Division looked very disorganised, desperate and miserable as they lacked food, fuel and uniform. They had also earlier lost most of the vehicles, tanks, and APCs that were destroyed by the rebels.

## Rebel Activities in Western Upper Nile

The rebels in Western Upper Nile used to cross from the Sudan into the remote rural villages of Waak and TuocLuak in the South of Nhialdiu where they used to camp as they waited to link up with other rebels around Leer, Adok base and Payinjiar area.

The route where their supplies that were carried on the head used to come from Liri in the Sudan to Wunkur and Tonga, down to Adok base and Payinjiar areas along the river Nile. Their second supply route was from Garia in the Sudan to Waak using different routes through the porous forests between Rubkona and Mayom counties by night or between Tharwangyiela and Tor -Abieth forests by day time.

On June 22, 2017, the rebels unsuccessfully attacked Pelieny outpost in Leer garrison but they were repulsed by our soldiers.

## Allied SPLM/A-IO Activities.

There were other government allied forces like SPLM/A-IO of Taban Deng that operated in Western Upper Nile. They had bases in Guit County with their command base at Kuerguiyna under Lt. Gen. Peter Dor Manjur. They occasionally created insecurity and committed atrocities in the areas under their control.

During the period, they carried out the following activities in the areas under their control: -

1) They conducted forceful recruitment of civilian populations in the areas under their control.
2) They occasionally set up road blocks.
3) They recruited some of our soldiers and promoted them to higher ranks.
4) They seized cows from the civilian populations when their soldiers visited their home villages.

## SSLA Activities.

The SSLA militia forces under Maj. Gen. Mathew Puljang in Mayom area committed the following atrocities in the area: -

- They forcefully recruited civil population into their army.
- They set up road blocks.
- They recruited some of our soldiers and afterwards promoting them to higher ranks.
- They seized cows from the civilians when their soldiers deserted to their home villages.

- They had a parade of 1,800 soldiers, that is less than the parade they reported to the SPLA Headquarters, but they were still being paid salaries for 12,000 soldiers from Juba.
- They set up civilian courts for trying cases rather than the local chiefs or Judges.
- They often conducted extra - judicial killings of civilians who are accused of stealing cows from Bahr El Ghazal and their soldiers, who are accused of crimes, without seeking approval or confirmation from the SPLA headquarters.

## General James Gai Yoac Militia Forces

These militia forces were recruits of Gen. James Gai Yoac in Western Upper Nile Leek, Nuer area. Gen. James Gai Yoac joined the government of South Sudan in 2016 from Khartoum after I had flushed him out of Wedekona in Upper Nile region.

Gen. Gai joined the government of South Sudan, but he never came with any forces to Western Upper Nile. He simply boarded a plane with five of his bodyguards and reported to the SPLA headquarters in Juba.

Having no forces on the ground, he planned to recruit civilians from his home clan, Leek Nuer area, whom he registered in readiness for integration into the SPLA. The new soldiers, however, did not stay in the barracks, but operated from their homes as they waited for the integration committee to integrate them into the SPLA with officer ranks. They spent their time minding their cattle camps and did not have any arms even.

## Armed Civilians in Western Upper Nile.

The armed civilians in the Western Upper Nile were a very hostile group that used to attack and rob lonely soldiers' weapons and killed them afterwards. Having no loyalties, they worked in collaboration with the rebels that occasionally would give them ammunition to fight with the government forces, but were also used by the government to fight the rebels.

Indeed, they also fought among themselves by raiding each other's cattle camps as well as crossing over to Bahr El Ghazal and Pariang for raiding more cattle. They did not abide by the peace agreement signed between the government and the rebels and occasionally attacked other civilians in the rebel-controlled areas, provoking fights even at times when peace talks were ongoing.

In February 2018, I was transferred from 4th Infantry Division that was based in Bentiu to command the SPLA 5th Infantry Division in Wau, from Maj. Gen. Majur Aleer. My transfer was triggered because of the differences I had with the Governor of North Liech State, Joseph Nguen Manytuil, who had told the SPLA headquarters that he would not go to Bentiu unless General Stephen Buoy was transferred from Bentiu.

Governor Manytuil did not want me to stay in Bentiu with him since people of Unity State preferred me and wanted me to replace him as their Governor. My superiors at the SPLA headquarters therefore decided to transfer me from the 4th Infantry Division to Wau to command the 5th SPLA Infantry Division. (More details in chapter 13)

The 5th Infantry Division was formed along other SPLA Divisions after the CPA in 2005, and was deployed in Western Bahr El Ghazal region in Wau and Raja areas. The Division shared a common border with Central Africa Republic (CAR) in the South of Raja and with Darfur, Sudan, in the West of Raja.

When I took over, I found out that there were some of our soldiers who were fond of harassing, killing civilians, looting people's properties and other forms of atrocities, especially at night on pretext of conducting patrols in Wau town.

I banned these activities that were mainly being perpetrated by the military intelligence and national security personnel and also stopped SPLA soldiers from carrying guns openly in the town while in uniform, unless they were on duty.

Strangely, my orders did not go down well and were defied by military intelligence personnel who stationed themselves at different checkpoints in Wau, collecting money from civilians and owners of private vehicles. Later on, we convened the state security committee meeting on the matter and an order was released that all soldiers manning checkpoints report to the barracks but the security forces still defied the order.

After seeing this habit continuing, I wrote to the Deputy Commander of 5th Infantry Division and Division Chief of Military Intelligence and requested that all military intelligence personnel be removed from the check points.

**My memo is reproduced here**

**From**: Maj. Gen. Stephen Buoy Rolnyang, Commander 5th Infantry Division
**To:** Maj. Gen. Arkanjelo Abanga, Deputy Commander of 5th Infantry Division

Cc: Cdr of Ground Force
CC: Governor Wau State
CC: Director National Security Wau State
CC: Commissioner of Police Wau State R/ Chief of M.I GHQS
CC: Ground Force Chief of Military Intelligence
CC: 5th Infantry division Intelligent Officer in Charge
CC: A/CDF for OPS, Intelligence and Training

**Subject:** Suspension of illegal military intelligence activities in Wau town and all Checkpoints. March 7, 2018.

We have discovered that there are some elements who are masquerading in the town and the checkpoints as Military Intelligence personnel from the 5th Infantry Division and are busy receiving handouts from civilians.

I have information that this group numbering 100 officers from different ranks had deserted duty from various SPLA divisions and have stationed themselves at Wau different checkpoints to extort money from civilians, while others were recruited by the former Military Intelligence officers of 5th Infantry Division and deployed them at the check points and markets in Wau town to collect money for them. They are charged with the followings;

1. Disobeying orders that all elements within military intelligence who are not Military intelligence personnel should report to division headquarters and, that genuine Military Intelligence personnel also officially deployed to the units and check points for security purposes.
2. For assigning themselves in the town and checkpoints in order to collect money from the people on a daily basis.
3. For causing insecurity in Wau town at night by shooting randomly and looting property of innocent civilians.
4. For conducting parallel patrolling in the town instead of being part of a joint security operation.
5. For threatening the Division Commander at gun point by cocking their

guns in the parade, an incident that was witnessed by all the officers of 5th Infantry division.

6. For running in the town with their guns as they refused to keep them in the armoury at the division headquarters.

That the Military Police are meant to operate in the town to arrest any SPLA soldier found carrying a gun and wearing uniform in public places in Wau town until Military Intelligence manages the situation. Those who will be found guilty will be executed.

You are hereby instructed to suspend all illegal joint operations at the checkpoints that are being conducted by the Military Intelligence personnel from the 5th Infantry Division until the government officially conducts an exercise to identify the real people who are involved.

***Note:*** The outcome of the security meeting was that all these forces must be screened and those found guilty to be suspended.

## Command Challenges:

During my tenure as the commanding officer of the SPLA 1st, 4th and 5th Infantry Divisions, I came across the following challenges;

- Our soldiers on the ground lacked food, medicines, uniforms and boots, and most soldiers in all the three divisions, did not have proper uniforms and walked half naked or with mismatched uniform.
- Our vehicles, tanks and APCs most of the time lacked spare parts and lubricants.
- We were short of different varieties of ammunitions and shells in our stores, since the rule was that the divisions acquire additional supplies only when the bases were attacked by the enemies.
- Lack of weapons such as 12.7mm, 14.5mm, PKM, RPG-7 guns, and 60mm, 81/82 mm mortars that were normally used for defensive operations.
- Lack of modern communication equipment.
- Lack of active, sober and qualified officers to command the units.

## Revitalised Peace Agreement.

On September 12, 2018, the peace agreement that was earlier signed but collapsed was revitalized by the IGAD with support from the international community.

Dr Machar was designated as the 1st Vice President, but this time around, there were other four proposed Vice Presidents included in the agreement to represent the following other parties. These were;

- Vice President for South Sudan opposition alliances (SSOA)
- Vice President (Woman) representing former Political Detainees, (FD)
- Two Vice Presidents representing the incumbent Transitional Government of National Unity (TGONU).

The agreement had an eight-month interim period that was extended two times, and ruled out several times.

All forces were to be cantoned, unlike the previous situation that led to the collapse of the 2015 deal with the events at J-1 in 2013. The SPLA in the government and SPLA – IO forces will be cantoned, organised, and trained together and deployed in all regions of South Sudan.

The parties agreed to release all the Prisoners of War (POW) and political detainees immediately under the supervision of the International Committee of the Red Cross (ICRC).

All the parties were tasked to ensure that all non-South Sudanese armed groups that are operating within the territory of South Sudan leave the country within the National Pre -Transitional Period (NPTC).

The parties were also supposed to refrain from outlawed actions such as;

1. Actions that may impede the provision of humanitarian assistance or protection of civilians and restrict free movement of the people.
2. Acts and forms of sexual and gender-based violence including sexual exploitation and harassment.
3. Offensive, provocative or retaliatory actions.
4. Acts of hostility, intimidation, violence or attacks against civilian population including IDPs, returnees, media, and UNMISS personnel. The parties agreed to the disengagement and separation of their forces which are in close proximity.

# Part III: From Grinti Barrack (Wau) to jail

## Chapter 13

*My differences with the NCP Group*

One of the defining facts of my senior military career is the enmity I elicited from some of my closest colleagues. In 2003, I was appointed commander of Western Upper Nile and served in the position up to 2005. My transfer there was necessitated by the fact that the late Gen. Paulino Matip Nhial demanded it as a condition to joining the SPLM/A.

This awful plan of my transfer was initiated by Maj. Gen. Thayip Gatluak Taitai, Dr Joseph Nguen Monytuil and Tut Keaw Gatluak, associates of late Gen. Paulino Matip who did not like me since they viewed me as a threat to their survival. They managed to convince Gen. Paulino Matip to request the top leadership of the SPLM/A to transfer me from Western Upper Nile to any of the SPLM/A area command.

Their hatred towards me developed into a witch-hunt due to the fact that I defected and left them in 1998 and re-joined the SPLM/A under the command of the late Dr Garang' ahead of them.

President Kiir sent the former Chief of General Staff Gen. Oyai Deng Ajak and his senior staff officers to my command in Western Upper Nile to inform me that Gen. Paulino Matip is ready to join the government of South Sudan and that he does not want you in Western Upper Nile.

The delegation informed me that I have been transferred to Kapoeta area to command the SPLA mobile force Infantry brigade that was deployed in the area. After listening to them attentively, I accepted the order and handed over the command to Brig. Gen. Konyi Didi. I immediately went and reported to my new assignment in Kapoeta area.

Once the news went round that I had reported in Kapoeta, Gen. Paulino Matip finally joined the Government of South Sudan. Despite getting into the crosshairs of Gen. Paulino Matip's group, I was delighted that the SPLA was becoming the single national army in the country.

I commanded the mobile forces in Kapoeta for one year and thereafter I received new orders from the office of the Chief of General Staff, Gen. Oyai Deng Ajak, that soldiers I was leading would be transferred to Western Upper Nile region and that I should not move with them to Western Upper Nile. He instructed me to report to SPLA headquarters (Juba) because Gen. Paulino Matip still did not want me back in Western Upper Nile. He, therefore, transferred me to the SPLA headquarters in Juba. I obliged and handed over the command of the Mobile Infantry Brigade to Brig. Gen. Kongor Reech Gak, who later led the Mobile forces from Kapoeta to Western Upper Nile.

Upon handing over, I proceeded to SPLA headquarters in Juba where I was deployed to establish the command of the SPLA Military Police for the first time after the (CPA) as there was no military police unit in South Sudan at the time. As previously highlighted in previous Chapters, I successfully structured and established the Military Police Unit along with the SPLA Commando elite unit, making the two units Special Forces within the SPLA command.

## Transfer to Lanya

When Gen. Paulino Matip came to Juba with his associates who had a beef with me in 2005, they again insisted that I should be transferred out of Juba for the reason that I had bad blood with Gen. Paulino Matip and I could harm him. Since they knew how to manipulate their way through the SPLA leadership at the headquarters, I was transferred to Lanya command base to command a commando as a separate unit from the military police. Brig. Gen. Simon Madit Ngor took over from me and became the new Commander of the Military Police unit based in Juba.

When Gen. James Hoth Mai was appointed as the SPLA Chief of General Staff in 2009, he transferred me back from Lanya command base to Juba to command the Military Police Unit for the second time. Gen. Mangar Buong Alueng replaced me as the commander of the commando unit in Lanya.

Gen. Paulino Matip's associates were at it again, and in 2013, they convinced the SPLA headquarters one more time to transfer me from Juba to 1st Infantry Division in Upper Nile region as deputy Commander of that division.

I took over the command of 1st Infantry Division from Maj. Gen. Angelo Jongkuc who was viewed as inept based on the weakness traits that he showed during the battle at Malakal in which 10 SPLA tanks under his command were captured by the rebels during the 2013 conflict.

Despite all the witch-hunt and regular transfers, I prayed to God often and I managed to control the forces of the 1st Infantry Division and fought tribal allied tendencies within the SPLA forces that were previously known for unnecessary fights between the soldiers in our units.

While serving as the commander of this force, I was contacted by some SPLA-IO senior officers to join them, but I turned down their request simply because I thought and believed that the 2013 incident was not a tribal war but political and that there was no need to encourage hatred and internecine wars among the people of South Sudan along the tribal line. This is so because the 1st Infantry Division was made up mostly of soldiers from the Nuer community, I tried and maintained inclusivity of all tribes and this led to peaceful and harmonious cooperation within the forces. Internal fights within the military under my command reduced to zero though some officers, NCOS and men from Nuer defected eventually to the rebel side.

By a stroke of luck, the bulk of the Nuer soldiers, who numbered 60 percent of the total soldiers ain the division, remained loyal to the government. The defectors were mostly the militia forces that re-joined the SPLA with Gen. Paulino Matip and other armed groups that were operating in Northern Upper Nile and who got deployed in the Upper Nile region when they joined the SPLA and government of Southern Sudan (GOSS).

## Transfer to 4th Infantry division

On December 2nd, 2015, I was transferred from the 1st Infantry to 4th Infantry Division to unify the remnants of the 4th Infantry Division soldiers with the forces that Gen. Bapiny Manytuil came with from Sudan in 2013 when he joined the government of South Sudan.

The forces loyal to Gen. Manytuil were commanded by Maj. Gen. Mathew Puljang and the bulk of the forces of the 4th Infantry Division joined the rebellion with Maj. Gen. Koang Chuol Ranleay who was the former Commander of the Division before the crisis of 2013 and later defected with most of the forces during the crisis that took place in Juba in December 2013.

Only a few soldiers remained in 4th Infantry Division command HQS, plus forces that were in Ruweng County. These soldiers were mainly made up of Panaru Dinka and other Dinka tribesmen, and only a few were from other tribes. The soldiers formed and operated in small groupings as if there was no proper command to unify and organise them into one supreme command base.

Other militias under the command of Gen. Bapiny Monytuil and direct field command of Maj. Gen. Mathew Puljang Top also joined the government in 2013. These forces were stationed in Bul Nuer, Mayom County but they were not integrated with other SPLA forces, though their leader Gen. Bapiny Monytuil was integrated into the SPLA as Lieutenant General and assigned as Deputy Chief of General Staff for Moral Orientation (M.O).

Upon my arrival in Bentiu town, the headquarters of the 4th Infantry Division, to take up my new assignment as a Commander to unify all the forces, little did I know that there were other plans to make forces of General Bapiny Manytuil remain independent in Mayom area, separate from the SPLA 4th infantry division that I was coming to unify.

Some politicians, Presidential Advisor for Security Affairs, Tut Keaw Gatluak and North Liech State, Governor Dr Joseph Monytuil, went to the Chief of Gen. Staff Gen. Paul Malong Awan to cancel my deployment.

They further recommended that Maj. Gen. Thayip Gatluak should continue as the commander of the remnant forces of the 4th Infantry Division, and that forces that came with Gen. Bapiny Monytuil should be led independently by Maj. Gen. Mathew Puljang Top.

Gen. Paul Malong refused to cancel my transfer, but accepted that the forces of Gen. Bapiny Monytuil be led as a separate independent force under the direct command of Maj. Gen. Puljang with direct supervision from the SPLA headquarters and under the influence of honourable Tut Keaw Gatluak, the national Security advisor of President Kiir and Dr. Joseph Nguen Monytuil, the governor of unity state

I accepted the new directive from the Chief of General Staff and took over the command of the two units, remnant forces of former 4th Infantry Division and the forces of Panaru from Maj. Gen. Thayip Gatluak Taitai and Maj. Gen. Deng Mayik Mai respectively.

But Governor, Dr Nguen also gave condition that he would not go to Bentiu until I was transferred from Bentiu to another location. While his demand was ignored by the SPLA command, he did not stop his agitation to remove me, only opting for alternative means of ensuring that I got transferred from the area.

He hatched another plot with Lt. Gen. Gabriel Jok Riak, who was then the former commander of SPLA Sector-1, which included the 3rd, 4th and 5th Infantry Divisions in Northern Bahr El Ghazal, Unity, and Western Bhar El Ghazal (Wau-Raja) states respectively.

The Governor met with Lt. Gen. Gabriel Jok Riak and made unfounded allegations against me that could see me removed from the area. They alleged that I was intending to join the SPLA-IO faction led by Dr Machar, that I had surrendered parts of the areas of the 4th Infantry Division to SPLA-IO, and had supplied the SPLA-IO with ammunitions and food.

When Gen. Paul Malong Awan got the information, he reported the issue to the Commander-in-Chief (Kiir), who then immediately instructed the COGS to arrest me and be put under a close Military Police Surveillance. I was summoned to Bilpam headquarters on March 18, 2016, by Gen. Paul Malong Awan and Gen. Mangar Buong Alueng, the then deputy Chief of Gen. Staff for Operations.

They arrested me, along with Maj. Gen. Joseph Manyuat Manydhol, on charges that we were planning to join the SPLA- IO. We remained in custody for six months until when the COGS asked Lt. Gen James Ajongo Mawut, who was the deputy Chief of Gen. Staff for Administration, to form an investigation committee to investigate our case.

Lt. Gen. Ajongo formed the investigation committee that was to be chaired by Maj. Gen. Ernest Dut and other six officers as members. The committee did their work but did not find us guilty. He, therefore, recommended that we would be released immediately, without charges, which the President did.

I was put under surveillance in my house for six months before Lt. Gen. Ajongo recommended to the COGS to appoint me to take up the portfolio of Director General for Procurement in the Ministry of Defence and Veterans' Affairs. Upon this recommendation, the COGS officially appointed me in the position on December 17, 2016.

On May 9, 2017 Lt. Gen. Ajongo was appointed COGS but strangely Gen. Paul Malong Awan refused to hand over to him. The former COGS fled to Yirol at night by vehicles on his way to his home town Mading Aweil in order to launch an attack against the government.

His motive of defecting from the government, however, did not go as he had planned. Prominent leaders and elders from his Jieng community convinced him to return to Juba and take up his new role. He obeyed the advice and went back to Juba and reconciled with President Kiir, before leaving for Nairobi to seek some medical treatment.

Unknown to many, while in Nairobi, he formed his own movement - the South Sudan United Front/ South Sudan United Army (SSUF/A) – which launched a war with the government.

On June 29, 2017, Gen. Ajongo, now the Chief of Gen. Staff, redeployed me as commander of the 4th Infantry Division for the second time. I took over the command of the division for the second time on July 2, 2017 from Maj. Gen. Yohanis Yoal Bath who was appointed as acting commander of 4th Infantry Division when I was under arrest in 2016.

The Governor of North Liech, Dr Joseph Nguen Monytuil, still refused to come down to Bentiu from Juba on hearing that I was redeployed there. He stayed in Juba for almost one year, demanding that I should be transferred from Bentiu to another division, but the COGS could not be cajoled. Instead, the Governor was accused of interfering with the internal operations within the military.

On November 30, 2017, Capt. Ruot Jiath, the officer in charge of the headquarters of the Governor, escorted honourable Ministers of the state, namely, Nyachieng Biey Tuel and Rebecca Gey Majok, on a visit to Unity oil fields. While on their way, they were stopped by the Military Police who were manning the checkpoint and were asked to report to my office to be given enough protection since the rebels were always ambushing convoys between Bentiu and Unity oil fields. We had developed a plan whereby we often provided additional security to government officials because rebels were fond of ambushing convoys on the road. Capt. Ruot Jiath was furious and he wanted to fight with the Military Police at the checkpoint, but the Ministers advised him to cool down and come to the office of the division commander.

When they came over, Capt. Ruot Jiath was politely asked by my bodyguards to hand over his guns at the entrance, as was the tradition, but he refused to do so, forcing my bodyguards to stop him from walking in. A commotion ensued at the entrance while I was already with the Ministers in my office, and I had to get out to find out what was happening.

By then, the situation was fast getting out of hand, with Capt. Ruot Jiath still adamant. He refused to listen to my orders, upon being told of the procedure. I, therefore, ordered that he and his soldiers who were rowdy and could not follow our laid down procedures be arrested. I subsequently asked the Ministers to return to the State headquarters until we resolved the issue.

The Ministers went back to the state headquarters and on their arrival at the Governor's headquarters, they informed the governor that all his bodyguards that were escorting us were arrested by Gen. Stephen Buoy. On hearing this, the Governor went to the President's office and reported the incident to the President Kiir. The President ordered the COGS to investigate the matter immediately and report to him. As part of his investigation, the COGS asked me to state what had transpired and I explained to him exactly all what had happened and he ordered me to release Capt. Ruot Jiathh and all the Governor's bodyguards. Due to the intimidation and accusations that was directed at my person, I decided to write the following letter:

## MESSAGE NO. 1

**From:** **Maj. Gen. Stephen Buoy Rolnyang**
**To:** Gen. James Ajongo Mawut, SPLA Chief of Defence Forces
CC: Commander of the Ground Forces
CC: File

**Subject: Resignation from the SPLA. Date: December 2, 2017**

Comrade, on March 18, 2016, I was arrested by the former SPLA Chief of Defence Forces Gen. Paul Malong Awan because the Governor of North Liech State Dr Joseph Nguen Monytuil and the Presidential Advisor Tut Keaw Gatluak, reported to him several times that I was planning to defect to the SPLA–IO. The two have been having a prolonged hatred that has developed into witch-hunt towards me.

I was placed in the custody for six months, but I was eventually released after it was found out that the allegations were cooked up, baseless and false.

Today, December 2, 2017, you have asked me to report to Juba after having been accused again of being involved in planning defections simply after I arrested Capt. Ruot Jiath, who is in charge of the Governor's headquarters, who came to our headquarters and threatened me at gun point. It is after this incident that Dr Joseph Nguen Monytuil, Governor went direct to report me to the President Kiir, upon which you were directed to call me to Juba.

Comrade, looking at the above, and in reference to the SPLA rules and regulation article 27, I hereby submit my resignation letter from the SPLA to your comradeship office.

I am resigning from the SPLA to leave the Governor and the Presidential Advisor do their work in peace. I am proceeding home to peruse my other interests like any other citizen.

I have given my best service in the SPLA under your good guidance in defending our nation over the years, and God can bear me witness for the contributions I have made over the years. I will never betray my people and country by joining opposing faction. For this matter, let Dr Joseph Nguen Monytuil and Tut Keaw Gatluak work with ease as they make their contributions too.

My warmest and heartfelt greetings to all the SPLA gallant force wherever they are, especially the units that I was commanding such as the Commando (the maroon cap), Military Police (the red cap) SPLA 1st Infantry Division (strong animal Jamus) and the SPLA 4th Infantry Division (Petrol Division).

They know my capability in leadership command and my position on ethnic and tribal ideology.

I greet all the martyrs who served in the units but perished either in action or under natural causes during my command. Those who died in executing my orders did not die in vain, but died while defending our nation.

My heartfelt greetings to all my colleagues, especially all former SPLA chiefs – of - staff and also to you, the current SPLA Chief of Defence Forces for guidance and leadership.

Finally, accept my final salute to my Commander-in-Chief Gen. Kiir, the President of the Republic of South Sudan, for his wise leadership and guidance. Comrade, in the light of the above, I ask your comradeship to appoint a new Commander to take over the command of 4th Infantry Division.

Thank you and May God bless South Sudan.

Upon receiving my resignation letter above, the COGS called for an emergency meeting to discuss the issues that I had addressed. He was advised by the Assistant Chief of Defence Forces for Operations Lt. Gen. Malual Ayom Dor, and Commander of Ground Force Lt. Gen. Marial Cinuong Yoal that they needed to talk to me with the aim of dissuading me against my planned resignation.

Indeed, the two Generals called me on phone and persuaded me not to resign from the SPLA. I listened to them and I withdrew the resignation letter that I had dispatched to the Chief of Defence Forces.

## Transfer to 5th Infantry Division

Due to the Governor's animosity towards me, the COGS, with orders from the President, transferred me from Bentiu 4th Infantry Division to Wau 5th Infantry Division on January 2, 2018.

On February 27, 2018, I took over the command of the 5th Infantry Division from Maj. Gen. Majur Aleer. I was accompanied by one full company from the 4th Infantry Division that was approved by the COGS and Commander of Ground Forces in line with the new military requirement that was adopted after the war of 2013.

The new rule required that senior military officers be accompanied by reliable force for personal protection when on a mission. During the period that I was transferred to 4th Infantry Division from 1st Infantry Division, I came with a company that was approved by the former COGS.

When I reported to Wau, I found out that the Military Intelligence Unit personnel were the ones manning the checkpoints and were collecting money from commercial trucks. I also found a few soldiers in the division since most had deserted and either went to work within their home areas or were recruited in other divisions of their choice. I also realised that most of the Nuer soldiers defected and joined the SPLM/A-IO.

After settling down, I recalled all the Military Intelligence personnel back to the barracks and directed that all checkpoints be manned by the Military Police, limited number of military intelligence personnel, Police and National Security officers. Strangely, the orders were defied and the Military Intelligence personnel refused to leave the checkpoints following incitement from the Military Intelligence Chief of the Division, Col. Bona Malual Agiu. As I understood it, Col. Agiu went to an extent of inciting the Military Intelligence personnel to assassinate me during a military parade.

When I came to the parade ground one day, I tried to assign them roles including reporting to the division headquarters, but they refused and threatened me at gun point. I managed to contain the commotion, but I still insisted that they should listen to my orders as commander of the division.

After protracted negotiations, they finally obeyed my directives and cooled down, but to my surprise, they resorted to looting civilian properties at night in Wau town. I reported the matter to the SPLA headquarters in Juba to investigate the incident and punish the perpetrators accordingly.

From their behavior, I concluded that the soldiers were not properly trained and cultured in military intelligence service. I was later informed that some of them had deserted from other divisions and entrenched themselves in military intelligence unit in order to loot from civilians and also collect money from moving vehicles and travelers at checkpoints.

I pleaded with the SPLA Military intelligence senior officers at the headquarters to transfer Col. Bona Malual and his team to Juba and deploy disciplined officers to serve in Wau town, but my request fell on deaf ears. It reached a point where I sent a memo, published below, to the headquarters:

## MESSAGE NO. 2

**From:** **Maj. Gen. Stephen Buoy Rolnyang**
**To:** Chief of Military Intelligence
CC: Ground Forces, Chief of Military Intelligence
CC: Commander Ground Force
CC: Assistant Chief of Defence Forces for OPS, Intelligence and Training
CC: SPLA Chief of Defence Forces

**Subject: Military Intelligence Activities in the 5th Infantry Division**
Date: March 8, 2018

I am writing to you to inform you that whereas I am the leader here, a few officers have refused to listen to my instructions and continue to disobey me openly.

To make matters worse, they are sabotaging my plans and also beginning to form tribal alliances within the military, yet our rules require that all soldiers should mix-up with one another irrespective of their tribe.

The officers incited the Military Intelligence personnel that threatened me at gun point during a parade in front of all the officers of the 5th Infantry Division.

They have defied the orders issued by the state security committee that requires all checkpoints to be manned by one Military Intelligence personnel, one Military Police, one National Security personnel, one Policeman and one from the Criminal Investigation Department (CID) personnel. They insist in having more than a platoon at each checkpoint with an intention of collecting money from passers-by and motorists.

They do not work under "one command policy" and are running a parallel force to the 5th Infantry Division command. They have also refused a directive that trained Military Intelligence personnel must be deployed to various units where there are no Military Intelligence personnel ranging from (Coy) up to division headquarters due to lack of Military Intelligence personnel in the units.

They are further harbouring more than 100 non-Military Intelligence personnel that deserted from various SPLA units and other organised forces in their units and deploying them in Wau town checkpoints as Military Intelligence in order to loot and collect money from innocent civilians on pretext of defending Wau town from rebels.

I am hereby informing your comradeship that the following Military Intelligence officers Col. Bona Malual Agiu, 1st Lt. Ayok Mathiang Akol and 2nd Lt. Aliza Akucnyir Majak have failed to take my directives, and are therefore undermining my command in this division.

I am recommending that you transfer these Military Intelligence officers and replace them with trained and disciplined officers who are conversant with the rules and regulations of our military service and are ready to defend them in totality.

For your comradeship, acknowledgment

After sending the letter, the Chief of Military Intelligence Maj. Gen. Chokrac Alith Kudum, informed Col. Bona Malual that I had requested that he be transferred to the SPLA headquarters in Juba, but he declined my request. From sources, Col. Bona Malual thereafter started bad mouthing me and further made false allegations that I had contact with Gen. Paul Malong Awan.

On May 10, 2018, I asked the Commander of Ground Forces Lt. Gen. Santino Deng Wol for permission to enable me go home to attend an earlier planned traditional rite that was to be done after the burial of our father.

I wrote the following message to Santino Deng Wol.

## MESSAGE NO. 3

**From:** 5th Infantry Division Commander
**To:** Ground Force Commander
CC: Commander North West area command
CC: The SPLA CDF Date May 10, 2018

**010/5/2018,** may your comradeship grant me five (5) days leave to go to Tuoc -loka near Akotong on Ajak Kuac and Mayom border in Mayom. This will enable me go home to attend an earlier planned traditional rite that was to be done after the burial of our father.

Your comradeship's positive response will be highly appreciated.

## MESSAGE NO. 4

**From:** Ground Force Commander
**To:** 5th Infantry division commander
CC: SPLA CDF Date May 12, 2018

**021/5/2018, your 014/5/2018 is received.** The ammunition will be brought to you soon to enable you to prepare your forces. Ensure that you use the ammunition well by keeping the rebels far from your base.

Ref. to your 013/5/2018, Brig. Ring Akuei is to stay with Maj. Gen. Butros Bol-Bol in North West area command headquarters.

Regarding your 007/5/2018, you have to wait for a while to receive the ammunition you had asked for first and clear the area, after that you will be granted days to go home.

When Chief of Defence Forces Gen. James Ajongo Mawut died on April 20, 2018, he was replaced with Gen. Gabriel Jok Riak.

On May 2, 2018, Gen. Gabriel Jok Riak took over the command of the SPLA. He met Tut Keaw, Governor of North Liech State, Dr Joseph Nguen Monytuil and Maj. Gen. Thayip Gatluak Taitai on May 12, 2018 at Dembish Hotel in Juba. They discussed how to get rid of me, but agreed to transfer me first from the 5th Infantry Division to the SPLA headquarters then they shall plan what to do with me afterwards.

**On May 22, 2018,** the Chief of Defence Forces was convinced by Tut Keaw and Governor of Unity State Dr Joseph Nguen Manytuil and he issued an order that transferred me from 5th Infantry Division to the SPLA defence headquarters as Director of Military organisation.

When I received my transfer letter, I instructed all units under 5th Infantry Division to prepare their handing over reports to be handed over to the new incoming commander of 5th Infantry Division.

I then called the Ground Force Commander and the Deputy Chief of Defence Forces Johnson Juma on the phone to remind them of my previous request for a permission to go home on a five days leave. I had also requested that I be allowed to hand over the command of 5th Infantry Division to the new commander when I come back from home, thereafter I could proceed to Juba to take over my new assignment.

Upon my reminder, the Commander of Ground Force went to the Deputy

Chief of Defence Forces to ask for approval because the Chief of Defence Forces was away on an official mission to Tanzania. The Deputy Chief of Defence Forces approved my leave as I had requested and agreed that I should hand over in Wau after five days.

**On May 26, 2018**, I left Wau for Mayom at 4 pm and spent the night at Ajak Kuac, resumed my journey the following day and arrived in Mayom the same day. I was received by Maj. Gen Mathew Puljang, the area commander and we proceeded to his headquarters to spend the night there.

**On May 28, 2018**, I asked Maj. Gen. Puljang to accompany me to my home and attend the ceremony together, but he told me that he had scheduled a meeting with a committee that was sent from the SPLA military headquarters who had come to Mankien to inspect a parade of his forces.

He authorised that his Deputy, Maj. Gen. Joseph Manyuat, to go with me and we arrived home safely, and in the morning on May 29, 2018. The following day, our celebration started in earnest, which lasted the whole day and night. We slaughtered animals in a ceremony that was also attended by elders from our community.

**On May 30, 2018,** Maj. Gen. Joseph Manyuat returned to their base leaving me behind as I spent the night with the elders from my clan for the second day. I left my village the following day for Mayom and arrived in the afternoon.

I passed through Mankien military headquarters to greet Maj. Gen. Puljang and his officers and they welcomed me and even prepared a cup of tea to drink. As we were talking, Maj. Gen. Puljang told me that those of Juba headquarters were looking for me on phone and your phone was off. I told him that there was no network in my village and my phone had also run out of power. I then asked him to call them so that I should talk to them through his phone.

He called Lt-Gen. Thoi Chany who told me that he would be coming to meet me the following day in regard to rumours that I was not happy with my latest transfer and that I had planned to rebel against the government, accusations that I denied.

I confirmed my availability to him following his request and I assured him that I will be waiting for him in Mayom as agreed to discuss the issue further. I then thanked Maj. Gen. Puljang for hosting me and I left for Mayom.

When I arrived in Mayom, Maj. Gen. Puljang was ordered by the SPLA headquarters in Juba to disarm and arrest me. Maj. Gen. Puljang sent his soldiers after I had left for Mayom with an intention of attacking me as ordered by the SPLA command in Juba.

As I was in my pyjamas, sleeping in a guest house in Mayom, to my amazement, soldiers armed with four tanks and three heavily mounted trucks arrived. When I came out and saw soldiers surrounding the guest house, I instructed the few bodyguards that were with me to board their cars to go and confirm from Maj. Gen. Puljang why he had sent his army to surround the compound. As we started moving to Maj. Gen. Puljang base, they also followed us at a distance.

We got into an ambush that had been laid ahead of us as we headed towards the direction of the headquarters of Maj. Gen. Puljang. We took a left turn towards the river and they continued chasing and firing at us, until we stopped at Cuolpi river side and crossed the river to report to Taban Deng's base at Tomor area, to enable me establish contact with the SPLA headquarters in Juba what the harassment and planned arrest was all about.

Before making any progress, we got into another ambush and this time the soldiers who were chasing us captured and chained me and took me to Mayom. During the scuffle, they killed three of my bodyguards and wounded other two soldiers from my headquarters.

I later learnt that Maj. Gen. Puljang had sent a message to Commander of Ground Forces informing him that Gen. Stephen Buoy wanted to rebel against the government. The Commander of Ground Forces thereafter directed Maj. Gen. Puljang to pursue me by all means.

The messages are stipulated below:

**MESSAGE NO. 5**

**From:** Special Operation Cdr (Mathew Puljang)
**To:** SPLA CDF
CC: Ground Force Commander
CC: 4th Infantry Division Cdr
CC: Special Operation Intelligent Officer
CC: Military Intelligence Ground Force
CC: Chief for Military Intelligence GHQS
CC: A/CDF for Admin, Personnel and Finance
CC: A/CDF for Operation, Training and Intelligent
CC: D/CDF and Operation Supervisor

**Date - May 31, 2018**

**032/5/2018,** Following the coming of Maj. Gen. Stephen Buoy Rolnyang to

Mankien on his way to his home in Bieh and back this morning at 10:20 am to my headquarters, we spoke through phone with A/CDF for Administration, personnel and finance and he was instructed to be here and wait for a committee from the headquarters, but he refused and instead proceeded to Mayom.

I have observed from his views that he is no longer an SPLA officer and I am right away going after him in Mayom.

**Regards.**

## MESSAGE NO. 6

**From:** Ground Force Cdr
**To:** Special Operation Cdr
CC: 4th Infantry Division Cdr
CC: Lion Division Cdr
CC: Chief for Military Intelligence GHQS
CC: SPLA CDF

**Date March 31, 2018**

059/5/2018, Maj. Gen. Stephen Buoy Rolnyang has rebelled this morning against the Government of South Sudan (GOSS). On receipt of this message, organise your forces and pursue him from Mayom to wherever he is going.

The division 3 Commander has been directed to put his soldiers on alert at Abiemnom, Majak Kon and Abyei to block the route leading to Awerpiny.

### Arrest and Prosecution

On June 1, 2018, they chained my legs and hands and flew me to Juba where I was manhandled and thrown in the national security van on arrival at Juba International Airport (JIA). I was driven in a van that did not have any ventilation save for a few small holes that were created to let in air as they led me to an underground bunker that was manned by the military intelligence.

The bunker was used by SAF when they were in South Sudan, but when they left, the bunker was abandoned and it instead became a dwelling ground for snakes and rats. I was holed up in this room for three days without food, water and nothing to sleep on as I was lying on the rough floor. Sometimes, I could see snakes and rats moving around.

When snakes and rats fought and ran towards me at night, I rolled on my belly to the other side of the bunker while in the dark without seeing anything around me even at day time there was no adequate air or ventilation at the same time. I urinated in my pants for three days until I was transferred from the military intelligence bunker under a cruel military intelligence officer Brig. Gen. Kuel Garang' Kuel to a military police custody, where the handcuffs were removed following orders from the commander of Military Police Maj. Gen. Zakaria Akoi Yak.

I was treated well under the Military Police custody as I was allowed to go out every evening to sit under a tree within the compound for two hours and then back to confinement. I considered this as a rare opportunity having gone through bad treatment previously.

**On June 16, 2018,** the Chief of Defence forces formed an investigation committee under Major Gen. Michael Manok Kot to look into my case. They investigated my alleged rebellion against the government and whether I was in contacts with Gen. Paul Malong Awan.

The charges were framed by Maj. Gen Puljang and politicians of Bul Nuer, especially Tut Keaw Gatluak and Dr Joseph Manytuil, the Governor of Unity State in order to get rid of me from the military politically.

The committee recommended to the Chief of Defence Forces that they did not find me guilty of the alleged offences and suggested that I should be released immediately. But the Chief of Defence Forces was very furious with the committee's outcome and he ordered the committee to sit again and investigate further until they find me guilty. The committee upon being forced to conduct a fresh investigation assumed that they found me guilty and recommended that I should be taken to face the General court martial (GCM) to answer the charges.

On January 3, 2019, the Chief of Defence Forces formed a General Court Martial that consisted of seven members namely;

Maj. Gen. Thiik Achiek Hol – Chairman
Brig. Riak Tiop Deng - Member
Brig. Duol Gony - Member
Brig. Nhial Arou - Member
Brig. Angui Geng - Member
Brig. Hillery Oduho - Member
Brig. Abubaker Mohamed – Judge

On February 4, 2019, I appeared before the General Court Martial (GCM) and was asked if I had any objection to the formation of the members of the panel. I told the court that I had reservation with the whole panel due to the following reasons.First the SPLA Act of 2009, Article 35 Paragraph 4 says, in all cases, the presiding officer shall be a senior in rank to the accused and that all members of the panel be at least equivalent in rank to the accused. Therefore, in my case, the presiding officer should have been a Lieutenant Gen. and six Major Generals.

Secondly, the SPLA Act 2009, Article 36 Paragraph 2, says that the General Court Martial (GCM) shall be convened by the Commander-in-Chief when the person being tried is in the rank of a Brig. Gen. and above and the Chief of Defence Forces should convene a court in respect of other officers in the lower ranks.

I told the court that it had been wrongly constituted and had to be overhauled in conformity with the above legal procedures. The court adjourned until February 7, 2019, but when we came back to court on the very day, the court adjourned again indefinitely. I later learnt while writing this book that the court was reconstituted by President Kiir himself.

It's membership includes;

1. Maj. Gen Thiik Achiek Hol - Court President
2. Maj. Gen. Atem Duot Atem
3. Maj. Gen. Peter Gatwech Gai
4. Maj. Gen. Akuei Ajou Akuei
5. Maj. Gen. Isiah Paul Lotole
6. Brig. Abubaker Mohamed – Judge, advocate

The court conducted 17 sessions upon which it collected views from witnesses. The last session was held in a closed door where closing arguments and mitigations were held.

The court dropped some of the charges such as Article 60 that relates to treason and Article 61 for offences relating to security that had been levelled against me earlier.

The only charge that remained was disobeying lawful orders from my superiors that were found in Article 67 and Standing Order 69.

The jail terms for the charges according to SPLA Act 2009 are as follows;

1. Article 60 on treason is life imprisonment.

2. Article 61 on offence relating to security is 14 years' imprisonment.
3. Article 67 on disobedience of lawful orders from the superior officer is five years' imprisonment.
4. Article 69 on Standing Order is three years' imprisonment.

The court looked at Articles 67 and 69 and voted to pass the following judgment against me:

- Demoted me from the rank of Major General to Private
- Dismissed me from the SPLA military service to civilian service
- Sentenced me for one year imprisonment that started from the date of my arrest which elapsed on May 31, 2019.

After reading the ruling, the Judge asked me if I have any appeal to make. This was my response,

**To:** Gen. Court Martial (GCM)
**Subject:** My statement about the (GCM) verdict
**Date:** October 21, 2019

In reference to your Honourable court's verdict on Article 69 (Standing Orders) SPLA Act 2009, in which you have passed the following judgment as follows;

1. You have demoted me from the rank of Major General to Private
2. You have dismissed me from the SSPDF service to become a civilian
3. You have sentenced me to one year imprisonment starting from the date of my arrest on May 31, 2019, that has already ended as I was arrested last May 2019.

Your Honour, first of all, I am grateful that the Honourable Court has not found me guilty of treason and other charges on Articles 60, 61 and 67 of the SPLA Act 2009, which went viral on social media with intention to tarnish my image and dignity. The Honourable Court has also asked me whether I need to appeal or not following the ruling.

## Response to the court's verdict

When I moved from Wau to my home in Mayom, I asked for permission from the Commander of the Ground Forces on phone and he gave me five days and directed that I immediately proceed to Wau and hand over the command of 5th

Infantry division to the new Commander once I am back from my home.

The Commander of the Ground Forces came to this Honourable Court and denied that he did not grant me permission to go home. I requested the Honourable Court to contact the Mobile Telecommunication Company (MTN) to provide this Honourable Court my audio with the Commander of the Ground Forces, but this Honourable Court turned down my request in favour of the Commander of the Ground Forces.

I talked with the Commander - in - Chief, General Salva Kiir, in Mayom through the phone of Gen. Akol Koor on the allegations that reached the President's office that I wanted to defect and join the rebels. But when the Commander-in-Chief found out that the allegation was not true and that I went home to attend a ceremony in honour of my late father, the Commander-in-Chief gave me five more days to spend at home before going back to Wau. The Commander-in-Chief told me that he would inform the CDF that he had given me five days off.

I was attacked by Maj. Gen. Mathew Puljang without orders from the SSPDF headquarters and his forces went ahead and killed three bodyguards and wounded two others that were attached to me. Interestingly, you have not arrested or demoted him to a private like what you have just done to me yet I did not fight back because I knew that they are the government forces and I had to surrender to them knowing that they might have been ordered by the SSPDF headquarters to arrest me.

It has appeared at this honourable Court that nobody ordered Maj. Gen. Mathew Puljang from the SSPDF to attack and arrest me. Maj. Gen. Puljang was acting on his own without being ordered by the SSPDF headquarters to do so, but to my surprise, no action was taken against him by the SSPDF command.

Instead, I am the one who has been arrested and charged with treason and other charges, while Maj. Gen. Puljang was the one who killed three of my bodyguards and wounded two others yet we did not fight them back in self-defence.

If I had fought Maj. Gen. Puljang in self-defence, I wouldn't have been arrested as there would have been a lot of deaths on both sides in Mayom town. That is why my soldiers were killed and wounded simply because I did not fight him and his forces back.

Honourable Court, the verdict that you have given me, that is a one-year imprisonment sentence starting from the date of my arrest on May 31, 2018, elapsed last May 2019, yet you are still keeping me in jail. This is very humiliating to my person.

The Honourable Court, this case is politically motivated by a few politicians from my own community Bul Nuer who are conspiring and colluding with some Bul Nuer SSPDF senior officers in order to get rid of me.

Therefore, I feel betrayed by these politicians and officers from my community in the face of the SSPDF command despite the immense contribution that I have made in defence of our country and its constitution.

I would like to ask this Honourable Court the following question. Where on earth in the military or in the history of the SPLA, has a General been demoted to the rank of a Private and given dismissal orders from the service on administrative charge like indiscipline that is purely an administrative and not even a crime?

Your Honourable Court, in the light of the above-mentioned reasons, I would like to say that I have no appeal to make against the verdict, because even if I appeal against the verdict, the same politicians will still influence the next outcome.

Let me leave it to H.E the President and Commander-in-Chief of the SSPDF to consider my case. Thank you very much.

After this session, the court decision was supposed to be taken to the President for confirmation according to the SPLA Act 2009, Article 89 (2), that states, "The findings and sentence of a General Court Martial (GCM), shall be confirmed by the President and Commander-in-Chief or by any officer authorised in his or her behalf by a warrant issued and signed by the President and Commander-in-Chief".

In my case, the President did not approve or confirm the court decision. Neither did he delegate a warrant to any officer to do so on his behalf. It was the legal advisor in the office of the President, (Molana) Majok Mading, working in concerts with Tut Keaw, Gen. Jok Riak, who wrote to Gen. Jok Riak that the verdict was confirmed by the President.

The court forwarded its decision to the Commander-in-Chief of the SSPDF, (SPLA). However, there was no warrant signed by the President to indicate that he delegated his powers to Gen. Jok Riak for the confirmation of my sentence. The letter of Molana Majok Mading to Gen. Jok Riak is here below:

**Gen. Gabriel Jok Riak,**

SSPDF Chief of Defence Forces, Republic of South Sudan, Juba
**Subject:** Confirmation of the Verdict of General Court Martial (GCM) Verdict on Criminal Case No. 22/2018 of Maj. Gen. Stephen Buoy Rolnyang

I refer to the referenced letter Number GCM/J/351/2019, of the President of the General Court Martial Maj. Gen. Thiik Aciek Hol dated October 21, 2019, addressed to H.E. the President and Commander-in-Chief of the SSPDF, in which the GCM read out the verdict to the above-mentioned convict.

According to the documents on record, and after the court ruling, the convict was asked as to whether he wishes to exercise his right of appeal or not in accordance to the provisions of Section 88 (2) of the SPLA Act, 2009, read together with Section 263 of the Code of Criminal Procedure Act, 2008.

The Convict is on record as having been satisfied by the verdict and hence did not intend to appeal.

Therefore, H.E. the President has confirmed the verdict of the GCM in totality and he has further directed that the convict should be released forthwith.

Have the assurance of my highest regards and consideration.

**Molana Majok Mading,**
Legal advisor Office of the President,
Republic of South Sudan, Juba

# Chapter 14

## I joined the rebellion on May 3, 2021

### *Root cause of conflicts in South Sudan*

In 2005, the founding father of the SPLM/A, Dr John Garang' de - Mabior signed the Comprehensive Peace Agreement (CPA) with the Sudan government under Omar Hassan El Bashir, that ended the longest Sudanese civil war that dated back to the mid-1950s, when the Southern insurgents took up arms against the Islamist government in the Sudan. Between 1983 and 2005, the war resulted in the deaths of more than 2 million people.

Unfortunately, Dr Garang' was killed in a Uganda helicopter crash on 30/7/2005, and as a result of his tragic death, President Salva Kiir who was an SPLA battlefield commander with little knowledge of the democratic governance and rule of law, was shortly installed to lead the South Sudan, home to over 12 million people drawn from 64 tribes or ethnic groups with diverse cultures, religion and languages.

President Kiir appointed his longtime rival Dr Riek Machar as his 1st Vice President. Both leaders (Kiir/Riek) failed to meet the expectations of the people of South Sudan who were fighting for freedom, justice and equality because they felt they were being oppressed by the Arabs, but now the oppression of Kiir/Riek is worse than the oppression of the Arab.

The South Sudanese people expected President Kiir and Machar to guide them towards a genuine democratic system of governance in the country. The two leaders failed to establish a viable state and to build vital institutions right away from the independence of the republic of South Sudan. The only institutions that exist in South Sudan are the army (SSPDF) and the national security forces which are predatory institutions.

After being in the presidency for two years after the independence of the Republic of South Sudan, the two leaders (Kiir/Riek), revealed their own true colours of President Kiir being a demi – dictator and Machar a vicious self –aggrandizing who care for their own selfishness.

In 2013, President Kiir accused Machar of attempting a coup, the move which plunged the country into a civil war. The war resulted in the death of nearly 400,000 people, and displacement of over 2 million people.

Later, the two leaders were forced by the international community to sign a power sharing agreement in Addis Ababa in 2015. The signed agreement was violated in 2016, by both leaders in tragic circumstances when fighting erupted in J-1 dubbed the J-1 dogfight. Machar thereafter fled to DR Congo in a hot pursuit which lasted for 41 days. During the civil war, several of Machar's fighters were killed on the way.

In 2018, the peace that was violated in 2016, as a result of J-1 fight, was revitalized under the auspices of the IGAD countries and another agreement was signed in Khartoum known as the revitalized agreement on the resolution of the conflict in the Republic of South Sudan (R –ARCSS) that reinstated Machar as 1st Vice President and this time around with other more Vice Presidents which resulted in the formation of the fragile and embattled Revitalized Transitional Government of National Unity (RTGONU), and it was agreed controversially to hold elections in 2022 or 2023, with the recent reconstitution of the Revitalized Transitional National Legislative Assembly (RTNLA), while the formation of the unified command and graduation of the unified forces as stipulated in the provision of the security arrangement is far from over.

President Kiir has established a private paramilitary security, which intimidates, tortures, executes people, and lynches political dissidents. President Kiir's associates in government are also too corrupt. They have embezzled millions of dollars from the U.S.A in grants and donations for over 12 million poor people of South Sudan. After staying in power for 16 years, President Kiir's report card indicates his dictatorial and kleptocratic tendencies. President Kiir has indeed failed to resolve crisis bedevilling the country in areas that include;

## Governance Crisis

The SPLM bureaucrats and kleptocrats in South Sudan, together with their affiliated remnants of the National Congress Party (NCP), are not only lacking in vision for the country, but also hell-bent on looting and murdering everyone who holds alternative ideas.

After realizing that they lack the vision and leadership required to manage the state of South Sudan, the SPLM/NCP Kleptocrats have resorted to war, silencing dissidents, perpetrating severe human rights crimes, and impoverishing residents in order to stay in power for the next 100 years.

Because of the country's governance vacuum and poor security institutions, there is widespread insecurity. Civilians resort to arming themselves for their own security and survival. Even in Juba, the nation's capital, "unknown gunmen" (who are recruited and paid) are on the loose.

Several peace agreements were signed to reroute the country to prosperity, but the same elites worked so hard to frustrate effort that could stop the war, build a modern state and put the country on the path of development. The country is run by decrees that keep recycling the same kleptocrats who are robbing the country and its citizens with impunity. Since the independence, state and nation building efforts were sabotaged at will. Subsequently, South Sudan became a failed state just two (2) years following its independence despite massive petrodollars.

The army (SSPDF), Diplomats, and Civil Servants have gone for months, if not years without pay, yet a soldier receives a salary of an equivalent amount of US$4 per month. Widows, children of freedom fighters and wounded heroes who sacrificed their lives for the independence of South Sudan are the beggars you could find at every corner of South Sudan. They are left in limbo and denied medical care, clean water, school, food and shelter for their families.

Consequently, most SSPDF forces if not all have deserted their units and mixed with civil population causing chaos and anarchy among communities in the countryside, indulged in inter-communal violence and bartering government ammunition and weapons with cattle. Those who are resilient and loyal to their units' resort to burning and selling charcoals in the nearby markets for their families' survival, action which does not only undermine climate change adaptation and mitigation efforts but contributes to environmental destruction and desertification.

The rural populations who financed and logistically supported the liberation war of 21 years for the independence of South Sudan do not enjoy the fruits and dividends of their struggle. The current SPLM elites have surrendered the SPLM Party and the governance of the nation to the NCP power brokers and kleptocrats.

The people of South Sudan did not only provide logistics but also offered their sons and daughters to fight the war. They did so, to enjoy freedom and public goods and services such as, clean water, food, electricity, education, health, shelter and security. What they got in return is poverty and dehumanization.

The government of South Sudan (GOSS) has rightly been given a name as the government of self service. After deviating from the SPLM vision, the current SPLM elites have surrendered the governance of the nation to the NCP power brokers and kleptocrats.

## Economic crisis

The oil that is being produced in Upper Nile and Unity States respectively is enough to support the economy and finance the governments' business. Instead, the crude oil has been sold in advance for several years by individuals within the SPLM elites for their personal gains. The elites have put their families in charge of marketing the crude oil and control national parastatals such as Nile Petroleum Corporation (Nilepet) and other financial institutions.

For example, the Nilepet is exclusively run by relatives of President Kiir and his inner circle. The SPLM elites are also running parallel markets selling the US dollars in black market to undermine national currency, loot the Central Bank of South Sudan to the core and depleted the foreign exchange reserves.

Blessed with arable land and natural resources, South Sudan still imports almost everything ranging from beef, vegetables, fruits, maize and other consumable goods from neighbouring countries. With more than 40 million livestock, the country is still importing beef from other countries which is a mockery and insult on the people of South Sudan. This is not surprising as the SPLM elites do not only lack vision to develop the economy, they are incompetent and whatever they do to improve their plights are undermined.

## Dire Humanitarian situation

The SPLM elites have looted the country and displaced more than 50 percent of the population of the displaced, 2.5 million are refugees in neighbouring countries and million more as internally displaced persons sheltering inside the United Nations Mission in South Sudan Protection of Civilian (POCs) sites. About 70 percent of the remaining population are in needs of humanitarian assistance.

## Destruction of the environment

The oil explorations and production have significant impacts on the environment. Water, pastures and the entire ecosystem of the people living along oil fields have been completely, if not, irreversibly damaged. Reports of fish, animals and people dying of strange illnesses have gone to deaf ears. The SPLM elites and NCP remnants are only interested in Petro- dollars. The 3 percent meant for oil producing communities to cushion them from the oil impact, has never reached the poor communities. Recent audit report by the Auditor General of South Sudan Audit Chamber highlighted broad daylight robbery of the money meant for the communities.

## Corruption.

Public resources are being looted with impunity. Anyone who is a sycophant and loyalist to the elite SPLM/NCP bureaucrats and kleptocrat is viewed as patriotic. The oil has been flowing, but no single road has been built. The only asphalt road which is 180 KM was built with the help of the American government. The elites have looted income the country generates. Yet they are not satisfied and have been engaged in undertaking massive debts. As if those are not enough, the elites went further by selling the crude oil underground to enrich themselves and their families to the detriment of the upcoming generations.

## Gross human rights violation.

Thousands of innocent South Sudanese are languishing in prisons in different parts of the country and have no access to justice, thousands have been subjected to extra-judicial killings, many women and girls have been raped. Cases of sodomization have been also reported. These are acts of dehumanization that must be challenged with the available force they deserve.

## Stalled Revitalized Peace Agreement.

President Kiir has failed to implement the 2018 Revitalized Peace Agreement for the Resolution of the Conflict in the Republic of South Sudan (R-ARCSS). The President and the NCP orphans in Juba have tactically and technically delayed the implementation of the agreement so that the elections will not take place in time as stipulated in the agreement. In addition, the elites are deliberately frustrating the unified forces and denies them food and medicines.

The elites are seriously engaging in bribing the opposition forces to join the SSPDF as sabotage to the implementation of security arrangement. The opposition leaders in Juba are under tactical arrest and some of their forces get frustrated.

The clashes and skirmishes that took place around Kajo-Keji, Yei, and Maban areas between the SSPDF and the SPLA-IO, the defection of the opposition forces to the government that was welcomed and encouraged by the SSPDF leadership, and the delay to constitute the hybrid court to try war criminals are indication of lack of political will by the government to fully implement the peace agreement.

## Entrenched tribalism

President Kiir has instilled enmity and tribalism among the people of South Sudan by separating the country into 32 states and carving away and favouring Dinka areas from the rest of the country, thereby making them separate states from the rest of the country. For years, Dinka people have lived as neighbours with their South Sudanese brothers, but President Kiir is attempting to undermine and disrupt this magnificent harmony and cooperation.

## The National Congress Party.

The presidential palace of this country has been captured by the elements of the National Congress Party group led by Security Advisor Tut Gatluak and his team including Dhieu Mathok, Joseph Monytuil Wicjang, the Governor of Unity State, Tong Akeen, the Governor of Northern Bahr El Ghazal, Dak Duop Bichok and Mayik Ayii. The group controls the President Kiir through Gen. Akol Koor and they have sidelined the real SPLM members from interacting with him. They have managed to manipulate the President into issuing erroneous decrees daily to sack who they don't want and appoint who they want, especially those who cannot challenge them before the President

On the 3rd of April, 2021, they met and discussed that they were given a broad hint by a medical doctor that the President will not live for the next six months, and that he will die from liver cancer. They were discussing how they will take over when the President dies. They agreed that first, the President should remove Nhial Deng Nhial, the minister in the office of the president, Commander of Defense Forces of the SSPDF and Gen. Thomas Duoth Guet External Security. They then recommended Marial Benjamin to replace Nhial Deng Nhial, and Gen. Santino Deng Wol to replace Gen. Johnson Juma Okot as a new CDF and Gen. Simon Yien Makuac to replace Gen. Thomas Duoth Guet in the External Security.

They say, when the President dies, the army and other organized forces will take over the leadership of the country and form a military transitional council (MTC) that will be led by Gen. Akol Koor for two years and be deputized by Security Advisor Tut Gatluak before going for the elections. They brought Gen. Simon Yien Makuac to rally Lou Nuer behind the would-be new leadership. The group has briefed Khartoum about their plan and assured them of their support in terms of the military in case the SPLM members try to challenge their action plan,

President Kiir's security advisor, Tut Gatluak, has corrupted the mind of President Kiir with money by scamming millions of dollars from financial institutions. Tut solicits millions of dollars in the name of the President's family from the Arab rich countries and takes the greater part of the money while President Kiir and Gen. Akol Koor are given the least. So far, Tut has mortgaged South Sudan oil to some countries in advance from 2018 up to 2027. For the next six years, there will be no money for the citizens of this country.

Due to corruption President Kiir has left many of his SPLM colleagues in the cold. For instance, when Omar Hassan El Bashir was being removed from power in Sudan, he sent his wife to hide in Juba, and she carried millions of dollars. She was received at the Juba International Airport by Security Advisor, Tut Gatluak and Gen. Akol Koor. Tut Gatluak sent President Bashir's wife to one of the Middle East friendly countries. The money remained with him in Juba as he promised to send it after her.

Unfortunately, he didn't send the money, he divided the loot with President Kiir and Gen. Akol Kor. Secondly, Tut Gatluak is more trusted than any SPLM member because he has promised and assured the President Kiir that no South Sudanese rebel movements would be harboured in Sudan again to challenge his leadership. Thirdly, President Kiir receives millions of dollars from corrupt individuals through Tut Gatluak, the money which he never had before.

Tut Gatluak and his group have plans to annex areas of Northern Bahr El Ghazal, Raja, Twic, Abyei, Unity State, Ruweng, and the whole of Upper Nile to Sudan. This was confirmed on April 24, 2021, when the Sudan armed forces under the command of a Brig. General came to Mayom County in Unity State with twelve military armored vehicles without the knowledge of the SSPDF HQS. They brought more ammunition, uniforms and new weapons for the militia forces being organized in Bul Nuer Mayom County under the leadership of Chuol Gatluak, the brother of Tut Gatluak, the new Mayorn County Commissioner.

Tut Gatluak and his team have been scheming to remove Vice President Taban Deng Gai and replace him with Dak Duop Bichok. President Kiir told them to wait for a while citing Taban Deng as being a notorious person who can cause another havoc in the country.

President Kiir has handed over control of the SPLM to the National Congress party. Tut Gatluak has purchased a magnificent home for President Kiir and opened a bank account in one of the Middle East countries that Tut Gatluak has chosen as President Kiir's retirement location. Tut has encouraged President

Kiir to retire and relocate to one of the Arab countries rather than East Africa, claiming that he will not be treated well in East Africa when he retires and that his property may not be safe after his reign.

# Appendix A

**From**: Major Gen. Stephen Buoy Rolnyang
**To**: Lt. Gen. James Ajongo Mawut

**Subject: Operations plan for Manyo County (Wedekona)**
Comrade it is now clear that the 7th Infantry division will not be able to liberate Manyo county from the rebels without the involvement of Sector-2 and SPLA headquarters physically, because the presence of the rebels across the river while drinking the same water with them, becomes a big threat to 1st Infantry division and Renk population due to their constant shelling on Renk town. This is not because they are more powerful than us, but because we lack boats to carry our equipment across the river Nile from Renk to Wedekona. We are careful not to cross the river from any point as the rebels may cross behind us to take over Renk once we cross.

Comrade, the area of 1st Infantry division is engulfed by the rebels from the Eastern directions especially the rebels that are being harbored by the Sudan army at Tibun, and Buoth areas. This is why we have always concentrated on the Eastern side more than the Western side, even though they always attack us from all directions and we manage to repulse them.

Therefore, I have proposed and developed the following operational plan in managing the operations of Manyo county for your comradeship approval;

**(A)** Mobilization of forces and equipment: -

1. 1st Infantry division shall contribute an infantry full battalion of 700 officers, NCOS and Men to be supported with the following equipment: -
2. One APC
3. Three Mounted Jeeps.
4. One Anti-Tank Gun mounted.

**(B)** 6th Infantry division shall contribute a full battalion of 700 officers, NCOS and Men with the following equipment: -

1. One APC.
2. Three mounted Jeeps.
3. One Anti-Tank Gun mounted.

**(C)** 7th Infantry division shall contribute two Battalions of 1000 officers, NCOS and Men combined with Gen. Ayuok Ugot forces with the following equipment.

1. Five APCS.
2. Five Mounted Jeeps.
3. Three Anti-Tank Guns mounted.

**(D)** White Army of Melut and Renk shall Mobilize 300 white men.

**(E)** SPLA HQS can send one Battalion of 700 officers, NCOS and men with the following equipment.

1. One APC.
2. Three mounted Jeeps.
3. Three anti-tank Guns mounted.
4. Two or three Tanks.

**Logistics requirements for operations**

(1) 500 big boxes of AKM ammos
(2) 300 shells of RPG-7 Guns
(3) 300 big boxes of PKM Ammos
(4) 600 shells of grenade launcher
(5) 5 fuel tanker trucks to carry fuel
(6) 5 water tanker trucks to carry water
(7) 30 trucks for transporting forces
(8) Three ferry boats for crossing the forces to Kaka
(9) 30 Motorola for effective communication
(10) 5 Thuraya communication phones
(11) Quantity of food of dry ration, flour, Jenyjario and oil for three weeks
(12) 3000 pairs of Uniform if necessary

**Command and Control**

1. I suggest that Sector-2 or SPLA headquarters can select a competent senior officer who can conduct that operation temporarily for possible short period of time.
2. Time frame should be first week of March 2015 if there is no peace agreement so far.
3. The forces should be assembled and organized at Molbok for rehearsal before they move on to the mission,

Comrade, after liberating Manyo County, I suggest that the same forces can even be used to liberate Pagak or any place under Sector-2 command.
The above is for your c/ship acknowledgement.

**From:** Major Gen. Stephen Buoy Rolnyang
**To:** Lt-Gen Johnson Gony Biliu-Sector-2 Commander
Info All Units Sector-2
Info Director for OPS
Info Director for M.I
Info Deputy Chief of Gen. Staff for OPS
Info Deputy Chief of Gen. Staff for M.O
Info SPLA Inspector Gen.
Info SPLA Chief of Gen. Staff

020/7/2015.
Ref your c/ship 009/7/2015, dated 19/7/2015, 005/7/2015 dated 15/7/2015, 007/7/2015 dated 17/7/2015, all asking me to explain why I did not write a message to the units of Sector-2 about your arrival in Sector- 2.

Comrade, I have already informed Sector-2 units about your arrival in the area in my message 040/7/2015, dated 17/7/2015. If there is any unit commander who is still directing his messages to me, he has to explain why he is still directing his messages to me.

Secondly, Ref to your c/ship 007/7/2015, concerning your question of who told me to organize the white army in Akoka, Melut, Renk and Maban areas. Comrade, I think it is not a bad idea to do that. I did this when you were in Egypt and the commissioners of Baliet, Akoka, Melut and Renk and some state Ministers from these communities including the State Minister of Finance took permission from the Governor of Upper Nile to approach me so that Jamus division can organize the armed youths of these counties into SPLA like what we did to Abushok forces who are now absorbed and are ready to fight as soldiers unlike the white army who can fight on voluntary basis without being controlled. I thought that this is a golden chance, if the community leaders can ask us to organize their armed youths into the SPLA as this will reduce our burden of asking for reinforcement from Juba.

I have formed the committee under Brig. Yagub Simon deputized by Col. Tor Ajuot the commander of the white army of these counties to organize only those with guns into the SPLA and come with the lists to be forwarded to your c/ship office to pass them to SPLA HQS for approval.

But I am surprised by your message that says I am intimidating yet I thought that there is nothing bad in writing to all units of Sector-2 about your arrival in the sector. First of all, I am not a sector commander who can refuse to hand over to you the sector and what did I gain from being an acting sector commander in your absence? I think you are trying to find a way to create a misunderstanding between us and this is not the first time to have received such a message from your c/ship. Therefore, this can really frustrate the efforts and activities of your subordinate commanders.
For your c/ship information.

From: Major Gen. Stephen Buoy Rolnyang
To SPLA Chief of Gen. Staff
Info Sector-2 Commander
Info Deputy Chief of Gen. Staff for Operations
Info Deputy Chief of Gen. Staff for Administration
Info Deputy Governor Upper Nile
Info Director National Security Renk
Info Director of M.I
Info Governor of Upper Nile State
Info Minister of Defence

003/11/2015.

**Subject: Attack by Renk commissioner**
Yesterday on 2/11/2015, at 2:00 PM, I received a call from Col. Mayol of Renk wild life department that there were Padang elders who needed to meet me to thank me for the recent scores made by 1st Infantry division at Wedekona and Gabat. I told Col. Mayol that there is no problem, so they have to come and get me at the river side transporting forces across the river to Wedekona and Gabat.

When Padang elders arrived, they were accompanied by Renk commissioner. I welcomed them under a big tree and they started addressing me over their visit.

All the elders appreciated the role of Jamus and promised to make contribution in honor of Jamus. When the commissioner was given a chance to talk, he insulted and accused me of the following,

That I am the enemy from within, and any time I could join the rebel like Olony and Yuanis Ukic did.

That Renk white army to be deployed inside the town to protect him because there is insecurity in Renk town.

- He accused me of not reporting to his office daily because he is senior to me by protocol.
- He accused me of not respecting him because I allowed night training where trainees fire bullets at night without his knowledge and ordered my deputy to stop firing range shooting.
- He accused me of conducting shelling to rebel positions at Kuek without his knowledge.
- He said that I stayed long in this division without being transferred.
- He said that I am the threat to the security of Apadang people in Upper Nile.
- He accused me also of closing the border because he ordered last time that there were 8,000 Arab traders who trade in Gum Arabic to be allowed to come to Renk through the border main gate to pick gum Arabic in area of Renk, but when I consulted the D/COGS for operations, he told me not to allow them to come because there is no trade movement agreed yet by the two countries.

With all the above white lies, comrade, I got annoyed and asked the elders to postpone the meeting until further notice, but the commissioner insisted that the meeting should continue whether I like it or not. So, I got fed up and wanted to fight with him physically, but the elders plus the guards intervened and separated us.

I called the Governor of Northern Upper Nile and explained what had happened and gave the phone to Col. Mayol who was facilitating and coordinating the meeting to explain further what transpired to the Governor. Comrade, when the Governor appointed this commissioner, I told him in his office that, this commissioner will bring disaster to Renk because he is pursuing the interests of Brig. Guot Akuei plus some Abiliang politicians who do not want the presence of Nuer in this state. Their plan is to clear Nuer out of Upper Nile government-controlled areas by the use of their white army.

They see me as a Nuer not as a National Army Commander. They see me as a problem to them for preventing them from killing Nuer and Shilluk who are here. They need a Dinka officer to command this division and to be deputized by Brig. Guot Akuei from Abiliang.

I told him that the white army should be deployed where there is a threat like Jalaak from Torguang, and Shilluk rebels that cross and kill civilians at Jalaak.

So, if there are armed youth, they can be deployed at Jalaak to protect civilians instead of deploying them inside Renk town to protect the house of the commissioner while SPLA soldiers are inside Renk for protection of everybody.

The people of Renk have been accusing Nuer in Division -1 of being rebels despite their diehard support which they owe every day in protection of Renk people.

For your c/ship information.

**From:** Major Gen Stephen Buoy Rolnyang
**To:** SPLA Chief of Gen. Staff

**Subject: Situation report on Western Upper Nile, Date 23/6/2017**

### Security situation: Rebel activities

The security situation in Western Upper Nile is normal at the moment with limited movements of rebels crossing from Garia in the North of Sudan and camp at the remote areas of Waak and Toch- Luak South of North Liech State to link up with rebels around Leer and Adok base areas. They have bases in Payinjiar areas.

Their supply routes in Western Upper Nile are through the river from Liri in the Sudan to Wunkur then to Tonga down to Adok bar and Payinjiar areas by river.

Another supply route is from Garia in the Sudan to Waak using different routes through the porous forests by night between Rubkona and Mayom counties mainly Tharwangyiela and Tor-Abieth forests, but with limited logistics because they carry them on their heads.

On 22/6/2017, they attacked Pilieny outpost of Leer area and they were repulsed. One of our soldiers was wounded and none of their soldiers was killed. The outpost is manned by two SPLA platoons.

### Forces of SPLA- IO for Taban.

Our relationship with forces of SPLM/A-IO that are allied to Taban is good but not so much very good due to the following reasons;

- They make forceful recruitment among civil populations.
- They set up road blocks.
- They recruit from our soldiers and promote them to higher ranks ranging from the rank of a Capt. to that of a Colonel.
- They seize civilians' cows when a soldier deserted.

- They loot randomly around the villages without having defined cantonments.
- Former Commander Yuanis Yoal Bath gave them the following areas to assemble:
- Kuerguiyna and Kuergeng in Guit area.
- Tharjiath in Koch area.
- Tomor in Mayom area.
- Ngop in Rubkona area.
- They frequently request Ammos even if there is no fighting.

**Forces of Major Gen. Mathew Puljang**

Our relationship with the forces under Major Gen. Mathew Puljang is good but lukewarm due to the following issues,

1. They make forceful recruitment among the population to cover up their less parade because their parade is 1800 including non- combatants.
2. They seize civilians' cows of those who refuse to be with them.
3. They see and bring the cases of civilians to their hands rather than being under the hands of civil local courts.
4. They fire squad civilians and soldiers without the knowledge of the top leadership of the country.
5. On my coming, Puljang called his officers for a meeting and told them not to accept his command to be combined or amalgamated with 4th Infantry division, but officers told him that it is good to combine us with 4th Infantry division to streamline the forces but he said he heard that he was put on reserve list without being given a job, and with that, the officers who were with him told him that let us wait first and maybe you will be assigned.
6. Major Gen. Mathew Puljang has been in contact with Manut or Dut Yai who is currently with the former Chief, and also the mind of Puljang is being spoiled by General Thayip Gatluak Taitai and the Governor of North Liech State by telling him not to accept to combine your forces with forces of 4th Infantry division because they want Thayip to be deployed in 4th Infantry division and Major Gen. Mathew Puljang would still be independent as usual as arranged earlier by the former chief of defence for his own intention and interest with those of governor Joseph Nguen Monytuil and Tut Keaw Gatluak when they promised the former chief to keep this force separate as his own special force to do anything that he may want to do.

1. Mayom civil population and intellectuals welcome the integration of the forces of Major Gen. Mathew Puljang into 4th Infantry division because they are tired of Mathew Puljang's activities in the area.
2. The main reason is that they want this force to be commanded by politicians themselves rather than the army HQS to threaten the leadership of the country against their removal and to remain as militia group within the government as in the case of Hezbollah militias in Lebanon and Hamas in Palestine.

**Forces of Lt. Gen. James Gai Yoay**

Gen. James Gai Yoay did not come with the forces when he joined the SPLA. He came with few officers from Khartoum to Juba, but he has recruited civilians from his section or clan called Leek and sent the officers who joined with him to command them. So now, he has forces in Nhialdiu and some in Rubkona counties, and frankly speaking, nothing bad was reported about their activities in those areas.

**Activities of the armed civilians in Western Upper Nile**

Our relationship with the armed civilians in western Upper Nile is good but not so much very good with the following issues:

They kill soldiers if found one moving alone and take his gun.

1. They raid each other's cattle.
2. They cause sectional fight or violence among themselves using guns.
3. They cross to Bahr El Ghazal and Panaru for cattle raiding.

**Activities of 4th Infantry division**

The 4th Infantry Division has been devastated by the rebellion of 2013 in which most of its forces joined the rebellion except forces in Jaw and Parieng areas.

When I took over this command of 4th Infantry division in 2015, I found about five different commands as follows:

1. Jaw forces under command of Brig. James Badeng Machar.
2. Parieng forces under command of Major Gen. Deng Mayik Mai.
3. Militia forces under command of Major Gen Joseph Manyuat.
4. Remnant of former 4th Infantry division forces under command of Major Gen. Thayip Gatluak.
5. And forces under Major Gen. Mathew Puljang in Mayom area.

I managed to combine the four different commands above except forces under Major Gen. Mathew Puljang that the SPLA headquarters said to be an independent force.

I organized four commands into three incomplete Bdes:

1. Bde 10 deployed at Panakuac and Unity oil fields.
2. Bde 11 deployed in Panaru and Jaw areas.
3. Bde 12 deployed in Leer area.

The parade was 11,000 with a lot of ghost names and including women, disables, old ages and martyrs and I reported to the SPLA headquarters that there were no forces in 4th Infantry division, but nobody responded to my report on what to do.

When I wanted to re-organize them, and that was eventually the time when my arrest occurred and I immediately got arrested and Major Gen. Yohanes Yoal Bath was brought in to command as my predecessor.

Now with my second deployment to 4th Infantry division, I got the command at zero level, all soldiers deserted and no enough forces to defend the area, but some of them reported back when they heard that I had arrived in Bentiu.

They have included their wives and relatives in the pay roll to replace those who have deserted. They have given them last pay certificate (LPC) and transferred them to units of wounded heroes to receive their salaries in their respective villages instead to recruit able men to fight.

The present salary parade is 10830 including non-combatants.

I have now formed the committee to register who is present to know the exact parade then to report it to your comradeship for further directives in case of ghost names and other non -combatants.

If it is not because of the presence of the reinforcement forces from 3rd and 5th Infantry divisions, the rebels would have taken western Upper Nile.

The parade of 3rd and 5th Infantry division forces that is present in Western Upper Nile is 2509 and may not also be complete because some of them have deserted their units back to Bahr El Ghazal.

Deployment of 4th Infantry division forces combined with reinforcement forces is as follows: -

1. Leer
2. Jaw
3. Parieng
4. Panakuac
5. Unity

6. Tor-Abieth
7. Tharwangyiela
8. Kaljak
9. Guit county HQs
10. Kilo 30
11. Bentiu town
12. Division HQS

**Achievements**

- Combination of four commands under one command.
- Renovation of command guest house.
- Renovation of command offices.
- Establishment of officers' mess and renovation of officers' mess hall.
- Training of two companies (Coys).
- Fencing of some barracks with barbed wires.
- Furnishing guest house and offices with sofa chairs and plastic chairs, TV sets, beds etc., but some of these items were sold out in the hands of Major Gen. Yuanis Yoal bath.
- Structuring command departments.

**Challenges**

- No heavy and light vehicles in the division, most of the vehicles or trucks have been privatized by former individual officers and commanders and some are grounded beyond repair.
- No tanks and APCS, most of the tanks and APC if not all, are grounded beyond repair.
- No weapons, most of the weapons if not all, were captured by the enemy and some taken by transferred commanders.
- Lack of Ammunitions and shells.
- No fuel.
- No food.
- Lack of uniform.
- No spare parts.
- Lack of medicines.
- Lack of well-trained officers, the officers who are here cannot command or be commanded.
- Lack of forces to defend greater western Upper Nile.

Most of our forces are not trained given the background of the integration of the forces from various Other Armed Groups (OAG) that were operating in former western Upper Nile and those recruited locally without being trained.

Presence of different other armed groups (OAG) within the area with different separate commands.

Recruitment of the SPLA soldiers by other armed groups and promote them to higher ranks so that our forces should desert the SPLA to the SPLM/A -IO for promotions.

Lacks of personal rifles, most of the soldiers if not all, are un-armed.

Lack of communication equipment.

Lack of running cost for administrative and operations purpose, the command depends only on unpaid salaries of deserters and absentees which sometimes are mismanaged by unit commanders for personal interests.

Lack of qualified moral orientation (M.O) and legal personnel at various units to carry out the work of M.O and justice.

Lack of cultivation equipment. The tractors that were given by the SPLA GHQS have been sold out in Juba by Major Gen. Yuanis Yoal Bath.

Most of our forces are deployed in states and counties HQS as bodyguards for governors and commissioners. They show up only during the salary payment.

**Recommendations**

Request for the provision of some of the above requirements if not all.

There is an urgent need for the integration of all other armed groups in western Upper Nile into the SPLA.

There is an urgent need for the forces of Mathew Puljang to be mixed with the forces of 4th Infantry division in order to streamline the organization of the forces.

There is an urgent need for the reinforcement forces of 3rd and 5th Infantry divisions in Western Upper Nile to be deployed fully with their LPC to be part of 4th Infantry division command.

There is a need to promote the SPLA senior NCOS to officers' rank to stop deserting to the SPLM/A -IO seeking for promotion.

Request for the maintenance of the grounded tanks, APC and fighting vehicles if there are no replacements.

Request for the approval of unpaid salaries to be used as running cost for administrative and operational issues.

There is a need to return our forces deployed in the counties and state HQS back to command. Request for a generator for 4th Infantry division command. There is no generator at all. I just borrow a generator from someone which we are using now but not yet paid. The owner needs 1,000,000 only one million SSP

I want your c/ship directives whether we should release them or keep them in prison until further directives.

Your c/ship response will be awaited.

**From:** Major Gen Stephen Buoy Rolnyang- Commander 4th Infantry division
**To:** Lt. Col Peter Lok Tang – SPLA –IO operation officer in Rubkona area

**Subject: Peace and reconciliation**
**17/12/2015.**

This is to inform your c/ship that, I have been transferred to Unity State as the commander of 4th Infantry division and I am writing this letter to your c/ship that, let us maintain peace so that our civilians get rest.

Our people have been suffering indeed because of this war. Let us observe peace among our communities.

I have instructed all the units to stay where they are and should not attack you anymore. I want you to do the same on your side so that we give peace a chance.

You are my friend that is why I write to you this letter and I hope you will understand me better than anybody else.

Greet Gen. Gathuoy Thak, Turuk Khor, my brother Turuk Bol, Kedol Thong and the rest of my friends, if they are with you there.

I am for peace, but not for war. We are the future of this country. Let us stop taking civilians cows and let us respect their properties. They are our people and people of Bentiu are one. So, let us stop tribalism and sectionalism among ourselves. I love people of Bentiu very much and their unity is our strength, as well as the same as the unity of all south Sudanese.

**Thank you all.**

**From**: Major Gen. Stephen Buoy Rolnyang- Commander 5th Infantry division.
**To:** Major Gen. Arkanjelo Abanga- Deputy Commander of 5th INF.
R/ Cdr of ground force
R/ Governor Wau State
R/ Director National security Wau State
R/ Commissioner of Police Wau State
R/ Chief of M.I GHQS
R/ Ground force chief of M.I
R/ 5th Infantry division intelligent officer in charge
R/ A/CDF for OPS, Intel and TRG

7/3/2018

**Subject: Suspension of illegal military intelligence activities in Wau town and all checkpoints.**

You are instructed to suspend all illegal Military intelligence activities in Wau town joint operations and check-points until they are officially screened to know who are really Military intelligence personnel for 5th Infantry division and those who are operating illegally in the town and check points in the name of the military intelligence (M.I) for 5th Infantry division.

These groups are about 100 officers and other ranks who deserted from various SPLA divisions and self-deployed or recruited by former Military intelligence officers of 5th Infantry division and deployed them in check points and markets in Wau town to collect money from civilians for them. They are charged with the followings:

1. They disobeyed command orders that all elements within Military intelligence who are not Military intelligence personnel should report to Division HQs and the trained M.I personnel be officially deployed to the units and check points for security purposes.

They have imposed self-deployment in the town and checkpoints in order to collect money from the people daily.

They are the ones causing insecurity in Wau town at night by shooting randomly and looting property of innocent civilians. They conduct parallel patrolling in the town instead of security joint operations.

They threatened Division commander at gun point by cocking their guns in the parade witnessed by all the officers of 5th Infantry division and ran into the town with their guns refusing to put them in the store at division HQS.

Military Police are the ones to operate in the town to arrest any SPLA soldier found carrying a gun and wearing uniform in public places in Wau town until M.I case settled.

For execution.

**From**: Major Gen. Stephen Buoy Rolnyang- Commander 4th Infantry division
**To:** Lt-Gen. Marial Cinuong Yol- A/CDF for OPS, TRG and Intel.
R/ SPLA Chief of defence forces

002/1/2018

**Subject: Report on my visit to Bul (Mayom area)**
Comrade, I moved from Bentiu (4th infantry division HQS) to Mayom on 19/12/2017 to meet Major Gen Mathew Puljang in Mayom and go together to visit all the shrines of Bul spiritual leaders for reconciliation between me and Puljang. We moved around Bul area for 9 days and finally, I came back to Division HQS on 28/12/2017.

We were warmly welcomed by all Bul civilians despite the order of the Governor asking former Mayom county government officials to prevent civilians from receiving and meeting us.

The security situation in Bul area is normal, especially Bul border with Warrap and Gogrial except individual criminals that cross the border of both sides to steal cows.

Some of Bul armed criminals kill people in revenge for old feuds and grudges due to a complete breakdown of law and order because the Police is doing nothing to maintain law and order. They also raid each other's cattle with Leek community of former Rubkona County.

Bul is seriously underdeveloped. The area has no health facility, no school and no good roads. Patient from the area have to walk to Anet in Twic or Bahr El Ghazal to get medical treatment. People are really suffering in greater Mayom despite the economic crisis in South Sudan.

Comrade, according to my view, Governor Nguen is totally rejected by the people on ground. There is an urgent need to remove him from the governorship. People stay without the government, because governor himself does not come down to be with the people. He stays in Juba. While his commissioners and other civil administrators are busy taking cows from the people and put them in their own houses to marry more wives with the cows, while nothing is done about the development of the state in order to deliver basic services to the people.

After he failed to prevent civilians from receiving us at the respective shrines of Bul spiritual leaders, he has now ordered the state government officials and commissioners to report to Juba on pretext to attend the workshop, but some officials refused to go to Juba, and still, he is threatening to remove them from their positions.

The governor sent a huge amount of money to government officials in greater Mayom to mobilize armed youth to go to Bahr El Ghazal to raid cattle and kill innocent people there, so that Juba may think that it is the unit of Puljang that carried out the raid on innocent civilians.

The governor has influenced the officers of the SPLM/A –IO for (Taban) Lt-Gen Peter Dor and Major Gen. Makal Kuol not to cooperate with 4th Infantry division and promised them to remain separate till the time of elections of 2018. He sent them money to confuse them. He encourages armed youth of greater Rubkona and Koch counties to attack and raid cattle from Southern Liech State communities of Haak and Adok in Leer and Mayendit counties.

The governor has also created serious border disputes between Ruweng and North Liech State by ordering commissioners of greater Rubkona counties to support armed youth activities to raid cattle and kill innocent people in Ruweng State.

Comrade, in fact, the governor is unhappy because the forces of Puljang have detached themselves from his direct command, because he was the one commanding Puljang forces, but not the ground force command. He wants to use that force to threaten the government in case he is removed from the governorship. Now, the force of Puljang is back to ground force command without any interference of politicians. This is the greatest achievement by the SPLA command.

This force was created by former Chief of General Staff, Paul Malong Awan with advice from the governor Nguen and presidential advisor Tut Keaw in order to have connection with Sudan to overthrow the government of the Republic of South Sudan with tangible evidences revealed to us by Major Gen Puljang. Those of Major Gen. Thayip Gatluak, John Maluk Matai and M.I. Col. Sabina Gatkuoth Geng are the group to implement this move if time could allow them before Malong was removed. The same group is still in contact with Malong up to now.

Major Gen. Thayip Gatluak ordered his HQS in Wau to report to his house in Mankien to stay there until he could get a chance to come down to Mayom and execute his plan with Malong. We conducted a search in his house in Mankien and found a big number of PKM, RPG-7, anti-tank and 12.7mm machine guns and we deployed all those guns and his bodyguards in the special operations unit.

**For your c/ship information.**

# Appendix B

The formation of the SPLA units since the inception of the SPLA in 1983.

1. **The SPLA 1st Infantry division.**

| S/n | Battalions | Year of passing out | Unit commander | Remarks |
|---|---|---|---|---|
| 1. | 104/105 | 1983 | William Nyuon Bany | |
| 2. | Jamus | 1983 | Kerubino Kuanyin Bol | |
| 3. | Tiger | 1983 | Salva Kiir Mayardit | |
| 4. | Tumsah | 1983 | Arok Thon Arok | |

**2. The SPLA 2nd Infantry division (Koryom)**

| S/n | Battalions | Year of passing out | Unit commander | Remarks |
|---|---|---|---|---|
| 1. | Zindia | 1984 | Peter Panom Thanypien | |
| 2. | Cobra | 1984 | Benjamin Nyankot | |
| 3. | Rhino | 1984 | Martin Aleyo | |
| 4. | Raad | 1984 | John Kong Nyuon | |
| 5. | Hadiid | 1984 | Francis Ngor | |
| 6. | Lion | 1984 | Deng Alony | |
| 7. | Agreb | 1984 | Nyaciegak Nyaculuk | |
| 8. | Bilpam | 1984 | Wilson Chol | |
| 9. | elephant | 1984 | Alfred Akuoc | |
| 10. | Hippo | 1984 | Francis Jago | |
| 11. | Commando | 1984 | Garang' Amor | |
| 12. | Red army | 1984 | | |
| 13. | Banat | 1984 | | |

## 3. The SPLA 3rd Infantry division (Mour-Mour)

| S/n | Battalions | Year of passing out | Unit commander | Remarks |
|---|---|---|---|---|
| 1 | Tuek-Tuek | 1985 | Daniel Awet | |
| 2 | Shark | 1985 | Bona Bang Dhol | |
| 3 | Eagle | 1985 | Kerubino Kuanyin Bol | |
| 4 | Wolf | 1985 | Riek Machar Teny | |
| 5 | Niran | 1985 | Tahir Bior | |
| 6 | Bee | 1985 | Martin Manyiel | |
| 7 | Badger | 1985 | | |
| 8 | Abushok | 1985 | Michael Miakol | |
| 9 | Nil | 1985 | Alfred Ajuong | |
| 10 | Red Army | 1985 | | |

## 4. The SPLA 4th Infantry division (Kazuk)

| S/n | Battalions | Year of passing out | Unit commander | Remarks |
|---|---|---|---|---|
| 1 | Zalan | 1986 | Andrew ANhiem | |
| 2 | Mut | 1986 | Elijah Hon Top | |
| 3 | Tingili | 1986 | Gelario Modi | |
| 4 | Kalany | 1986 | Elijah Akol | |
| 5 | Rajab | 1986 | Elijah Maduk | |
| 6 | Namus | 1986 | Maker Malou | |
| 7 | Yoany | 1986 | James Hoth Mai | |
| 8 | Mazlum | 1986 | Daniel Deng Alony | |
| 9 | Fashoda | 1986 | Oyai Deng Ajak | |
| 10 | Mukshasha | 1986 | Alfred Lado Gore | |
| 11 | Moonlight | 1986 | | |
| 12 | Hanka | 1986 | Mager Aciek | |
| 13 | Akoun | 1986 | Francis Jago | |
| 14 | Maiwut T.F | 1986 | Kuac Kang Rial | |
| 15 | Faustino Puok | 1986 | Makuac Tinec | |
| 16 | Boma T.F | 1986 | John Ajith Nhial | |
| 17 | Red Army | 1986 | | |

## 5. The SPLA 5th Infantry division (Zal-Zal-1)

| S/n | Battalions | Year of passing out | Unit commander | Remarks |
|---|---|---|---|---|
| 1 | Majunun | 1987 | Thuc Majok | |
| 2 | Lazim | 1987 | | |
| 3 | Takcin | 1987 | Adier Deng | |
| 4 | Songky | 1987 | | |
| 5 | Kasha | 1987 | Yusif Kuwa Maki | |
| 6 | Volcano | 1987 | | |
| 7 | Shakush | 1987 | | |
| 8 | Commando | 1987 | | |
| 9 | Red Army | 1987 | | |

## 6. The SPLA 6th Infantry division (Zal-Zal -2)

| S/n | Battalions | Year of passing out | Unit commander | Remarks |
|---|---|---|---|---|
| 1 | Petrol | 1987 | | |
| 2 | Nejda | 1987 | | |
| 3 | Winy | 1987 | | |
| 4 | Munshar | 1987 | | |
| 5 | Daniel Shoki | 1987 | | |
| 6 | Shamish | 1987 | | |
| 7 | Neshab | 1987 | | |
| 8 | Gerger | 1987 | | |
| 9 | Kokap | 1987 | | |
| 10 | Sunun | 1987 | | |
| 11 | Pas | 1987 | | |
| 12 | Gazal | 1987 | | |

## 7. The SPLA 7th Infantry division (Infijiar)

| S/n | Battalions | Year of passing out | Unit commander | Remarks |
|---|---|---|---|---|
| 1 | Maniir | 1988 | | |
| 2 | Marwii | 1988 | | |
| 3 | Talga | 1988 | | |
| 4 | Shambe | 1988 | | |
| 5 | Pibor | 1988 | | |
| 6 | Himir | 1988 | | |
| 7 | Bunia | 1988 | | |
| 8 | Dam | 1988 | | |
| 9 | Ali Guatala | 1988 | | |
| 10 | Malek | 1988 | | |
| 11 | Naam | 1988 | | |

## 8. The SPLA 8th Infantry division (Intifadha)

| S/n | Battalions | Year of passing out | Unit commander | Remarks |
|---|---|---|---|---|
| 1 | Mandela | 1989 | | |
| 2 | Nkurumah | 1989 | | |
| 3 | Taagig | 1989 | | |
| 4 | Samora | 1989 | | |
| 5 | Nyacigak | 1989 | | |
| 6 | Nasir | 1989 | | |
| 7 | Grader | 1989 | | |
| 8 | Lamumba | 1989 | | |
| 9 | Augustino Nito | 1989 | | |
| 10 | Commando | 1989 | | |

## 9. The SPLA 9th Infantry division (Intisaar)

| S/n | Battalions | Year of passing out | Unit commander | Remarks |
|---|---|---|---|---|
| 1 | Jamus | 1990 | | |
| 2 | Tiger | 1990 | | |
| 3 | Tumsah | 1990 | | |
| 4 | Agreb | 1990 | | |
| 5 | Lion | 1990 | | |
| 6 | Rhino | 1990 | | |
| 7 | Neshab | 1990 | | |
| 8 | Volcano | 1990 | | |
| 9 | Zahj | 1990 | | |

### The historical list of the SPLA Commanders

The highest rank in the SPLA during the bush war was a Commander (Cdr), and then alternate (A/Cdr) and followed by other conventional ranking system as:

1. Commander (Cdr)
2. Alternate Commander (A/Cdr)
3. Capt.
4. 1st Lt
5. 2nd Lt

This is the list of the SPLA commanders after Riek Machar and Lam Akol rejoined the SPLA.

| S/N | Rank | Name in full | Date of promotion | Remarks |
|---|---|---|---|---|
| 1. | Cdr | Dr. John Garang' De Mabior | 15/5/1983 | |
| 2. | Cdr | Salva Kiir Mayardit | 15/5/1983 | |
| 3. | Cdr | Dr Riek Machar Teny Dhur-gon | | |
| 4. | Cdr | James Wani Igga | 1/1/1986 | |
| 5. | Cdr | Daniel Awet Akot | 1/1/1986 | |
| 6. | Cdr | Kuol Manyang Juuk | 1/1/1986 | |
| 7. | Cdr | Lual Diing Wol | 1/1/1989 | |
| 8. | Cdr | Stephen Duol Chuol | 1/1/1988 | |
| 9. | Cdr | Pagan Amum Okiech | 16/5/1991 | |
| 10. | Cdr | Deng Alor Kuol | 16/5/1991 | |
| 11. | Cdr | John Kong Nyuon | 16/5/1991 | |

| | | | | |
|---|---|---|---|---|
| 12. | Cdr | Abdel; Aziz Adam El Hilu | 16/5/1991 | |
| 13. | Cdr | Samuel Abujohn Kabashi | 16/5/1991 | |
| 14. | Cdr | Nhial Deng Nhial | 16/5/1991 | |
| 15. | Cdr | Malik Agar Eyre | 16/5/1991 | |
| 16. | Cdr | Stephen Madut Baak | 1/11/1991 | |
| 17. | Cdr | Bona Bang Dhol | 1/11/1991 | |
| 18. | Cdr | Elijah Malok Aleng | 1/11/1991 | |
| 19. | Cdr | Cagai Atem Biar | 1/11/1991 | |
| 20. | Cdr | Mark Machiec Magok | 1/11/1991 | |
| 21. | Cdr | Kuot Deng Kuot | 1/11/1991 | |
| 22. | Cdr | Anthony Bol Madut | 1/11/1991 | |
| 23. | Cdr | Akec Koc Acieu | 1/11/1991 | |
| 24. | Cdr | Peter Wal Athieu | 1/11/1991 | |
| 25. | Cdr | Oyai Deng Ajak | 1/11/1991 | |
| 26. | Cdr | Dominic Dim Deng | 1/11/1991 | |
| 27. | Cdr | Salva Mathok Geng | 1/11/1991 | |
| 28. | Cdr | Bior Ajang Duot | 1/11/1991 | |
| 29. | Cdr | David Dual Palek | 1/11/1991 | |
| 30. | Cdr | Daniel Deng Monydit | 1/11/1991 | |
| 31. | Cdr | Garang' Mabil Deng | 1/11/1991 | |
| 32. | Cdr | Gier Chuang Aluong | 1/11/1991 | |
| 33. | Cdr | Majak Agot Atem | 1/11/1991 | |
| 34. | Cdr | James Oath Mai | 1/11/1991 | |
| 35. | Cdr | Obuto Mamur Mete | 1/11/1991 | |
| 36. | Cdr | Biar Atem Ajang | 1/11/1991 | |
| 37. | Cdr | Kennedy Gayin Ngare | 1/11/1991 | |
| 38. | Cdr | Joseph Akech Aciek | 1/11/1991 | |
| 39. | Cdr | Pieng Deng Kuol | 1/5/1992 | |
| 40. | Cdr | George Athor Deng | 1/5/1992 | |
| 41. | Cdr | Paul Malong Awan | 1/7/1992 | |
| 42. | Cdr | Santo Ayang Deng | 1/7/1992 | |
| 43. | Cdr | Justin Yac Arop | 1/3/1993 | |

| | | | | |
|---|---|---|---|---|
| 44. | Cdr | Ayuen Alier Jongroor | 1/3/1993 | |
| 45. | Cdr | Wilson Deng Kuoirot | 1/3/1993 | |
| 46. | Cdr | Patrick Ayiteng Lotwa | 1/3/1993 | |
| 47. | Cdr | Daniel Ayual Makoi | 1/3/1993 | |
| 48. | Cdr | Edward Lino Abiei | 1/3/1993 | |
| 49. | Cdr | Kuol Dim Kuol | 1/3/1993 | |
| 50. | Cdr | Scopas Loboro Kenyi | 1/3/1993 | |
| 51. | Cdr | Daniel Kodi Anjelo | 1/3/1993 | |
| 52. | Cdr | Ismail Khamis Jalab | 1/3/1993 | |
| 53. | Cdr | Peter Longole Kuam | 1/3/1993 | |
| 54. | Cdr | Thomas Cirilo Swaka | 1/3/1993 | |
| 55. | Cdr | Jadalla Augustino Jada | 1/3/1993 | |
| 56. | Cdr | Elias Waya Nyipuoc | 1/3/1993 | |
| 57. | Cdr | Yusif Kara Haruon | 1/1/1995 | |
| 58. | Cdr | Telephone Kuku Abujala | 1/1/1995 | |
| 59. | Cdr | James Ajongo Mawut | 1/7/1995 | |
| 60. | Cdr | Jok Reng Magot | 1/7/1995 | |
| 61. | Cdr | Michael Majok Ayom | 1/7/1995 | |
| 62. | Cdr | William Deng Garang' | 1/7/1995 | |
| 63. | Cdr | Stephen Anyak Chol | 1/7/1995 | |
| 64. | Cdr | Dr Dau Aleer Abit | 1/7/1995 | |
| 65. | Cdr | Telar Ring Takpiny | 1/7/1995 | |
| 66. | Cdr | Mading Deng Kuol | 1/7/1995 | |
| 67. | Cdr | John Ayii Manyok | 1/7/1995 | |
| 68. | Cdr | Akuei Deng Akuei | 1/7/1995 | |
| 69. | Cdr | Jurkuc Barac Jurkuc | 1/7/1995 | |
| 70. | Cdr | Malony Akau Nai | 1/7/1995 | |
| 71. | Cdr | Abraham Jok Aring | 1/7/1995 | |
| 72. | Cdr | Dr Akol Diing Duot | 1/7/1995 | |
| 73. | Cdr | Dr Atem Nathan Riak | 1/7/1995 | |
| 74. | Cdr | Dr Achol Marial Deng | 1/7/1995 | |
| 75. | Cdr | Dr Majok Yak Majok | 1/7/1995 | |
| 76. | Cdr | Louis Aliardo Paul | 1/7/1995 | |
| 77. | Cdr | Mayom Deng Biar | 1/7/1995 | |
| 78. | Cdr | Kuol Mayen Mading | 1/7/1995 | |

| | | | | |
|---|---|---|---|---|
| 79. | Cdr | Arok Isaiah Angeth | 1/7/1995 | |
| 80. | Cdr | Chol Gai Arok | 1/7/1995 | |
| 81. | Cdr | Gai Manyang Dot | 1/7/1995 | |
| 82. | Cdr | Paul Garang' Deng | 1/7/1995 | |
| 83. | Cdr | Matur Chut Dhuol | 1/7/1995 | |
| 84. | Cdr | Wuor Mabior Deng | 1/7/1995 | |
| 85. | Cdr | Maciek Akucpiir Cayar | 1/7/1995 | |
| 86. | Cdr | Peter Mading Duor | 1/7/1995 | |
| 87. | Cdr | Malek Ruben Riak | 1/7/1995 | |
| 88. | Cdr | John Mayik Jaw | 1/7/1995 | |
| 89. | Cdr | Malual Ayom Dor | 1/7/1995 | |
| 90. | Cdr | Ateny Ajak Makur | 1/7/1995 | |
| 91. | Cdr | Ayuel Jogak Deng | 1/7/1995 | |
| 92. | Cdr | Mangar Buong Alueng | 1/7/1995 | |
| 93. | Cdr | Francis Nyacidi Kukuol | 1/7/1995 | |
| 94. | Cdr | Babur Meze Dorongo | 1/7/1995 | |
| 95. | Cdr | Chol Thon Balok | 1/7/1995 | |
| 96. | Cdr | Gabriel Majok Riak | 1/7/1995 | |
| 97. | Cdr | Andrea Dominic Safar | 1/7/1995 | |
| 98. | Cdr | Angelo Taban Biajo | 1/7/1995 | |
| 99. | Cdr | Bullen Ayuen Mabior | 1/7/1995 | |
| 100. | Cdr | Taban Deng Gai | 1/7/1995 | |
| 101. | Cdr | Peter Bol Kong | 1/7/1995 | |
| 102. | Cdr | John Luk Jok | 27/1/1996 | |
| 103. | Cdr | Maker Deng Malou | 1/11/1996 | |
| 104. | Cdr | Edward Achuiny Dau | 1/11/1996 | |
| 105. | Cdr | Yar Chuol Ruei | 1/11/1996 | |
| 106. | Cdr | Peter Parnyang Daniel | 1/11/1996 | |
| 107. | Cdr | Pargol O. Alan | 1/11/1996 | |
| 108. | Cdr | Benjamin Majak Dau | 1/11/1996 | |
| 109. | Cdr | Johnson Gony Biliu | 1/11/1996 | |
| 110. | Cdr | James Malith Gatluak | 1/11/1996 | |
| 111. | Cdr | Moses Chot Riek | 1/11/1996 | |
| 112. | Cdr | Charles Lam Chol | 1/11/1996 | |

| | | | | |
|---|---|---|---|---|
| 113. | Cdr | Gabriel Maluth Kueth | 1/11/1996 | |
| 114. | Cdr | Peter Kuol Thiep | 1/11/1996 | |
| 115. | Cdr | Abiel Chan Anyang | 1/11/1996 | |
| 116. | Cdr | Paul Topic Liet | 1/11/1996 | |
| 117. | Cdr | Philip Chol Biowei | 1/11/1996 | |
| 118. | Cdr | James Yol Kuol | 1/7/1997 | |
| 119. | Cdr | Marial Chanuong Yol | 1/7/1997 | |
| 120. | Cdr | Akuei Adal Akuei | 1/7/1997 | |
| 121. | Cdr | Dau Aturjong Nyuol | 1/7/1997 | |
| 122. | Cdr | Bol Akot Bol | 1/7/1997 | |
| 123. | Cdr | Charles Madut Akol | 1/7/1997 | |
| 124. | Cdr | Santino Deng Wol | 1/7/1997 | |
| 125. | Cdr | Butros Bol Bol | 1/7/1997 | |
| 126. | Cdr | Joseph Natio Awan | 1/7/1997 | |
| 127. | Cdr | Kitchener Motan Alan | 1/7/1997 | |
| 128. | Cdr | Jacob Miyar Miyen | 1/7/1997 | |
| 129. | Cdr | Thiik Aciek Hol | 1/7/1997 | |
| 130. | Cdr | Aciek Anot Deng | 1/7/1997 | |
| 131. | Cdr | Chol Aleer Abit | 1/7/1997 | |
| 132. | Cdr | Marcel Stephen Babanen | 1/7/1997 | |
| 133. | Cdr | Malual Majok Chiengkuac | 1/7/1997 | |
| 134. | Cdr | Kur Kuol Ajiu | 1/7/1997 | |
| 135. | Cdr | Lual Chol Dhol | 1/7/1997 | |
| 136. | Cdr | David Manyok Barac | 1/7/1997 | |
| 137. | Cdr | Angelo Jongkuc Jol | 1/7/1997 | |
| 138. | Cdr | James Koang Chol | 1/7/1997 | |
| 139. | Cdr | Kuol Deng Abot | 1/7/1997 | |
| 140. | Cdr | Michael Manoah Kot | 1/7/1997 | |
| 141. | Cdr | Richard Babiro Mark | 1/7/1997 | |
| 142. | Cdr | Marcello Otwari Dominic | 1/7/1997 | |
| 143. | Cdr | Garang' Akok Adut | 1/7/1997 | |
| 144. | Cdr | Dr Lueth Garang' Kuany | 1/7/1997 | |

| | | | | |
|---|---|---|---|---|
| 145. | Cdr | Dr Henry Makeny Dhieu | 1/7/1997 | |
| 146. | Cdr | Tuar Alier Ajak | 1/7/1997 | |
| 147. | Cdr | Mac Paul Kuol Awar | 1/7/1997 | |
| 148. | Cdr | Samson Mabior Lual | 1/7/1997 | |
| 149. | Cdr | Bol Angara Dut | 1/7/1997 | |
| 150. | Cdr | Garang' Bul Pager | 1/7/1997 | |
| 151. | Cdr | Kiir Garang' De Kuek | 1/7/1997 | |
| 152. | Cdr | Magok Magok Deng | 1/7/1997 | |
| 153. | Cdr | Ajak Deng Biar | 1/7/1997 | |
| 154. | Cdr | Deng Tong Jok | 1/7/1997 | |
| 155. | Cdr | Deng Kuot Nyang | 1/7/1997 | |
| 156. | Cdr | Arop Mayak Monytoc | 1/7/1997 | |
| 157. | Cdr | Monydhang Deng Kuol | 1/7/1997 | |
| 158. | Cdr | Santino Ajiu Dau | 1/7/1997 | |
| 159. | Cdr | Zamba Michael Duku | 1/7/1997 | |
| 160. | Cdr | Philip Lomodong Lako | 1/7/1997 | |
| 161. | Cdr | Festo Kumba | 1/7/1997 | |
| 162. | Cdr | Kizikia Ruei Puot | 1/7/1997 | |
| 163. | Cdr | Daniel Kongor Aruai | 1/7/1997 | |
| 164. | Cdr | Assai Osman Assai | 1/7/1997 | |
| 165. | Cdr | Thon Duop Bol | 1/7/1997 | |
| 166. | Cdr | John Mayar Mayiik | 1/7/1997 | |
| 167. | Cdr | Aleu Ayieny Aleu | 1/7/1997 | |
| 168. | Cdr | Akot Deng Akot | 1/7/1997 | |
| 169. | Cdr | Dr Pius Vincent Subek | 1/7/1997 | |
| 170. | Cdr | Abraham Wani Yona | 1/7/1997 | |
| 171. | Cdr | Philip Thon Leek | 1/7/1997 | |
| 172. | Cdr | Edward Friday Lado | 1/7/1997 | |
| 173. | Cdr | George Garang' Deng | 1/7/1997 | |
| 174. | Cdr | Martin Ohuro Okeruk | 1/7/1997 | |
| 175. | Cdr | Okech Alaak Okech | 1/7/1997 | |
| 176. | Cdr | Martin Gumwel Mabior | 1/7/1997 | |

| | | | | |
|---|---|---|---|---|
| 177. | Cdr | Elesio Emor Ojetok | 1/7/1997 | |
| 178. | Cdr | Francis Atada Kerubino | 1/7/1997 | |
| 179. | Cdr | Louis Lobong Lojore | 1/7/1997 | |
| 180. | Cdr | George Echom Ekeno | 1/7/1997 | |
| 181. | Cdr | Deng Akecak Jok | 1/7/1997 | |
| 182. | Cdr | Elijah Biar Kuol | 1/7/1997 | |
| 183. | Cdr | Mabior Kuir Maketh | 1/7/1997 | |
| 184. | Cdr | Samuel Ojuku Kur | 1/7/1997 | |
| 185. | Cdr | Deng Rokdit Mayar | 1/7/1997 | |
| 186. | Cdr | Majier Deng Kur | 1/7/1997 | |
| 187. | Cdr | Ajak Yen Alier | 1/7/1997 | |
| 188. | Cdr | Chol Biar Ngang | 1/7/1997 | |
| 189. | Cdr | Ajak Arok Mabior | 1/7/1997 | |
| 190. | Cdr | Michael Nyang Jok | 1/7/1997 | |
| 191. | Cdr | Dr Sebur John Mansuk | 1/7/1997 | |
| 192. | Cdr | Deng Arop Kuol | 1/7/1997 | |
| 193. | Cdr | Beda Machar Deng | 1/7/1997 | |
| 194. | Cdr | Kasiano Lopir Lodea | 1/7/1997 | |
| 195. | Cdr | Mathew Mathou Deng | 1/7/1997 | |
| 196. | Cdr | Kuong Danhier Gatluak | 1/7/1997 | |
| 197. | Cdr | Thomas Duoth Guet | 1/7/1997 | |
| 198. | Cdr | Maguek Gai Majak | 1/7/1997 | |
| 199. | Cdr | David Reath Malual | 1/1/1998 | |
| 200. | Cdr | James Gatiek Diar | 1/1/1998 | |
| 201. | Cdr | Faustino Atem Koc | 29/1/1998 | |
| 202. | Cdr | Simon Madit Ngor | 29/1/1998 | |
| 203. | Cdr | Geatano Nyuol Atem | 29/1/1998 | |
| 204. | Cdr | Philip Bipean Machar | 1/5/1998 | |
| 205. | Cdr | William Manyang Mayak | 1/5/1998 | |
| 206. | Cdr | Stephen Buoy Rolnyang | 1/5/1998 | |
| 207. | Cdr | Deng Solomon Leek | 1/7/1998 | |
| 208. | Cdr | Joh Akuany Mayen | 1/7/1998 | |

| | | | | |
|---|---|---|---|---|
| 209. | Cdr | Juma Baba Kaka | 1/7/1998 | |
| 210. | Cdr | Ramadan Mathiang Akucjai | 1/7/1998 | |
| 211. | Cdr | Mamer Makuac Kuol | 1/7/1998 | |
| 212. | Cdr | Malual Aguer Diing | 1/7/1998 | |
| 213. | Cdr | Moses Dhieu Kur | 1/7/1998 | |
| 214. | Cdr | Rabbi Majunng Emannuel | 1/7/1998 | |
| 215. | Cdr | Deng Leek Deng Majook | 1/7/1998 | |
| 216. | Cdr | Zakaria Hakim Deng | 1/7/1998 | |
| 217. | Cdr | Deng Manyang Leek | 1/7/1998 | |
| 218. | Cdr | Aboi Arok Deng | 1/7/1998 | |
| 219. | Cdr | Garang' Mading Agok | 1/7/1998 | |
| 220. | Cdr | Orbano Oyet Jobojobo | 1/7/1998 | |
| 221. | Cdr | Paul Macuei Malot | 1/7/1998 | |
| 222. | Cdr | Paul Mayom Akec | 1/7/1998 | |
| 223. | Cdr | John Lat Zakaria | 1/7/1998 | |
| 224. | Cdr | Johnson Juma Okot | 1/7/1998 | |
| 225. | Cdr | Dhol Mathiang Dhol | 1/7/1998 | |
| 226. | Cdr | Atem Aguang Atem | 1/7/1998 | |
| 227. | Cdr | Malok Ring Kiir | 1/7/1998 | |
| 228. | Cdr | Malok Atem Aguer | 1/7/1998 | |
| 229. | Cdr | Ruben Thiong Atat | 1/7/1998 | |
| 230. | Cdr | Isaiah Alier Deng | 1/7/1998 | |
| 231. | Cdr | Edward Gai Garang' | 1/7/1998 | |
| 232. | Cdr | Moses Ngoth Jok | 1/7/1998 | |
| 233. | Cdr | Lino Lukuac Pac | 1/7/1998 | |
| 234. | Cdr | Kon Atem Biar | 1/7/1998 | |
| 235. | Cdr | Andrew Kuei Mabil | 1/7/1998 | |
| 236. | Cdr | Lueth Keer Ajak | 1/7/1998 | |
| 237. | Cdr | Garang' Ngang Abuoi | 1/7/1998 | |
| 238. | Cdr | Abendigo Majak Barkuei | 1/7/1998 | |
| 239. | Cdr | Natale Majak Lual | 1/7/1998 | |
| 240. | Cdr | Louis Agany Deng | 1/7/1998 | |

| | | | | |
|---|---|---|---|---|
| 241. | Cdr | Achol Mading Mayen | 1/7/1998 | |
| 242. | Cdr | Solomon Maker Deng | 1/7/1998 | |
| 243. | Cdr | Peter Manyang Cikom | 1/7/1998 | |
| 244. | Cdr | Lazarus Deutong Agot | 1/7/1998 | |
| 245. | Cdr | Abraham Malok Kot | 1/7/1998 | |
| 246. | Cdr | Bona Baak Bol | 1/7/1998 | |
| 247. | Cdr | John Riak Alier | 1/7/1998 | |
| 248. | Cdr | Garang' Dut Ngor | 1/7/1998 | |
| 249. | Cdr | Dut Yai Dut | 1/7/1998 | |
| 250. | Cdr | Samuel Deng Deng | 1/7/1998 | |
| 251. | Cdr | Albino Bol Akol | 1/7/1998 | |
| 252. | Cdr | Michael Ngor Mabior | 1/7/1998 | |
| 253. | Cdr | Aguer Kuac Dut | 1/7/1998 | |
| 254. | Cdr | Mathiang Garem Deng | 1/7/1998 | |
| 255. | Cdr | Emilio Aleu Wol | 1/7/1998 | |
| 256. | Cdr | Garang' Malong Koor | 1/7/1998 | |
| 257. | Cdr | Angelo Chan Angara | 1/7/1998 | |
| 258. | Cdr | Daniel Deng Akuot | 1/7/1998 | |
| 259. | Cdr | Autiak Kuac Kuac | 1/7/1998 | |
| 260. | Cdr | Joseph Akol Giir | 1/7/1998 | |
| 261. | Cdr | Albino Ater Reec | 1/7/1998 | |
| 262. | Cdr | Arkanjelo Athian Teng | 1/7/1998 | |
| 263. | Cdr | Aquilino Atak Akech | 1/7/1998 | |
| 264. | Cdr | Dok Machar Chol | 1/7/1998 | |
| 265. | Cdr | John Lorech Lele | 1/7/1998 | |
| 266. | Cdr | Morris Agany Wek | 1/7/1998 | |
| 267. | Cdr | Maker Thiong Mal | 1/7/1998 | |
| 268. | Cdr | Alpayo Dau Dut | 1/7/1998 | |
| 269. | Cdr | Ateny Mayen Jok | 1/7/1998 | |
| 270. | Cdr | Mayen Manyang Jok | 1/7/1998 | |
| 271. | Cdr | Manyok Chan Madol | 1/7/1998 | |
| 272. | Cdr | Gar Yuang Ajak | 1/7/1998 | |

| | | | | |
|---|---|---|---|---|
| 273. | Cdr | William Manyang Roor | 1/7/1998 | |
| 274. | Cdr | Victor Majok Amecrot | 1/7/1998 | |
| 275. | Cdr | Mario Mou Abiem | 1/7/1998 | |
| 276. | Cdr | Kernyang Cier Dut | 1/7/1998 | |
| 277. | Cdr | Luka Nyikero Majuc | 1/7/1998 | |
| 278. | Cdr | Malual Kuir Ajak | 1/7/1998 | |
| 279. | Cdr | Ateny Nyuon Yac | 1/7/1998 | |
| 280. | Cdr | Akuei Lual Ajok | 1/7/1998 | |
| 281. | Cdr | Kur Chol Bul | 1/7/1998 | |
| 282. | Cdr | Gabriel Gai Riak | 1/7/1998 | |
| 283. | Cdr | Philip Kot Wut | 1/7/1998 | |
| 284. | Cdr | Daniel Deng Lual | 1/7/1998 | |
| 285. | Cdr | Anei Angok Anei | 1/7/1998 | |
| 286. | Cdr | Thiep Agot Deng | 1/7/1998 | |
| 287. | Cdr | Morris Rehan Deng | 1/7/1998 | |
| 288. | Cdr | Gabriel Elijah Agau | 1/7/1998 | |
| 289. | Cdr | Isaiah Alier Machankok | 1/7/1998 | |
| 290. | Cdr | Daniel Makur Dol | 1/7/1998 | |
| 291. | Cdr | Bullen Panchol Awal | 1/7/1998 | |
| 292. | Cdr | Ajith Akuei Awan | 1/7/1998 | |
| 293. | Cdr | Thongjang Awak Thongjang | 1/7/1998 | |
| 294. | Cdr | Majak Nhial Nyuon | 1/7/1998 | |
| 295. | Cdr | John Along Ayur | 1/7/1998 | |
| 296. | Cdr | Thon Abraham Luk | 1/7/1998 | |
| 297. | Cdr | Mathew Mathiang Akucwel | 1/7/1998 | |
| 298. | Cdr | Simon Mawien Agoth | 1/7/1998 | |
| 299. | Cdr | Akuei Akuei Ajou | 1/7/1998 | |
| 300. | Cdr | Michael Majur Aleer Deng | 1/7/1998 | |
| 301. | Cdr | John Malith Monykuc | 1/7/1998 | |
| 302. | Cdr | Chol Abraham Kuckon | 1/7/1998 | |
| 303. | Cdr | Chol Lual Mac | 1/7/1998 | |
| 304. | Cdr | Deng Awuou Ader | 1/7/1998 | |

| | | | | |
|---|---|---|---|---|
| 305. | Cdr | Deng Atem Apet | 1/7/1998 | |
| 306. | Cdr | Joseph Mayen Akoon | 1/7/1998 | |
| 307. | Cdr | Abraham Panchol Mac | 1/7/1998 | |
| 308. | Cdr | Moses Majok Anyieth | 1/7/1998 | |
| 309. | Cdr | Peter Dau Kuany | 1/7/1998 | |
| 310. | Cdr | Joseph Gatluak Maluac | 1/7/1998 | |
| 311. | Cdr | Peter Garang' Angong | 1/7/1998 | |
| 312. | Cdr | Monykuer Mayen Anei | 1/7/1998 | |
| 313. | Cdr | Angon Ungom Chut | 1/7/1998 | |
| 314. | Cdr | Mathew Aluong Gai | 1/7/1998 | |
| 315. | Cdr | Malual Akol Ayiei | 1/7/1998 | |
| 316. | Cdr | Kongor Reec Gak | 1/7/1998 | |
| 317. | Cdr | Machar Geu Deng | 1/7/1998 | |
| 318. | Cdr | Makuei Matheyo Ruei | 1/7/1998 | |
| 319. | Cdr | Atem Duot Atem | 1/7/1998 | |
| 320. | Cdr | Chol Alaak Ajak | 1/7/1998 | |
| 321. | Cdr | Ajak Deng Reng | 1/7/1998 | |
| 322. | Cdr | Nathaniel Mayen Chol | 1/7/1998 | |
| 323. | Cdr | James Bol Nyok | 1/7/1998 | |
| 324. | Cdr | Samuel Nhial Akot | 1/7/1998 | |
| 325. | Cdr | James Thuc Akot | 1/7/1998 | |
| 326. | Cdr | Bol Ador Ader | 1/7/1998 | |
| 327. | Cdr | William Alier Kuer | 1/7/1998 | |
| 328. | Cdr | Ajok Awuor Ajok | 1/7/1998 | |
| 329. | Cdr | Alfred Nyal Chan | 1/7/1998 | |
| 330. | Cdr | Simon Jok Dau | 1/7/1998 | |
| 331. | Cdr | Mabil Chol Thiong | 1/7/1998 | |
| 332. | Cdr | Ayuel Garang' Deng | 1/7/1998 | |
| 333. | Cdr | James Anyop Kuer | 1/7/1998 | |
| 334. | Cdr | Joseph Duop Deng | 1/7/1998 | |
| 335. | Cdr | Awer Garang' Awer | 1/7/1998 | |
| 336. | Cdr | John Garang' Akoon | 1/7/1998 | |

| | | | | |
|---|---|---|---|---|
| 337. | Cdr | Dhieu Luac Akok | 1/7/1998 | |
| 338. | Cdr | Abraham Machar Thiong | 1/7/1998 | |
| 339. | Cdr | James Biel Ruot | 1/7/1998 | |
| 340. | Cdr | Isaac Marol Mangok | 1/7/1998 | |
| 341. | Cdr | John Garang' Mayen | 1/7/1998 | |
| 342. | Cdr | Kennedy Kot Thuc | 1/7/1998 | |
| 343. | Cdr | Chuti Deng Thoot | 1/7/1998 | |
| 344. | Cdr | John Mabut Arou | 1/7/1998 | |
| 345. | Cdr | Garang' Ngor Agany | 1/7/1998 | |
| 346. | Cdr | Longocho Amaci Logodor | 1/7/1998 | |
| 347. | Cdr | Mawut Wuoi Yuol | 1/7/1998 | |
| 348. | Cdr | Lino Garang' Malith | 1/7/1998 | |
| 349. | Cdr | Samuel Deng Agok | 1/7/1998 | |
| 350. | Cdr | Paulino Kon Dhieu | 1/7/1998 | |
| 351. | Cdr | Victor Akok Anei | 1/7/1998 | |
| 352. | Cdr | Daniel Deng Dau | 1/7/1998 | |
| 353. | Cdr | Akol Alith Akuei | 1/7/1998 | |
| 354. | Cdr | Machar Nhial Magok | 1/7/1998 | |
| 355. | Cdr | Deng Akuei Kur | 1/7/1998 | |
| 356. | Cdr | Maker Deng Mac | 1/7/1998 | |
| 357. | Cdr | Ajak Gureec Anyang | 1/7/1998 | |
| 358. | Cdr | Dhiak Chol Dhiak | 1/7/1998 | |
| 359. | Cdr | James Aguer Arok | 1/7/1998 | |
| 360. | Cdr | Louis Gatluak Luak | 1/7/1998 | |
| 361. | Cdr | Abendigo Ajak Anyieth | 1/7/1998 | |
| 362. | Cdr | Achol Deng Achol | 1/7/1998 | |
| 363. | Cdr | Deng Kuot Guut | 1/7/1998 | |
| 364. | Cdr | Kuol Ayuen Kuot | 1/7/1998 | |
| 365. | Cdr | Manaseh Mac Anyieth | 1/7/1998 | |
| 366. | Cdr | Dut Achuek Lual | 1/7/1998 | |
| 367. | Cdr | Sebit William Garang' | 1/7/1998 | |
| 368. | Cdr | Deng Til Ayuen Kur | 1/7/1998 | |

| | | | | |
|---|---|---|---|---|
| 369. | Cdr | Luka Dut Yel | 1/7/1998 | |
| 370. | Cdr | William Madut Deng | 1/7/1998 | |
| 371. | Cdr | James Gatjiath Thoat | 1/7/1998 | |
| 372. | Cdr | Garang' Mayol Deng | 1/7/1998 | |
| 373. | Cdr | Mam Chicko Loitko | 1/7/1998 | |
| 374. | Cdr | Chokrac Alith Kudum | 1/7/1998 | |
| 375. | Cdr | Abraham Jongroor Deng | 1/7/1998 | |
| 376. | Cdr | Ayuen Garang' Jok | 1/7/1998 | |
| 377. | Cdr | Zakaria Atem Manyok | 1/7/1998 | |
| 378. | Cdr | Abuoi Bul Dut | 1/7/1998 | |
| 379. | Cdr | Zakaria Kuol Yak | 1/7/1998 | |
| 380. | Cdr | Nyok Deng Tol | 1/7/1998 | |
| 381. | Cdr | Deng Aleer Chol | 1/7/1998 | |
| 382. | Cdr | Aciek Garang' Mac | 1/7/1998 | |
| 383. | Cdr | Mac Gai Kok | 1/7/1998 | |
| 384. | Cdr | Jok Aleer Deng | 1/7/1998 | |
| 385. | Cdr | Simon Manyuon Akol | 1/7/1998 | |
| 386. | Cdr | Maggot Piok Keer | 1/7/1998 | |
| 387. | Cdr | Michael Mabior Makuei | 1/7/1998 | |
| 388. | Cdr | Simon Idingo Alani | 1/7/1998 | |
| 389. | Cdr | Alier Mayak Kom | 1/7/1998 | |
| 390. | Cdr | Manaseh Monyluak Ajuot | 1/7/1998 | |
| 391. | Cdr | Khot Gak Atem | 1/7/1998 | |
| 392. | Cdr | Lul Chol Wictuor | 1/7/1998 | |
| 393. | Cdr | Morris Lokule Yoane | 1/7/1998 | |
| 394. | Cdr | Francis Lotio Michael | 1/7/1998 | |
| 395. | Cdr | Ayuen Alith Akuei | 1/7/1998 | |
| 396. | Cdr | Robert Ewat Okimo | 1/7/1998 | |
| 397. | Cdr | Pasqualle DImo Keer | 1/7/1998 | |
| 398. | Cdr | West Yugulu Kayuku | 1/7/1998 | |
| 399. | Cdr | Fancrasio Kueth Achuil | 1/7/1998 | |
| 400. | Cdr | William Deng Gai | 1/7/1998 | |

| | | | | |
|---|---|---|---|---|
| 401. | Cdr | Daniel Koang Chol | 1/7/1998 | |
| 402. | Cdr | Mohammed Siyeed Bazara | 1/7/1998 | |
| 403. | Cdr | Marial Anhiem Marial | 1/7/1998 | |
| 404. | Cdr | Jackson Tilian Garang' | 1/7/1998 | |
| 405. | Cdr | Isaiah chol Aruai | 1/7/1998 | |
| 406. | Cdr | Atem Garang' Deng | 1/7/1998 | |
| 407. | Cdr | James Acuil Malith | 1/7/1998 | |
| 408. | Cdr | Aleu Akecak Jok | 1/7/1998 | |
| 409. | Cdr | Thiep Deng Thiep | 1/7/1998 | |
| 410. | Cdr | Ayom Mac Jok | 1/7/1998 | |
| 411. | Cdr | Madhor kuot Guut | 1/7/1998 | |
| 412. | Cdr | Dr Manyang Agoth Thon | 1/7/1998 | |
| 413. | Cdr | Monyluak Alor Kuol | 1/7/1998 | |
| 414. | Cdr | Francis Bol Ayom | 1/7/1998 | |
| 415. | Cdr | Michael Makuei Lueth | 1/7/1998 | |
| 416. | Cdr | Benjamin Bulek Agakic | 1/7/1998 | |
| 417. | Cdr | Dr Monywiir Arop Kuol | 1/7/1998 | |
| 418. | Cdr | Kulang Mayen Kulang | 1/7/1998 | |
| 419. | Cdr | Eli Achol Deng Hot | 1/7/1998 | |
| 420. | Cdr | Dr Valario Ahoy Ngong | 1/7/1998 | |
| 421. | Cdr | Gabriel Malual Ayak | 1/7/1998 | |
| 422. | Cdr | Gerigory Deng Kuac | 1/7/1998 | |
| 423. | Cdr | Enok Majok Machar | 1/7/1998 | |
| 424. | Cdr | Peter Chol Marcelino | 1/7/1998 | |
| 425. | Cdr | Gabriel Alaak Garang' | 1/7/1998 | |
| 426. | Cdr | Mayen Ngor Atem | 1/7/1998 | |
| 427. | Cdr | Luka Yombe Duad | 1/7/1998 | |
| 428. | Cdr | Chat Paul Nul | 1/7/1998 | |
| 429. | Cdr | Riak Jereboam Machuor | 1/7/1998 | |
| 430. | Cdr | Makuei Philemon Majok | 1/7/1998 | |
| 431. | Cdr | Chol Atem Diing | 1/7/1998 | |
| 432. | Cdr | Peter Dut Kezikia | 1/7/1998 | |

| | | | | |
|---|---|---|---|---|
| 433. | Cdr | Awok Lam Ajak | 1/7/1998 | |
| 434. | Cdr | Dr Makuei Malual Kang | 1/7/1998 | |
| 435. | Cdr | Moses Mabior Deu | 1/7/1998 | |
| 436. | Cdr | Atem Kuir Jok | 1/7/1998 | |
| 437. | Cdr | Yol Akau Yol | 1/7/1998 | |
| 438. | Cdr | Ajang Majok Aguer | 1/7/1998 | |
| 439. | Cdr | Deng Bol Deng | 1/7/1998 | |
| 440. | Cdr | Scopas Juma Amba | 1/7/1998 | |
| 441. | Cdr | Deng Chuol Maleng | 1/7/1998 | |
| 442. | Cdr | Isaiah Alier Diing | 1/7/1998 | |
| 443. | Cdr | Bior Ajok Bior | 1/7/1998 | |
| 444. | Cdr | Juac Nathan Garang' | 1/7/1998 | |
| 445. | Cdr | Diing Adim Adim | 1/7/1998 | |
| 446. | Cdr | Mabior Runrac Lepiny | 1/7/1998 | |
| 447. | Cdr | Rebecca Nyandeng Chol | 1/7/1998 | |
| 448. | Cdr | Aluel Ayiei Chath | 1/7/1998 | |
| 449. | Cdr | Thon Agok Deng | 1/7/1998 | |
| 450. | Cdr | Alfred Manyang Agok | 1/7/1998 | |
| 451. | Cdr | Elijah Alier Ayom | 1/7/1998 | |
| 452. | Cdr | Deng Dau Deng Malek | 1/7/1998 | |
| 453. | Cdr | Deng Yiey Thanypiny | 1/7/1998 | |
| 454. | Cdr | Luka Achaya Barnaba | 1/7/1998 | |
| 455. | Cdr | Augustino Ali Lowaya Balaka | 1/7/1998 | |
| 456. | Cdr | Konyi Didi Kaka | 1/7/1998 | |
| 457. | Cdr | Simon Yien Makuac | 1/7/1998 | |
| 458. | Cdr | William Chol Piok | 1/7/1998 | |
| 459. | Cdr | James Guek Nyoac | 1/7/1998 | |
| 460. | Cdr | John Lam Dhioyier | 1/7/1998 | |
| 461. | Cdr | Peter Jany Ruot | 1/7/1998 | |
| 462. | Cdr | Samuel Hoth Dak | 1/7/1998 | |
| 463. | Cdr | Paul Aciek kon | 1/7/1998 | |
| 464. | Cdr | Mohammed Sadiq Leek | 1/7/1998 | |

| | | | | |
|---|---|---|---|---|
| 465. | Cdr | Lual Tut Lual | 1/7/1998 | |
| 466. | Cdr | Chuor Deng Mareng | 1/7/1998 | |
| 467. | Cdr | James Kok Ruea | 1/7/1998 | |
| 468. | Cdr | Michael Top Yai | 1/7/1998 | |
| 469. | Cdr | Peter Ruot Chuol | 1/7/1998 | |
| 470. | Cdr | Peter Par Jiekuic | 1/7/1998 | |
| 471. | Cdr | John Chuol Dhol | 1/7/1998 | |
| 472. | Cdr | James Tut Thuoc | 1/7/1998 | |
| 473. | Cdr | Peter Thok Chuol | 1/7/1998 | |
| 474. | Cdr | Yasir Siyeed Arman | 1/7/1998 | |
| 475. | Cdr | Daniel Deng Alony | 1/8/1998 | |
| 476. | Cdr | Dok Jok Dok | 1/8/1998 | |
| 477. | Cdr | Anyang Akol Akuei | 1/8/1998 | |
| 478. | Cdr | Abdelgadir Hamid Mahid | 1/7/1999 | |
| 479. | Cdr | John Jok Nhial | 1/9/1999 | |
| 480. | Cdr | James Gatluak Gai | 1/9/1999 | |
| 481. | Cdr | Samuel Gai Yirchak | 1/9/1999 | |
| 482. | Cdr | Karlo Kuol Ruac | 1/9/1999 | |
| 483. | Cdr | George Gathuoy Thaak | 1/9/1999 | |
| 484. | Cdr | Michael Chiangjiek Geay | 1/9/1999 | |
| 485. | Cdr | James Nhial Wathkak | 1/9/1999 | |
| 486. | Cdr | Stephen Chap Majuan | 1/9/1999 | |
| 487. | Cdr | Joseph Mathok Thiep | 1/9/1999 | |
| 488. | Cdr | Paul Dor Lampur | 1/9/1999 | |
| 489. | Cdr | James Yak Dayiem | 1/9/1999 | |
| 490. | Cdr | Stephen Gatgok Khor | 1/9/1999 | |
| 491. | Cdr | Monyjok Mabil Deng | 1/11/1999 | |
| 492. | Cdr | Alfred Deng Aluk | 1/1/2000 | |
| 493. | Cdr | John Jok Gai | 1/1/2000 | |
| 494. | Cdr | Jagood Mukwar Marada | 1/1/2000 | |
| 495. | Cdr | Izzat Kuku Angelo | 1/1/2000 | |
| 496. | Cdr | Adam Kodi | 1/1/2000 | |

| | | | | |
|---|---|---|---|---|
| 497. | Cdr | Simon Kallo Komi | 1/1/2000 | |
| 498. | Cdr | Yaguob Osman Kaklika | 1/1/2000 | |
| 499. | Cdr | Ibrahim Almulfa Miri | 1/1/2000 | |
| 500. | Cdr | Saed Kacho Komi | 1/1/2000 | |
| 501. | Cdr | Awad Jarballa Kuwa | 1/1/2000 | |
| 502. | Cdr | Neroun Philip Ajo | 1/1/2000 | |
| 503. | Cdr | Suliman Jabona Mohammed | 1/1/2000 | |
| 504. | Cdr | Malid Hamood Angelo | 1/1/2000 | |
| 505. | Cdr | Ezikiel Kuku Talodi | 1/1/2000 | |
| 506. | Cdr | Musa Abdelbagi Fadul | 1/1/2000 | |
| 507. | Cdr | Walid Hamid Mohammed | 1/1/2000 | |
| 508. | Cdr | Lomle Kuwa El Nawai | 1/1/2000 | |
| 509. | Cdr | Habil Katan Ariya | 1/1/2000 | |
| 510. | Cdr | Bolish Sharir Jori | 1/1/2000 | |
| 511. | Cdr | Philip Mundari Tutu | 1/1/2000 | |
| 512. | Cdr | Ramadan Hassan Nimir | 1/1/2000 | |
| 513. | Cdr | Abbas Haj- Hamed El Bardy | 1/1/2000 | |
| 514. | Cdr | Peter Luin Koma | 1/1/2000 | |
| 515. | Cdr | Joseph Tuka Ali | 1/1/2000 | |
| 516. | Cdr | Abdala Ali Fadul | 1/1/2000 | |
| 517. | Cdr | Sadiq Afendi Hamed | 1/1/2000 | |
| 518. | Cdr | Tenya Nyetho Nyalo | 1/1/2000 | |
| 519. | Cdr | Daniel Marzuk Hamed | 1/1/2000 | |
| 520. | Cdr | Dakin Juma El Faisal | 1/1/2000 | |
| 521. | Cdr | Fatima Abdelgadir Marjan | 1/1/2000 | |
| 522. | Cdr | El Thir Mohammed Idris | 1/1/2000 | |
| 523. | Cdr | Mohammed Yunis Babiker | 1/1/2000 | |
| 524. | Cdr | Dafalla Adam El Mardhi | 1/1/2000 | |
| 525. | Cdr | El Jundi Abdaraman | 1/1/2000 | |
| 526. | Cdr | Seif El Dowla Abdaraman Balu | 1/1/2000 | |
| 527. | Cdr | Jafer Juma Mohammed | 1/1/2000 | |
| 528. | Cdr | Ahmed Alomda Baada | 1/1/2000 | |

| | | | | |
|---|---|---|---|---|
| 529. | Cdr | Efisio Kon Uguak | 1/1/2000 | |
| 530. | Cdr | Alfred Majok Madut | 1/1/2000 | |
| 531. | Cdr | Gabriel Ayok AJeber | 1/1/2000 | |
| 532. | Cdr | Valentine Yak Kon | 1/1/2000 | |
| 533. | Cdr | Andrea Mayar Achor | 1/1/2000 | |
| 534. | Cdr | Santo Majok Urukel | 1/1/2000 | |
| 535. | Cdr | Akol Majok Nyigan | 1/1/2000 | |
| 536. | Cdr | Charles Kon Akot | 1/1/2000 | |
| 537. | Cdr | Dor Deng Dor | 1/1/2000 | |
| 538. | Cdr | Peter Law Madhieu | 1/1/2000 | |
| 539. | Cdr | Lousi Natale | 1/1/2000 | |
| 540. | Cdr | Dominic Manago Dabi | 16/5/2000 | |
| 541. | Cdr | Lanya Ulka Mei | 1/4/2001 | |
| 542. | Cdr | Butrus Batha Enno | 1/4/2001 | |
| 543. | Cdr | John Duoth Nhial | 28/5/2001 | |
| 544. | Cdr | Timothy Kueth Luak | 28/5/2001 | |
| 545. | Cdr | Isaiah Tut Gatpan | 28/5/2001 | |
| 546. | Cdr | Jacob Gatwec Chuol | 28/5/2001 | |
| 547. | Cdr | Peter Gatluak Mutdol | 28/5/2001 | |
| 548. | Cdr | Stephen Lony Deng | 28/5/2001 | |
| 549. | Cdr | Andrew Geany Gai | 28/5/2001 | |
| 550. | Cdr | Michael Wicyic Wang | 28/5/2001 | |
| 551. | Cdr | Jeremiah Kuol Chan | 28/5/2001 | |
| 552. | Cdr | Mary Stephen Reat | 28/5/2001 | |
| 553. | Cdr | John Puoljor Wicyoak | 28/5/2001 | |
| 554. | Cdr | James Nguen Tuong | 28/5/2001 | |
| 555. | Cdr | Michael Machar Nguen | 28/5/2001 | |
| 556. | Cdr | Peter Gatkuoth Wan | 28/5/2001 | |
| 557. | Cdr | John Koang Nyuon | 28/5/2001 | |
| 558. | Cdr | Chan Babuoth Jobar | 28/5/2001 | |
| 559. | Cdr | James Gatjok Wang | 28/5/2001 | |
| 560. | Cdr | John Buom Koryom | 28/5/2001 | |

| | | | | |
|---|---|---|---|---|
| 561. | Cdr | Peter Marpiny Guet | 28/5/2001 | |
| 562. | Cdr | Abraham Wal Nhial | 28/5/2001 | |
| 563. | Cdr | Tuong Majok Deng | 28/5/2001 | |
| 564. | Cdr | William Deng Monga | 28/5/2001 | |
| 565. | Cdr | Stephen Kueth Pathot | 28/5/2001 | |
| 566. | Cdr | James Liyliy Kuol | 28/5/2001 | |
| 567. | Cdr | Lawrence Lony Lueng | 28/5/2001 | |
| 568. | Cdr | John Turuk Khor | 28/5/2001 | |
| 569. | Cdr | Thomas Kerdol Thong | 28/5/2001 | |
| 570. | Cdr | Cypriano Idiongo Tisiano | 1/7/2001 | |
| 571. | Cdr | Victor Gira Silvator | 1/7/2001 | |
| 572. | Cdr | Jacob Laweko Angasi | 1/7/2001 | |
| 573. | Cdr | Elias Lino Jada | 1/7/2001 | |
| 574. | Cdr | Faustino Ochan Lawrence | 1/7/2001 | |
| 575. | Cdr | Mohammed Ahamed Omar | 1/7/2001 | |
| 576. | Cdr | Dr Ajak Bulen Alier | 1/7/2001 | |
| 577. | Cdr | Robert Deng Garang' | 1/7/2001 | |
| 578. | Cdr | John Deng Reng | 1/7/2001 | |
| 579. | Cdr | El Kana Gumlel Tiger | 1/7/2001 | |
| 580. | Cdr | Joseph Kon Akot | 1/7/2001 | |
| 581. | Cdr | Isaac Makur Buoc | 1/7/2001 | |
| 582. | Cdr | Peter Gatwech Lual | 1/7/2001 | |
| 583. | Cdr | Lual Tut Bol | 1/7/2001 | |
| 584. | Cdr | Tang Wal Lual | 1/7/2001 | |
| 585. | Cdr | Peter Pal Teny | 1/1/2002 | |
| 586. | Cdr | James Yiec Biet | 1/1/2002 | |
| 587. | Cdr | Daniel Biel Bol | 1/1/2002 | |
| 588. | Cdr | James Deng Chol | 1/1/2002 | |
| 589. | Cdr | Peter Keak Jal | 1/1/2002 | |
| 590. | Cdr | Samuel Lony Geng | 1/1/2002 | |
| 591. | Cdr | David Gatluak Domai | 1/1/2002 | |
| 592. | Cdr | Hoth Guor Luak | 1/1/2002 | |

| | | | | |
|---|---|---|---|---|
| 593. | Cdr | David Duoth Kon | 1/1/2002 | |
| 594. | Cdr | John Kutei Bayak | 1/1/2002 | |
| 595. | Cdr | Gabriel Puoc Chatiem | 1/1/2002 | |
| 596. | Cdr | Daniel Biel Jakook | 1/1/2002 | |
| 597. | Cdr | Simon Gatwech Majok | 1/1/2002 | |
| 598. | Cdr | Peter Gatbel Wei | 1/1/2002 | |
| 599. | Cdr | Simon Luk Tem | 1/1/2002 | |
| 600. | Cdr | Tut Pal Luak | 1/1/2002 | |
| 601. | Cdr | David Yien Bilieth | 1/1/2002 | |
| 602. | Cdr | Paul Ruot Yuol | 1/1/2002 | |
| 603. | Cdr | Top Riek Pany | 1/1/2002 | |
| 604. | Cdr | John Deng Jok | 1/1/2002 | |
| 605. | Cdr | David Rial Mut | 1/1/2002 | |
| 606. | Cdr | David Nyang Kuok | 1/1/2002 | |
| 607. | Cdr | Deng Deng Akoon | 6/1/2002 | |
| 608. | Cdr | Aziz Atari Aziz | 6/1/2002 | |
| 609. | Cdr | Sieko Ochan Riang | 6/1/2002 | |
| 610. | Cdr | James Koat Kuony Tut | 6/1/2002 | |
| 611. | Cdr | John Bol Wakoah | 6/1/2002 | |
| 612. | Cdr | Albino Gatluak Tai | 6/1/2002 | |
| 613. | Cdr | James Gai Gatluak | 6/1/2002 | |
| 614. | Cdr | George Kel Gatwec | 6/1/2002 | |
| 615. | Cdr | James Lieb Liah | 6/1/2002 | |
| 616. | Cdr | Peter Gatkuoth Chuol | 6/1/2002 | |
| 617. | Cdr | Doyak Chuol Dol | 6/1/2002 | |
| 618. | Cdr | Gideon Gatdor Manguet | 6/1/2002 | |
| 619. | Cdr | Simon Kun Puoc | 6/1/2002 | |
| 620. | Cdr | James Lul Tiem | 6/1/2002 | |
| 621. | Cdr | Exodus Mathiang Gok | 6/1/2002 | |
| 622. | Cdr | David Gai Chan | 6/1/2002 | |
| 623. | Cdr | John Luk Bayak | 6/1/2002 | |
| 624. | Cdr | Thomas Dut Gatkek | 6/1/2002 | |

| | | | | |
|---|---|---|---|---|
| 625. | Cdr | Peter Lim Bol | 6/1/2002 | |
| 626. | Cdr | John Madol Bitiem | 6/1/2002 | |
| 627. | Cdr | John Wicjial Banyuel | 6/1/2002 | |
| 628. | Cdr | Elijah Gatkuoth Ruea | 6/1/2002 | |
| 629. | Cdr | James Chuol Gatbuok | 6/1/2002 | |
| 630. | Cdr | James Gatluak Puoc | 6/1/2002 | |
| 631. | Cdr | John Wicyual Chuol | 6/1/2002 | |
| 632. | Cdr | Peter Gatwec Thor | 6/1/2002 | |
| 633. | Cdr | Gordon Banak Thon | 6/1/2002 | |
| 634. | Cdr | Peter Tap Gadet | 6/1/2002 | |
| 635. | Cdr | James Gatluak Chuol | 6/1/2002 | |
| 636. | Cdr | James Kuac Gaak | 6/1/2002 | |
| 637. | Cdr | Samuel Dok Wanjang | 6/1/2002 | |
| 638. | Cdr | Peter Lok Yol | 6/1/2002 | |
| 639. | Cdr | Tahir Bior Abdala Ajak | 14/1/2002 | |
| 640. | Cdr | Mathew Puljang Top | 16/1/2002 | |
| 641. | Cdr | Tito Biel Wic | 16/1/2002 | |
| 642. | Cdr | Michael Kolchara Nyang | 16/1/2002 | |
| 643. | Cdr | Garang' Mayar Ater | 16/1/2002 | |
| 644. | Cdr | Daniel Dut Mabeny | 16/1/2002 | |
| 645. | Cdr | Majok Deng Majok | 16/1/2002 | |
| 646. | Cdr | Daniel Marial Buot | 16/1/2002 | |
| 647. | Cdr | Mama Zeineb Mangok Mabok | 1/1/2003 | |
| 648. | Cdr | Kamilio Otwari Aliardo | 1/7/2003 | |
| 649. | Cdr | Joseph Victor Tambuwadi | 1/7/2003 | |
| 650. | Cdr | Edward Magot Zakayo | 1/7/2003 | |
| 651. | Cdr | Anthony Lemi Mambe | 1/7/2003 | |
| 652. | Cdr | Oliver Ali Diko | 1/7/2003 | |
| 653. | Cdr | David Ocheng Tokwaro | 1/7/2003 | |
| 654. | Cdr | Richard Muzari Marila | 1/7/2003 | |
| 655. | Cdr | Suzan Agum Abdon | 1/7/2003 | |

| | | | | |
|---|---|---|---|---|
| 656. | Cdr | Dr Ann Itto | 1/7/2003 | |
| 657. | Cdr | Tulio Odongi Ayahu | 1/7/2003 | |
| 658. | Cdr | Gabriel Mathiang Rok | 1/7/2003 | |
| 659. | Cdr | Abeny Nathaniel Anei | 1/7/2003 | |
| 660. | Cdr | Sarah Ayak Maketh | 1/7/2003 | |
| 661. | Cdr | Aker Deng Ayom | 1/7/2003 | |
| 662. | Cdr | Nyankiir Atem Manyang | 1/7/2003 | |
| 663. | Cdr | Ajith Chol Atem | 1/7/2003 | |
| 664. | Cdr | Victoria Adhardit Arop | 1/7/2003 | |
| 665. | Cdr | Bangot Amum Landit | 1/7/2003 | |
| 666. | Cdr | Martha Yom Jok | 1/7/2003 | |
| 667. | Cdr | Achol Garang' Adhuong | 1/7/2003 | |
| 668. | Cdr | Dr Alex Demitir | 1/7/2003 | |
| 669. | Cdr | Remy Oller Itorong | 1/7/2003 | |
| 670. | Cdr | Lazarus Lem Nicodimo | 1/7/2003 | |
| 671. | Cdr | Dr Margret Itto | 1/7/2003 | |
| 672. | Cdr | Ramadan Marko Jada | 1/7/2003 | |
| 673. | Cdr | Michael Okwaki Rogers | 1/7/2003 | |
| 674. | Cdr | Samuel Ohia Ademano | 1/7/2003 | |
| 675. | Cdr | Angelo Odong Longing | 1/7/2003 | |
| 676. | Cdr | Geatano Ofer Otawo | 1/7/2003 | |
| 677. | Cdr | Daniel Rodolfo Ngbabala | 1/7/2003 | |
| 678. | Cdr | John Taban Otino | 1/7/2003 | |
| 679. | Cdr | William Loki Lokirimoi | 1/7/2003 | |
| 680. | Cdr | Emilio Igga El mas | 1/7/2003 | |
| 681. | Cdr | Edward Zaremia Gongor | 1/7/2003 | |
| 682. | Cdr | Atansio Okeny Lado | 1/7/2003 | |
| 683. | Cdr | Michael Suro Yokwe | 1/7/2003 | |
| 684. | Cdr | Santo Lowonga | 1/7/2003 | |
| 685. | Cdr | Joseph Gaga Lolongo | 1/7/2003 | |
| 686. | Cdr | Wani Nyambur Bogota | 1/7/2003 | |
| 687. | Cdr | Jildo Oling Baranga | 1/7/2003 | |

| | | | | |
|---|---|---|---|---|
| 688. | Cdr | John Magga Ezikiel | 1/7/2003 | |
| 689. | Cdr | Michael Robert kenyi | 1/7/2003 | |
| 690. | Cdr | Peter Jirkis Jadan | 1/7/2003 | |
| 691. | Cdr | Ambros Ngbaringibe Mutan-wia | 1/7/2003 | |
| 692. | Cdr | Richard Remo Soro | 1/7/2003 | |
| 693. | Cdr | Gibson Rajab Benaya | 1/7/2003 | |
| 694. | Cdr | Repheal Geatiang | 1/7/2003 | |
| 695. | Cdr | Pasquale Joseph Ayan | 1/7/2003 | |
| 696. | Cdr | Anthony joseph Kpandu | 1/7/2003 | |
| 697. | Cdr | Morris Batist Peter | 1/7/2003 | |
| 698. | Cdr | Daniel Dut Mayan | 1/7/2003 | |
| 699. | Cdr | Lam Akol Ajawin | 31/10/2003 | |
| 700. | Cdr | Akuoc Mayong Jago | 31/10/2003 | |
| 701. | Cdr | Awec Akol Benyo | 31/10/2003 | |
| 702. | Cdr | Yorlong Kur Chol | 31/10/2003 | |
| 703. | Cdr | Majowuok Deng Aloker | 31/10/2003 | |
| 704. | Cdr | Chok Kuer Wai | 31/10/2003 | |
| 705. | Cdr | Johnson Otto Kuol | 31/10/2003 | |
| 706. | Cdr | Gabriel Chol Akol | 31/10/2003 | |
| 707. | Cdr | Mayo Nyikang Kur | 31/10/2003 | |
| 708. | Cdr | Akutien Yor Akol | 31/10/2003 | |
| 709. | Cdr | Nyakwan Padiet Along | 31/10/2003 | |
| 710. | Cdr | Kon Majok Kon | 31/10/2003 | |
| 711. | Cdr | William Ongu Otien | 31/10/2003 | |
| 712. | Cdr | Ajang Mudhir Aker | 31/10/2003 | |
| 713. | Cdr | Samuel Okoth Ajang | 31/10/2003 | |
| 714. | Cdr | Oyath Amum Ajang | 31/10/2003 | |
| 715. | Cdr | Gordon Oyai Diing | 31/10/2003 | |
| 716. | Cdr | Peter Dak Otong | 31/10/2003 | |
| 717. | Cdr | William Obul Othow | 31/10/2003 | |
| 718. | Cdr | Obwonyo Awin Nyikuac | 31/10/2003 | |

| | | | | |
|---|---|---|---|---|
| 719. | Cdr | Obac Kur Jago | 31/10/2003 | |
| 720. | Cdr | Gwang Robert Nyiker | 31/10/2003 | |
| 721. | Cdr | Ngor Wunthow Ayang | 31/10/2003 | |
| 722. | Cdr | Nyidhok Ochol Nyidhok | 31/10/2003 | |
| 723. | Cdr | Kuleiker Kur Kuleiker | 31/10/2003 | |
| 724. | Cdr | Tito John Awak | 31/10/2003 | |
| 725. | Cdr | Abraham Joseph Payiti | 31/10/2003 | |
| 726. | Cdr | Dut Malual Arop | 1/12/2003 | |
| 727. | Cdr | Nyal Chan Nyal | 1/12/2003 | |
| 728. | Cdr | Tito Biel Chuor | 7/12/2003 | |
| 729. | Cdr | James Liah Dieu Deng | 7/12/2003 | |
| 730. | Cdr | George Mut Nyang | 7/12/2003 | |
| 731. | Cdr | Simon Kot Thian | 7/12/2003 | |
| 732. | Cdr | James Puy Yak | 7/12/2003 | |
| 733. | Cdr | James Ruei Deng | 7/12/2003 | |
| 734. | Cdr | James Leek Machar | 7/12/2003 | |
| 735. | Cdr | Stephen Loar Gatluak | 7/12/2003 | |
| 736. | Cdr | Peter Hoth Chuol | 7/12/2003 | |
| 737. | Cdr | David Hoth Monyjoak | 7/12/2003 | |
| 738. | Cdr | James Ruathdheal Tut | 7/12/2003 | |
| 739. | Cdr | Peter Latjor Gai | 7/12/2003 | |
| 740. | Cdr | Simon Mani Kuol | 7/12/2003 | |
| 741. | Cdr | John Mabieh Gar | 7/12/2003 | |
| 742. | Cdr | James Tut Gatluak | 7/12/2003 | |
| 743. | Cdr | Daniel Deng Nuer | 7/12/2003 | |
| 744. | Cdr | John Majok Nhial | 7/12/2003 | |
| 745. | Cdr | Peter Kuol Gatbuok | 7/12/2003 | |
| 746. | Cdr | Kong Kong Yoacjobar | 7/12/2003 | |
| 747. | Cdr | Riek Moang Deng | 7/12/2003 | |
| 748. | Cdr | Simon Kuany Chatiem | 7/12/2003 | |
| 749. | Cdr | James Mut Riekah | 7/12/2003 | |

| | | | | |
|---|---|---|---|---|
| 750. | Cdr | David Makuol Ruot | 7/12/2003 | |
| 751. | Cdr | Martin Tereson Kenyi | 26/12/2003 | |
| 752. | Cdr | Emannuel Ambros Ocholimoi | 26/12/2003 | |
| 753. | Cdr | Mathew Arop Obuoya | 26/12/2003 | |
| 754. | Cdr | Ben Bilal Mamur | 26/12/2003 | |
| 755. | Cdr | Marko Gabriel Tiberious | 26/12/2003 | |
| 756. | Cdr | Elio Benson Otome | 26/12/2003 | |
| 757. | Cdr | Edward Bilo Levi | 26/12/2003 | |
| 758. | Cdr | Elia Paulino Isara | 26/12/2003 | |
| 759. | Cdr | Jacob Orisa Bosco | 26/12/2003 | |
| 760. | Cdr | Ben Taban Marcello | 26/12/2003 | |
| 761. | Cdr | Kasimiro Okomos Gaitano | 26/12/2003 | |
| 762. | Cdr | Kornelious Abel Ochara | 26/12/2003 | |
| 763. | Cdr | Ruai Kuol Jal Thor | 1/1/2004 | |
| 764. | Cdr | Riek Dogor Juer | 1/1/2004 | |
| 765. | Cdr | Peter Laat Manyuek | 1/1/2004 | |
| 766. | Cdr | Osman Mathoat Dhuong | 1/1/2004 | |
| 767. | Cdr | Kur Yai Nyop | 1/1/2004 | |
| 768. | Cdr | Simon Riek Kuol Jal | 1/1/2004 | |
| 769. | Cdr | Michael Pajok Nyok | 2/2/2004 | |
| 770. | Cdr | Ruben Dak Chaak | 2/2/2004 | |
| 771. | Cdr | Gai Both Gai | 2/2/2004 | |
| 772. | Cdr | Oboch Ngirro Korok | 24/2/2004 | |
| 773. | Cdr | Paul Ngari Murolo | 24/2/2004 | |
| 774. | Cdr | Korok Nyal Lokoriyo | 24/2/2004 | |
| 775. | Cdr | Batros Lomich Keng | 24/2/2004 | |
| 776. | Cdr | Monjor Kolong Korok | 24/2/2004 | |
| 777. | Cdr | Ngot Maperdit Thiik | 1/3/2004 | |
| 778. | Cdr | Jok Dau Kachuol | 1/3/2004 | |

# Appendix C: Historical Pictorials

*Gen. Stephen Buoy plays Chess game with Capt. Mabor Malith in Prison 2018.*

*Gen. Stephen Buoy Rolnyang rests on bed inside his Solitary Confinement room at Giade military Police Custody in 2018.*

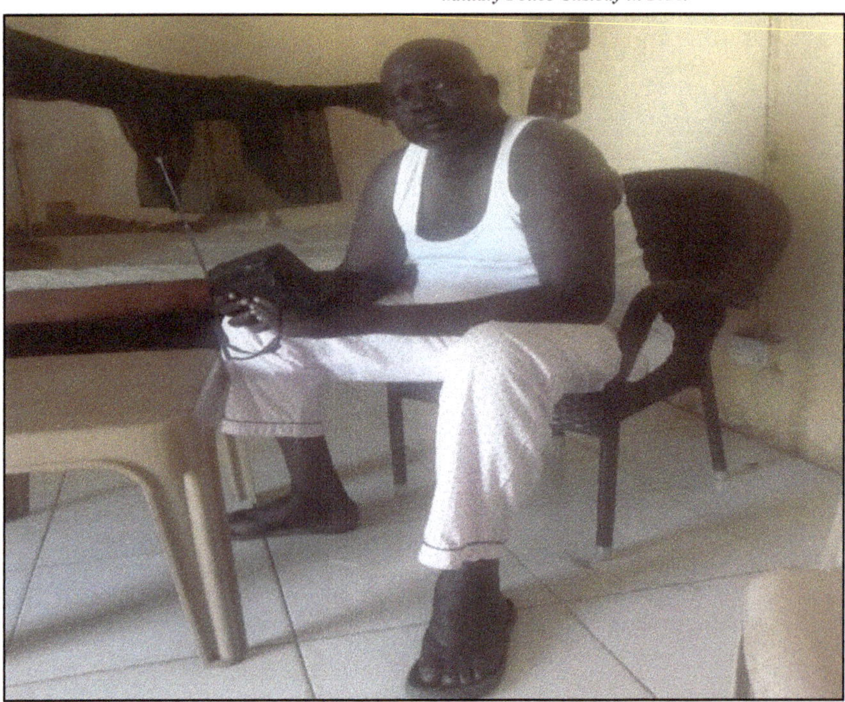

*Gen. Stephen Buoy Rolnyang llistens to the radio while in confinement cell at Giade Military Police in 2018.*

Gen. Stephen Buoy Rolnyang with late Gen. Ajonga Mawut (Melut operations in 2015).

*Gen. Stephen Buoy Rolnyang when serving as the Commander of SPLA Mobile Forces Brigade in Kapoeta area in 2006.*

*Gen. Stephen Buoy Rolnyang as the Commander of W.U.N (Bentiu) 2003.*

***Gen. Stephen Buoy Rolnyang (right), Commander of Military Police in 2009.***

***Gen. Stephen Buoy Rolnyang (above), Commander of Military Police in 2007.***

***Gen. Stephen Buoy Rolnyang inspects ammunitions at the headquarters of the SPLA 4th Infantry division (Bentiu) 2018.***

***Col. Justice Riek Bim and Lt. Col. Stephen Kuiyna Gatjiek visit Gen. Stephen Buoy Rolnyang during his first arrest at Bilpam prison in 2016.***

***Gen. Stephen Buoy Rolnyang arrested in Mayom and brought to Juba on handcuffs on June 1, 2018.***

***The Author (Left) with Gen. JJ (left.***

***Gen. Stephen Buoy Rolnyang salutes the officers after inspecting a Guard of Honor at the SPLA 1st Infantry division headquarters 2015.***

***Gen. Stephen Buoy Rolnyang takes a walk with the Governor of Tonj State Anthony Bol Madut at Division HQS (Wau) in 2018.***

*Stephen Buoy briefs the forces at the 4th Infantry division in Bentiu (2017).*

***Fighting vehicles of the SPLA 1st Infantry division.***

***Different types of guns captured from renegade Olony's barge at Melut***

***The barge captured from renegade Gen. Olony at Melut battle.***

***Gen. Stephen Buoy Rolnyang briefs forces at the 1st Infantry division in 2014.***

***Gen. Stephen Buoy Rolnyang poses for a photo with commando officers at Lanya area in 2009.***

***Gen. Buoy briefs commando forces at Newsite (Juba) in 2008.***

***Gen. Stephen Buoy inspects the Military Police on parade ground in 2009 at New Bilpam.***

***South Sudan President Salva Kiir Mayardit casts his vote during the election day.***

***Riek re-joins the SPLM/A. Salva Kiir (Left), John Garang' (Centre) and Riek Machar (Right) celebrate the re-unification of the two movements.***

***Maper- Akuar pose for a photo after signing a Peace Agreement with Twic commissioner Yol Kuol and Abyei commissioner Ajing Path.***

*A/Cdr Stephen Buoy*

***Stephen Buoy flanked by his bodyguards in 1994***

***Brig. Omar Hassan El Bashir (Left) holding spear poses for a photo on the top of Armored personnel carrier (APC) with Brig. James Koang Ruac (right) in the center in Mayom operations in 1987.***

***Stephen Buoy while still a student in Khartoum (1986).***

***Gen. Gabriel Tang Ginye Deputy Commander to Bol Nyathony in Eastern Upper Nile, when Gordon Koang defected to the SPLM/A in 1988.***

*Gen. Paulino Matip Nhial.*

*The founding members of the SPLM/A, from left to right Kerubino Kuanyin Bol, Arok Thon Arok and William Nyuon Bany.*

*The founding members of the SPLM/A*

*Vincent Kuany Latjor*

*Anya Nya Veteran Joseph Oduho.*

*Anya Nya veteran Samuel Gai Tut.*

*Gen. Stephen Buoy Rolnyang during the Raja Operations.*

# References

1. Douglas H. Johnson (1994): The Nuer prophets
2. Douglas H. Johnson: African Issues, the root causes of Sudan civil war. (2003)
3. James Bandi Shimanyula (2005): John Garang' and the SPLA
4. James Copnall (2014): A poisonous thorn in our hearts
5. M.H Kanyane, JH Mai, DA Kuok (2009): Liberation struggle in South Sudan
6. Monani Alison Magaya (2014): The Anya Nya movement in South Sudan
7. Lam Akol, SPLM/A: insider an African revolution, Khartoum, 2009
8. Peter Adwok Nyaba, South Sudan: Politics of Liberation, 1998,
9. Abel Alier: too many agreements dishonoured.
10. SPLM manifesto, July 31, 1983

www.ingramcontent.com/pod-product-compliance
Lightning Source LLC
Chambersburg PA
CBHW041256040426
42334CB00028BA/3038

* 9 7 8 0 6 4 5 4 5 2 9 5 2 *